# Social Media

# Social Media

## *How to Engage, Share, and Connect*

Regina Luttrell

*Rowman & Littlefield Publishers*
Lanham • Boulder • New York • London

Published by Rowman & Littlefield
A wholly owned subsidiary of The Rowman & Littlefield Publishing Group, Inc.
4501 Forbes Boulevard, Suite 200, Lanham, Maryland 20706
www.rowman.com

16 Carlisle Street, London W1D 3BT, United Kingdom

British Library Cataloguing in Publication Information Available

**Library of Congress Cataloging-in-Publication Data**

Luttrell, Regina, 1975–
  Social media : how to engage, share, and connect / Regina Luttrell.
    pages cm
  Includes index.
  ISBN 978-1-4422-2611-1 (cloth : alk. paper) — ISBN 978-1-4422-2612-8 (pbk. : alk. paper) — ISBN 978-1-4422-2613-5 (electronic)  1.  Online social networks. 2.  Social media.  3.  Public relations.  I. Title.
  HM742.L874 2015
  302.23'1—dc23                                                        2014013880

∞™ The paper used in this publication meets the minimum requirements of American National Standard for Information Sciences—Permanence of Paper for Printed Library Materials, ANSI/NISO Z39.48-1992.

Printed in the United States of America

# CONTENTS

CONTENTS

## PART III
THE SOCIAL MEDIA PLAN

# FOREWORD

## Ryan Schram

*Social marketing.*

It is a vehicle that has profoundly changed the way consumers engage with brands and with one another—the effects of which the marketing world has only begun to distinguish and understand in the past several years.

These amazing platforms are a springboard for the world's creators, with billions of pieces of new content posted and exchanged every single day.

However, there are far more profound, societal trends as well:

- One-third of women aged eighteen to thirty-four say they check Facebook when they first wake up in the morning—even before going to the bathroom![1]
- One in six marriages globally now happen because of people who met through online social networks.[2]
- If Facebook were a country, it would be the third most populated in the world based on the size of its user base.[3]
- Adults who use Twitter on an active basis rank it as the most timely source for news events, largely surpassing "traditional" outlets like cable news channels.[4]

All of these indelible impacts, and "social" is merely a "teenager" in terms of how long it has been around as a concept, let alone actively in the lives of the people who participate in it.

As a result, now more than ever, chief marketing officers, public relations directors, social media strategists, and professionals throughout our profession recognize that they must have their brands in the middle of this ongoing "conversation" across social channels. Yet their team members are vastly unprepared to engage.

Why? Because, more than any other medium in the history of marketing and advertising, social methods have transcended the traditional thinking that previously ruled the educational landscape. The siloed, often myopic, approaches of yesteryear simply do not apply in an ecosystem that moves so quickly and intimately involves so many across a brand organization.

Modern-day social marketing is a true juxtaposition unlike anything else. Digitally enabled and mobility-native, it is a real-time, evergreen vehicle that consumers themselves not only willingly participate in but also constantly update and improve over time. Through the eye of the marketer and practitioners alike, these dynamics provide multidimensional opportunities:

A platform for brand building and storytelling through content marketing.

A terminus to interact with current and prospective customers through the channels of their choice.

An opportunity to provide world-class service experiences (and, hopefully, solve some world-class problems a customer might run into).

The possibilities are limitless. But so are the potential pitfalls for the brands that miss the proverbial boat on where the best opportunities are to maximize their involvement or, worse yet, do not even know where to begin with their strategy.

Unlike a thirty-second spot that's produced in private and then broadcast to viewers unidirectionally, social is a nonstop bilateral collaboration between consumer and marketer.

And it has changed the world forever.

In *Social Media: How to Engage, Share, and Connect*, my friend, Dr. Gina Luttrell, approaches prospective social practitioners in a straightforward and common sense way: by allowing the content to be consumed as a stand-alone topic or as a series of topics that can immediately be put to use—in your planning, in a conversation, or in the boardroom.

She is uniquely qualified as one of the rare educators who has solely focused her research on the growth of social marketing, but who has also spent time in the "real world" as a marketer and public relations practitioner.

All too frequently, the people writing books like this are individuals who have never actually had to roll up their sleeves, do the work for a brand, and receive the practical knowledge that comes along with that.

Dr. Luttrell is the antithesis of this image. She has leapt headfirst into the subject matter, enabling her to create this body of work in a way that is meaningful for its readers—whether they are an everyday practitioner or an aspiring one.

This book is a useful, daily resource that will find its way not only in the classroom but also on the bookshelves and desks of public relations and social marketing leaders as a go-to guide that can be read in its entirety or by topic.

What I found to be particularly relevant was Dr. Luttrell's holistic organization of the "Circular Model of SoMe" and how it challenges the industry to create a new way of looking at "tried and true" marketing and public relations principles.

While sharing, optimizing, managing, and engaging are ways the industry has been doing offline for many decades, doing so in conjunction with a real-time, fluid medium such as social media is something that is often overlooked and, unfortunately, underplanned.

As chief operating officer at IZEA, a pioneer in sponsored social marketing technology, I am awed by these profound changes in the overarching marketing ecosystem and, correspondingly, the way humanity is helping shape it.

Think about it: More than half of the human race on Earth is under the age of thirty. They've never known life without the Internet existing. Being on Snapchat, Instagram, and Twitter isn't just something fun for those individuals to do. It's something they have been programmed to do for as long as they can remember.

As brands covet to build relationships and engage in dialog with these important young adults, the investment toward doing so continues to increase. eMarketer estimates advertisers will invest $38.82 on social networking advertising per social network users in North America alone in 2014—up from $26 only a year before. That figure only includes paid advertising that appears on social channels, not to mention nonadvertising investments such as creation of content, management of brand pages, or social customer service.

In other words, the interest surrounding the social marketing space—and the investment made within it—has only just begun.

Enjoy *Social Media: How to Engage, Share, and Connect* and utilize it in your daily efforts to shape the next generation of marketing innovation.

Onward!

## Notes

1. Ben Parr, "The First Thing Young Women Do in the Morning: Check Facebook [STUDY]," *Mashable* (blog), July 6, 2010, http://mashable.com/2010/07/06/oxygen-face book-study/.

2. Chadwick Martin Bailey and Match.com, "Match.com and Chadwick Martin Bailey 2009–2010 Studies: Recent Trends: Online Dating," last modified March 2010, accessed January 28, 2014, http://cp.match.com/cppp/media/CMB_Study.pdf.

3. Graeme McMillan, "If Facebook Was a Country, It'd Be Larger Than China in Three Years," *Digital Trends*, http://www.digitaltrends.com/social-media/facebook-could-be -larger-than-china-in-three-years-time/.

4. Amy Mitchell and Dana Page, Pew Research Center, "Twitter News Consumers: Young, Mobile and Educated," last modified November 2013, accessed January 28, 2014, http://www.journalism.org/files/2013/11/Twitter-IPO-release-with-cover-page.pdf.

# PREFACE

The profound effect that social media has had on the communications industry is arguably even more important to the field of public relations. The emergence of social media technologies inspired the development of a new marketing model—one that promotes the user as an integral part of the conversation rather than merely an onlooker.

Written in a relaxed and pragmatic tone, this book is succinct and practical in nature. The intent is for the publication to serve as a guide to better understand, create, and develop sound social media strategies. The reader can either choose to complete the book in its entirety or refer to single chapters related to a topic of interest to them. With that in mind, it is my hope that the book presents itself as a unique practical guide and a "go-to" reference related to all things social media. Each individual chapter is meant to introduce and expose the reader to a specific topic; however, when combined with topics presented within other chapters, the entirety of the book is able to guide practitioners throughout the process of creating successful social media campaigns.

## Audience for the Text

This book is useful for both students and public relations and social media practitioners. Students are presented with an applied approach to social media that is rooted in the history of the industry, as well as exposed to the supporting theories. Ideally, theory should inform practice within the field. I have selected the best from social media management and also introduce students to new models, allowing further insights into processes and practice. Practitioners will gain valuable practical insights into the applications of social media and enhance their understanding and execution of social media technologies. The design of this publication is intended to help those who are, or intend to become, part of social media planning within an organization. Individuals with a background in public relations, marketing, advertising, corporate communications or management may find themselves pulled into social media strategies at some point in their careers. The information provided within these pages should help guide these inputs and decisions on social media strategy, ultimately resulting in a more effective and robust process.

## Organization of the Text

This text is broken into three sections, with part I, "The Advancement of an Industry," covering the first three chapters. Chapter 1 introduces readers to the Four Quadrants of Public Relations and how social media integrates within each area. Chapter 2 provides the historical context of social media. Readers are presented with a new social media model, the Circular Model of SoMe for Social Communication—*Share, optimize, Manage, engage*—and the role it plays as a central function in social media planning. Finally, chapter 3 highlights how social media and public relations work together with marketing and advertising.

Part II, "Formulating a Strategy," includes chapters 4–12, which focus on the various social media tools available to develop creative, engaging, and meaningful social media plans. From social networking sites to photo sharing and crisis communication strategies, these chapters are filled with nuggets of information and practical examples that every practitioner will benefit from.

Last, part III, "The Social Media Plan," contains the concluding chapter, chapter 13, which outlines the different aspects of a social media plan. Each step that contributes to the strategic planning of a social media plan is explored, including key metrics. Comprehensive case studies are also provided as learning tools and can be analyzed, deconstructed, and applied within the framework of your own organizational social media planning.

## Unique Features of the Text

There are various "Theory into Practice" case studies scattered throughout the chapters of the text. Each case study provides the reader with real-world examples of successful campaigns related to the topics presented within the chapter. This feature is intended to help guide practitioners toward a contemporary understanding of the public relations profession as it stands today, as well as provide a foundation to create a comprehensive social media plan based on a practical, professional basis.

Quick links are also provided in each chapter to help readers connect more deeply with the presented topics. I invite readers to join me in the conversation on Twitter (@ginaluttrell) by using #LRNSMPR to discuss the book, ask questions, or chat about the links provided.

Finally, a book such as this would not be complete without interviews from professionals. You will find commentary from some of the greatest minds in the industry dispersed throughout the book, including a series of videos that further enhance content presented within the material. Readers who are using the interactive ebook can simply click on a link and watch. Print readers can find the videos at http://ginaluttrellphd.com/videos/.

## Acknowledgments

A project such as this could not be completed without a great deal of support from others. First, thank you to Rowman & Littlefield Publishers for believing in my manuscript. Thank you to my executive editor, Charles Harmon, for patiently ushering me into the world of book publication, and to his assistant, Robert Hayunga, for quickly providing the right answers.

When I asked, you said "yes," and for that I will be eternally grateful to each of you: Ryan Schram, Howard Rheingold, David Weinberger, Eastern Michigan University, Ronn Torossian, SHIFT Communications, Christopher Penn, Todd Defren, Don Bartholomew, Barry Leggetter, Airfoil Group, Overit Media, the College of Saint Rose, Kayla Germain, Ben Marvin, Paul Conti, Rosemary Sheridan, Joanna Clark, Hannah Mosher, Melissa Meyer, Leah Rodriguez, Alyssa De Gilio, Johnalyn Scarati, Chad Wiesbeck, Laura Jackson, Mike Carroll, Phil Keays, and my mom and dad for cheering each step of the way. Finally, many thanks to my husband, Todd, for his unending support and confidence in me, my two precious beans, and Coco—my faithful companion.

To the students and professionals who will read this book—I thank you as well. I hope my passion for social media, public relations, marketing, and communications shines through. Feel free to connect with me on Twitter, @ginaluttrell. I can't wait to chat with you!

**Part I**
# THE ADVANCEMENT OF AN INDUSTRY

# THE FOUR QUADRANTS
# OF PUBLIC RELATIONS

> This chapter explores the four quadrants public relations professionals work in: *media*, *community*, *business*, and *government*, paying particular attention to their interrelationship and how social media plays an ever-present, integral role.

## The Four Quadrants of Public Relations Explained

In 1944 Rex Harlow wrote "Public Relations at the Crossroads," wherein he summarized the duties of public relations professionals. In essence, Harlow highlighted that public relations professionals contend with a myriad of relationships including internal and external relations, personal relations, personnel relations, industrial relations, stockholder relations, board of directors' relations, customer relations, government relations, supplier-creditor relations, community relations, trade relations, opinion surveys, advertising, and publicity. Additionally, Harlow also noted that public relations responsibilities of the time generally included press, radio, motion pictures, printing, public speaking, and professional writing.[1]

Even in today's fast-paced work environment, Harlow's insights still ring true as those of us in the public relations profession know that we have to be able to do it all. In fact, it is now expected that we become experts in multiple arenas within the field to be triumphant in supporting the companies and organizations that we represent.

What is implied, but not directly stated in Harlow's summary of the profession, are the Four Quadrants of Public Relations. The idea is simple.

Within these four quadrants, all functions of public relations fall. To be well versed in each quadrant, while also understanding each individual element, is critical to the development of today's public relations practitioners. The Four Quadrants of Public Relations include:

1. *Media*—inclusive of publicity, as well as traditional and social press
2. *Community*—inclusive of internal, external, online, employee, consumer, and personal interactions
3. *Business*—inclusive of investor relations, C-level executive advisement, and social care (customer service)
4. *Government*—inclusive of political, lobbying, public affairs, and issues management

Public relations practitioners should think of these as completely interrelated and strive to incorporate aspects of all four quadrants into their daily activities to develop a higher level of strategic implementation.

The Four Quadrants of Public Relations (courtesy of Regina Luttrell)

Success is seen when public relations professionals include all four quadrants into the public relations planning process. However, the supporting concepts behind the Four Quadrants of Public Relations are not new. *The novelty lies in how these quadrants are grouped and explained in an interrelated fashion.* Public relations practitioners have a defined responsibility to mediate between an organization and its public to build relationships with a variety of stakeholders by disseminating information to the public as well as seeking or collecting information. This information, or feedback, often provides public relations practitioners and their organizations with insight as to how the public perceives the organization and its operations. Utilizing this open, two-way, symmetrical communication, as exemplified in the Grunig-Hunt model, allows for a higher level of mutual understanding and offers a more balanced approach to consumer-company interactions.[2] Communication should move between an organization and its publics effectively. The symmetrical communication model is one of the more robust models that public relations professionals practice because this model promotes a greater sense of engagement with an organization's targeted audience by listening, connecting, and facilitating through action rather than merely pushing messages out.[3] A continual, open line of communication between a public relations practitioner and the publics being served is essential in our digital age of socially driven public relations activities.

Historically speaking, the idea of open communication has been at the cornerstone of defining public relations.[4] Going forward, it will become increasingly important to focus on sustaining an open model of communication with the public. The theory behind the Four Quadrants of Public Relations relies heavily on this type of engagement in order to interact with various publics, and since social media is also founded on the open communication concept, this communication model will take on considerable importance.

With that in mind, it is significant to understand how the four-quadrant model relies on any single segment building upon another, yet maintaining its interconnectedness with all of the other segments. Let's examine how each segment works individually and then how they work together.

## Quadrant I: Media Relations

In practice, public relations professionals work closely with the media to distribute their messages to the public. The media (specifically news sources inclusive of online, television, print, radio, and electronic media) has long since been viewed by the public as a trustworthy and highly regarded source.[5] It is the job of public relations professionals to build strong, mutually respectful relationships with journalists. Traditionally, public relations practitioners manage their media relations responsibilities by sending press releases, pitch emails, arranging interviews, organizing press conferences, and responding to media inquiries.[6]

It is easy to recognize the outcome of these efforts each time we turn on the television to watch the nightly news. The information that is displayed within these telecasts is carefully, tactfully, and strategically "placed" by public relations practitioners across America. To the untrained eye, all of the news presented may seem as though a journalist researched the story, gathered the interviewees, and put the thirty-second TV news spot together. In truth, many of these news stories are actually the fruit of diligent public relations practitioners. It is our job as professionals to identify a newsworthy trend and capitalize on it.

As an example, the American Bar Association (ABA) is frequently reported on in the news. This organization has been regularly referenced within news stories in both local and national news outlets, as well as major printed publications. Responsibilities of the media relations division within the ABA include serving as the organization's press secretary with local and national news outlets, as well as ensuring that the messages and issues of the ABA are reported on accurately by providing the correct resources to journalists transmitting the stories.[7]

When the ABA launched Operation Enduring LAMP, a mobilization of America's lawyers to help those called up for active military service, the timing and focus of the news conference were established by the public relations practitioner to ensure the best possible results for placement and coverage. Because of their relationships with the media, the event generated national network and newspaper coverage, which, in turn, benefited the association by swelling its ranks with a large number of new pro-bono lawyers to help in the effort.[8] The newsworthy trend here relates to services offered to active military personnel as the timing of this initiative coincided with the onset of the war in Iraq.

When Downsize Fitness, a consortium of fitness centers that exclusively caters to overweight clientele, reached out to Zapwater Communications to assist in creating a media campaign focused on increasing awareness about the fitness centers and subsequently driving an uptick in membership applications, the results turned into front-page national news. The challenge was to differentiate Downsize Fitness from your typical run-of-the-mill fitness centers. With the focus of the media pitches being based on the owner's own struggle with weight loss, Zapwater Communications dedicated its efforts to reaching out to daily newspapers and broadcast media. The initial media win came in the form of securing a feature article in the *Chicago Tribune* by health and fitness writer Julie Deardorff. Publication of this article spurred a flurry of additional media hits, and the story was ultimately syndicated in more than 120 news outlets.[9] *PBS Nightly Business Report* ran a segment on the founder and the newest fitness trend to hit America.[10] This publicity campaign, dubbed "Downsize Fitness: Downsizing the Obesity Epidemic," won the Grand Prize at the 2013 Bulldog Awards for Excellence in Media Relations and Publicity.[11]

Typically, campaigns like Operation Enduring LAMP and Downsize Fitness are built on a coordinated use of varied communication techniques and tools used by public relations practitioners and the instinct to know what stories are perfect to pitch. Pitching the perfect story is dependent upon a practitioner's ability to spot and capitalize on newsworthy trends occurring in the world. Practitioners work with the media to place editorials in newspapers; produce video and audio news releases; arrange radio, TV, print, and social media interviews; promote websites for their organizations; and offer easy access to additional materials that complement the news stories. By leveraging a company or organization's best assets, including subject-matter experts, and seizing the news of the day, media relations can be used to strategically build a favorable image, to educate the public, or to use the ensuing public opinion as a court of appeal.

It would be cliché to state that practitioners must be "out-of-the-box thinkers," but if we are to assess issues and trends successfully to identify the correct demographics within the public, then we must look beyond the typical confines previously presented.[12] The aforementioned examples highlight not only the importance of the relationship between the public relations practitioner and the media but also the varied job duties and skills required of a practitioner within their daily activities. It can be seen that the public relations practitioner is no longer responsible solely for delivering the message, but also for creating the message, maintaining the message, and cultivating the message.

**#LRNSMPR**

Learn More about Media Relations Campaigns

Quick Links

- Dunkin' Donuts, http://bit.ly/1851sUK
- AKA Central Park, http://bit.ly/13qM3tx
- Macaroni Grill, http://bit.ly/110VaPK

## Quadrant 2: Community Relations

In addition to media playing a pivotal role in public relations, community relations also play an equally important role in the road to success for public relations practitioners. With that in mind, the buzz surrounding corporate social responsibility (CSR) has become an integral component in community relations. With greater frequency, companies and organizations are giving back to the communities in which they reside, which in turn require public relations practitioners representing these organizations to further cultivate the relationships between the organization and the community. The responsibility of community relations is the second quadrant in the four quadrants we will explore.

We must remember that "community" no longer means just the physical community, but also the online community. Today's public relations practitioners live with one foot in the real world and one in the virtual community. Public relations campaigns now require a great deal of effort from the public relations practitioner to support the organization's online activities often promoted on Facebook pages, Pinterest boards, Twitter feeds with specific hashtag identifiers, videos, and photo-sharing sites (including Flickr and Instagram). Engaging the targeted audience online should now be considered a natural component of any public relations campaign planning process. A recent GAP study revealed that social media monitoring accounted for an average of 70 percent of a company's core public relations or communications budget.[13] Separately, participants of the study further indicated that overall social media activities accounted for 66 percent of an organization's public relations and communication allocations. These results illustrate that social media responsibilities have significantly increased and have emerged as a mainstream responsibility of public relations professionals.[14] Keep this idea in mind as we examine quadrant two more closely.

As a rule, this role of "community liaison" helps develop crucial relationships within the community. Community relations practitioners are being asked to perform a multitude of tasks including the ability to create, implement, and manage the organization's community awareness initiatives.[15] This means that they are the individuals who promote community initiatives and programs inclusive of resource sharing, community education programs, workshops, events, and symposiums identified as key corporate areas for promotion. They are also the employees who create strategic alliances with representatives of consumer, employee, and public interest groups; key provider practices; vendors; governmental agencies; and prominent community organizations.[16] Community relations practitioners may even participate in community activities surrounding corporate issues, including serving on committees, meeting with elected officials and politicians, sitting on various planning boards, speaking at and attending community board and similar meetings, creating timelines, attending various networking events and symposiums, and other tasks.[17]

Corporations including General Electric, TOMS Shoes, IBM, Starbucks, Cisco, and Verizon are just a few examples of companies that are leading the way in a revolution toward corporate citizenship by contributing to the transformation and empowerment of the communities in which they are an integral part. This is beneficial not only for the communities but also for the corporations. It is the intention of the corporation to uphold its image and reputation within the community while contributing positively.

With this idea of corporate citizenship in mind, a variety of corporations have committed themselves to improving public education around the world. IBM, for example, is focused on preparing the next generation of leaders and workers as it supports community priorities and concerns. Through the program KidSmart Early Learning, IBM exposes many of the world's remotely located and underprivileged students to new and exciting technologies that they would not normally have the chance to experience. Reading Companion, also part of IBM's initiatives, is an interactive software application that assists in learning to read.[18] By making this software available to the neediest populations, IBM is attempting to solve education's toughest problems with solutions that draw on advanced information technologies. To achieve its goals, IBM forms partnerships with states and school districts located in the United States, as well as in developing countries, to better research technology solutions designed to help support school reform efforts and raise student achievement.[19] Another example of a company that prides itself on giving back to the communities that it conducts business with is Cisco. The company has developed a community service campaign designated "GETideas" that establishes a global community focused on transforming trends within the educational sector. This program affords its communities a forum wherein education leaders can share resources, brainstorm ideas, and establish best practices related to evolving educational philosophies within schools.[20] Getideas.org establishes an online platform for educators to engage with and learn from one another, all the while informing and preparing the current generation more effectively than previous generations. Participants can visit the organization's website to gain valuable information, but, equally important, they also have the opportunity to connect with other educators utilizing the initiative on Twitter, Pinterest, Facebook, and through the organization's YouTube channel.

Kraft Foods Group also understands the importance of working with the community to achieve its goals. The company gives back to the community in various ways. In April 2013, the company kicked off its Make an Impact 2013 community service campaign. Employees worked on two hundred various volunteer projects that supported the company's community involvement priorities: fighting hunger and promoting healthy lifestyles.[21] When asked why in an email interview, Leah Bradford, associate director for Corporate Community Involvement and vice president of the Kraft Foods Group Foundation, said, "Community Involvement is part of our heritage. Our employees have always had a passion for service and they share their time, talent and resources to support nonprofit organizations all year long. There are a number of issues facing our communities. We focus our efforts on areas where we can make the most impact. Hunger and obesity are serious challenges for society and our business. As a food company, we use our expertise in food and nutrition to fight hunger and promote healthy lifestyles across North America." Employees planted community gardens, sorted and packed donated items at food banks, and led activities that supported nutrition, education, and active play for children during their week of giving back. Consumers were able to interact with the company on its Facebook page to not only peruse photos of employees giving back at various locations across the United States and Canada but also engage in conversations about the campaign. Additionally, Kraft Twitter followers participated by tweeting what they did to help out in their local communities during National Volunteer Week. In essence, responsibilities such as managing the company social networking sites fall directly to the public relations practitioners.

These examples aim to highlight that a company's donation of capital or services, either within the actual community or online, become important contributions from a public relations standpoint. This is related to the positive impact for the population and communities they touch, and also for the organization in fostering good relationships in communities that directly impact brand and image.

---

**#LRNSMPR**

Learn More about Corporate Social Responsibility

Quick Links

- Starbucks Community Service, http://bit.ly/YNyUMO
- GE Citizenship, http://invent.ge/17Ch04I
- Zappos Community Involvement, http://bit.ly/1088I67
- IBM's KidSmart Early Learning Program, http://bit.ly/1OU9kZ0

---

## Quadrant 3: Business Relations

In general, there are few successful organizations in business today that are exempt from establishing some degree of a relationship with the surrounding community and populations. Organizations must strive to interact and connect with the public in a positive manner, which, in turn, affects the image presented to the public. In today's business landscape, there is an increased level of responsibility expected of the public relations practitioner to guide the CEO, or other executive officials, through the organization's public relations plan, reputation management, and brand management. The 2013 Edelman Trust Barometer survey revealed that a mere 43 percent of global publics trusted organizational CEOs as credible, and less than one-fifth of the same population believe that business leaders tell the truth.[22] This perception can have obvious ramifications for a company's brand, image, bottom line, and ultimate ability to build trusting relationships with its consumers.

By participating in the model of corporate citizenship, it is evident that one of the key responsibilities of a business is to be a good citizen. It is extremely important to understand that the function of the public relations department is to help businesses achieve a desired level of citizenship within the community. *Therefore, public relations must be a part of every department within a business.* This is an important takeaway. As a result of this idea, it is easy to see how business relations play a critical role in the daily lives of public relations practitioners.

Within the process of conducting daily business, organizations perform a variety of public relations activities to stay involved with their publics. CEOs are being held accountable for the company's strategic plan. Public relations has always been responsible for closely monitoring its implementation, including assessing and addressing factors impeding successful execution of planned activities. Strategic thinking should include—in addition to customary market and competitive obstacles—significant nation-state cultural, social, and political biases. To connect with consumers, many times companies will sign up as cosponsors of various events designed to advance human rights or address environment opportunities.[23] Unfortunately, in recent years many companies have faced scandals that have tarnished the image of corporations. The messaging regarding the outcomes of these scandals also fall to the public relations practitioners to manage, but we will touch on that topic in the "crisis" chapter.

Corporate scandals have had an overwhelming impact on how the public assesses corporations, their leaders, and their securities.[24] Companies today must give back to society to begin to regain public trust. Accountability and responsibility are differentiators in today's global workforce. Results from a recent Reputation Institute's Pulse Study indicated that a company's character is responsible for more than 40 percent of a company's reputation.[25] Corporate responsibility and accountability are interwoven. Public relations practitioners around the globe are being called on to help both for-profit and nonprofit businesses ensure "accountability" on all levels. As large corporations expand throughout the world, the ability to do business in other countries will be judged by how well these corporations conduct business in their home countries.[26]

The good news is that there has been a recent uptrend in businesses addressing these "mishandlings" of corporate citizenship scandals. This trend has been aided by organizations onboarding and incorporating government officials or oversight entities within their public relations plans. Some experts feel that having a government tie-in lends authenticity to the work the organization is trying to accomplish. This scenario may also be part of why the fourth quadrant of public relations, government relations, is on the rise.

## Quadrant 4: Government Relations

Government relations have long been the foundation of the public relations industry dating back to the ancient Roman and Greek civilizations.[27] While not acknowledged as "public relations" at the time, the activities performed by these individuals could unarguably be considered public relations tools and tactics. The use of persuasion through writing public speeches, publicity events, and meeting with public officials would be interpreted as public relations activities as the role is characterized today.[28]

As it stands today, practitioners in government relations are also known as public affairs officers or public affairs specialists. These practitioners frequently possess the difficult job of supporting the company's public policy initiatives as well as developing legislative and regulatory proposals on behalf of the company (all the while simultaneously practicing effective public relations strategies). It is within their job responsibilities to maintain positive relationships with the legislature, since they work so closely with these elected officials. Responsibilities within this discipline of public relations practitioners include lobbying of the legislature to advocate on behalf of legislation important to enhancing an organization in a strategic manner.

One example of note, "Rock the Vote," will help clarify this concept. This public relations campaign was endorsed by politicians and political groups from both major political parties. More than twenty years ago, prior to the 1992 and 1996 presidential elections, a nationwide public relations campaign was launched that focused on the mass registration of young voters (ages eighteen to twenty-four). After the inaugural success of the 1992 Rock the Vote campaign, governmental agencies took notice and wanted to achieve an even higher level of registered voter participation from this same demographic of voters. In 1996, Rock the Vote came to life again and has been a mainstay political initiative every election year since.

When this public relations campaign was rolled out in the early 1990s, young voters only had the option of signing and addressing two types of

*Original "Rock the Vote" poster used in the 1992 elections (courtesy of Regina Luttrell)*

postcards pledging to vote. If we fast forward to the current period, the emergence of social media has provided participants a myriad of convenient avenues allowing new voters to register.

Originally, in promoting the Rock the Vote initiative, the public relations practitioners utilized mass media and community events as their main avenues of distribution—specifically MTV. (Note the connection to media relations, community relations, and obviously government relations here.) The public relations agency responsible for this successful public relations campaign created various public service announcements that were aired on MTV around the clock, including nationwide radio announcements, coordinated traveling bus tours to register young voters, and famous personalities hired to endorse the importance of voting.[29] The campaign also targeted community events that younger voters would likely attend such as concerts on college campuses. Voter registration tables were set up at these events, which allowed for convenient registration. The public relations campaign garnered great attention and was a huge success. Efforts exhibited by the public relations practitioners during these two public relations campaigns reaped two million new young voters—the most new young voters in history at the time.[30] This public relations initiative ended a twenty-year cycle of declining voter participation and was proven a success with a 20 percent increase in youth turnout compared to the previous 1988 presidential election.[31] Metrics related to success for the campaign were established by comparing the number of new voters with previously registered voters. Rock the Vote is still active today.

It should be mentioned that politicians also use public relations tactics to benefit themselves as they conduct their daily activities and annual campaigns. These tactics become important in instances wherein a politician desires to raise money or attract votes. When politicians are successful at the ballot box, they use public relations to promote and defend their service in office, with an eye toward the next election. Public relations practitioners are responsible for leading the way in shaping these carefully worded messages as they coordinate speaking engagements; plan special events at nursing homes, churches, or daycare centers; write press releases; and ensure that the politician is on message each time. This is often accomplished by providing the political speaker with carefully thought-out talking points related to the key messages being conveyed.

## Applying an Interconnected Approach

We can see that there are a great number of responsibilities and outcomes that rely on the skills that a public relations practitioner possesses. There is not a single formula for success. Specifically, let's look at media relations. This segment of public relations can be considered a free-standing, specialized function within the world of public relations, as could any of the Four Quadrants of Public Relations for that matter. However, in understanding each quadrant, the overlap between the quadrants, how to work within each quadrant, and incorporating a diverse range of essential skills, we can see a pattern for successful public relations planning, process, and implementation. Aspects of each of the four quadrants rely on one another to be successful.

Within media relations, practitioners must have the ability to successfully conduct outreach to the news media on behalf of an organization or company. It is essential to have the right communication skills to complete this task along with superior writing abilities. It is also essential to know how to reach out to the media in the appropriate way and through the appropriate channels, what to say, and what will or will not be effective in having a story picked up by a news outlet. These skills related to media relations should be inherent within a public relations practitioner.

When working with the community, practitioners take on the role of enhancing an organization's participation and position within the community by establishing outreach efforts that mutually benefit the organization and the community. This aspect of a public relations practitioner's role cannot be accomplished without the correct set of skills. The public relations practitioner must know how to build those relationships.

In parallel with community relations, the approach to business relations is also executed in a similar manner. Public relations practitioners ultimately build and continually foster relationships within the business community. Organizations today want to make sure the actions they take are interpreted as being "good citizens." It is the job of the public relations practitioner to have the appropriate skills to accomplish this aspect of developing these relationships.

Finally, public relations practitioners have also taken on the role of involving their respective organizations within the development of public policy and government relations. Being able to represent an organization's interests to governing bodies and regulatory agencies with the expectation that the governing body will understand the needs of your organization falls under the responsibilities of a public relations practitioner or, as we mentioned previously, a public affairs professional. Knowledge in public speaking and governmental issues and having the ability to communicate effectively are essential when working in government relations.

The profession of public relations aids an organization in establishing mutually adapted relationships with external entities—be that with the media, the community, other businesses, or the government. It is the role of the public relations practitioner to foster these relationships within each quadrant of public relations. Being able to interconnect and apply the required skill sets from each quadrant to gain an increased understanding of the organization's "big picture" is equally important. As evidence, public relations practitioners must have a variety of skill sets to accomplish their job duties, and this set of skills falls within the Four Quadrants of Public Relations: *media*, *community*, *business*, and *government*.

## Theory into Practice

How the Coca-Cola Company and its global initiative to fight obesity employs the Four Quadrants of Public Relations successfully.

### Overview

In May 2013, the Coca-Cola Company launched a global initiative to help fight and prevent obesity. By offering lower-calorie and no-calorie beverage alternatives, a higher level of transparency regarding the nutritional information displayed on packaging, and ceasing to advertise to children less than twelve years of age, the company announced it would also support projects that reinforced the importance of physical activity in countries around the world where Coca-Cola conducts business. This includes the corporate headquarters located in Atlanta, Georgia.

This is an example of a public relations campaign that has utilized the Four Quadrants of Public Relations effectively.

### Media

To launch the global initiative, Coca-Cola scheduled a press event wherein a pledge of $3.8 million was made on behalf of the Coca-Cola Foundation to support statewide programs that aided in promoting an active lifestyle. One such program included a local organization, Georgia SHAPE, which is spearheaded by the governor of Georgia.

Within the Coca-Cola Company's press center, information was provided to the media, including press releases related to the global initiative; partnerships with local organizations such as Georgia SHAPE; b-roll; photos of the chairman and CEO of the Coca-Cola Company, Muhtar Kent, Georgia governor Nathan Deal, and City of Atlanta mayor Kasim Reed; and other pertinent information ready-made for the media to use.

## Community

By partnering with local organizations, the initiative promoted a number of company-coordinated public events wherein community members, families, and children participated in activities supporting physical activity. During each event, Coca-Cola provided participants with branded T-shirts and took photos and video footage that was used in its media kit, referred to as "Coming Together." The photos and videos were also used on the company website.

## Business

Organizations across Georgia were awarded grants that supported Coca-Cola's global initiatives. Each business gained acknowledgment of its commitment to help foster a healthier lifestyle by being mentioned at events, as well as in the Coca-Cola Company press releases. Georgia SHAPE, supported by Governor Deal, was the center of the press highlights by being included in the public event and on all written press releases.

## Government

Georgia governor Nathan Deal took part in a press event where he publicly supported the efforts of the Coca-Cola Company. Within the company press release, Governor Deal is quoted as saying, "Working with Coca-Cola and others to strengthen programs such as Georgia SHAPE and Walk Georgia gives Georgians of all ages and abilities more opportunities to become physically active."

The governor's presence at the event, as well as the inclusion of his quote in the press release, implies to the public that the governor supports both the Coca-Cola brand and the initiatives it has launched. This partnership establishes a strong bond between the company and local government.

By taking a step back to see how this example integrates each of the Four Quadrants of Public Relations, it is easier to see how each independent quadrant contributes to a fully coordinated, successful public relations campaign executed by the Coca-Cola Company that benefits not only the local communities but also the company itself. Initiatives such as this help reinforce the Coca-Cola brand in a positive light. Additionally, partnering with a local nonprofit like Georgia SHAPE to launch an initiative of this type is a natural fit considering the new initiatives Coca-Cola supports.

Ultimately, the success of these types of initiatives is only as good as the public relations practitioners' ability to see the bigger picture. If any of the four quadrants are used independently rather than as an integrated effort, achievement of the overall goal can quickly dissipate.

View the full Coming Together press kit to read the official press release and to download b-roll, photos, and infographics: http://bit.ly/14nlAiq.

## Notes

1. R. Harlow, "Public Relations at the Crossroads," *Public Opinion Quarterly* (1944): 551–56.

2. D. Wilcox, G. Cameron, B. Reber, and J. Shin, *THINK Public Relations* (Upper Saddle River, NJ: Pearson Education, 2013).

3. D. Moss and B. DeSanto, "What Do Communications Managers Do?" *J&MC Quarterly* (2005): 873–90; L. Wernet-Foreman and B. Devin, "Listening to Learn: 'Inactive' Publics of the Arts as Exemplar," *Communication World* (2006): 287–94.

4. F. Seitel, *The Practice of Public Relations* (Upper Saddle River, NJ: Pearson, 2014); Wilcox et al., *THINK Public Relations*.

5. Wilcox et al., *THINK Public Relations*.

6. Wilcox et al., *THINK Public Relations*; Seitel, *The Practice of Public Relations*.

7. R. Stein, "Our Media Pros," *ABA Journal*, no. 12 (2003).

8. Stein, "Our Media Pros."

9. T. Sinkinson, "Lessons in Landing Front Page Placement: Zapwater Communications Downsizes the Obesity Epidemic for Downsize Fitness," *Bulldog Reporter* (2013), http://www .bulldogreporter.com/dailydog/article/lessons-in-landing-front-page-placement-zapwater -communications-downsizes-the-obesi (accessed May 20, 2013).

10. Sinkinson, "Lessons in Landing Front Page Placement."

11. Sinkinson, "Lessons in Landing Front Page Placement."

12. D. Anderson, "Identifying and Responding to Activist Publics: A Case Study," *Public Relations Research*, no. 1 (1992): 151–65.

13. University of Southern California Annenberg School for Communication and Journalism, Strategic Communication and Public Relations Center, GAP IV: Seventh communication and public relations Generally Accepted Practices study (Q4 2011 data), 2011. Retrieved from the University of Southern California Annenberg School for Communication and Journalism Strategic Communication and Public Relations Center website: http://ascjweb .org/gapstudy/corporations/.

14. University of Southern California Annenberg School for Communication and Journalism, Strategic Communication and Public Relations Center, GAP IV: Seventh communication and public relations Generally Accepted Practices study (Q4 2011 data).

15. K. Keller, *Best Practice Cases in Branding* (Upper Saddle River, NJ: Pearson, 2007).

16. Wilcox et al., *THINK Public Relations*.

17. Seitel, *The Practice of Public Relations*; Keller, *Best Practice Cases in Branding*.

18. IBM, "Citizenship Initiatives. Focused on Issues Where We Can Apply IBM's Technology and Talent," accessed May 20, 2013, http://www.ibm.com/ibm/responsibility/initiatives/citizenship.shtml.

19. Keller, *Best Practice Cases in Branding*.

20. Cisco, "Corporate Social Responsibility," accessed May 20, 2013, http://csr.cisco.com/casestudy/getideas.

21. Kraft, "Kraft Launches First Celebration of Community Service," accessed May 20, 2013, http://files.shareholder.com/downloads/ABEA-3QV6OO/2459222506x0x653268/a734c1e6-1ade-4df0-943c-642060d36fac/Make_an_Impact_2013_release_FINAL_4.12.13_.pdf.

22. Edelman, "Global Results: 2013 Edelman Trust Barometer," accessed May 20, 2013, http://www.edelman.com/trust-downloads/executive-summary/.

23. J. Budd, "Opinion . . . Foreign Policy Acumen Needed by Global CEOs," *Public Relations Review* (2000): 123–34.

24. IBM, "Citizenship Initiatives."

25. Reputation Institute, "Pulse Study," accessed May 20, 2013, http://www.reputationinstitute.com/advisory-services/reptrak-in-country.php.

26. Keller, *Best Practice Cases in Branding*.

27. Wilcox et al., *THINK Public Relations*.

28. Seitel, *The Practice of Public Relations*.

29. Keller, *Best Practice Cases in Branding*.

30. D. Burgess, B. Haney, M. Snyder, et al., "Rocking the Vote: Using Personalized Messages to Motivate Voting among Young Adults," *Public Relations Quarterly* (2000): 29–52.

31. Keller, *Best Practice Cases in Branding*.

## CHAPTER TWO

# THE EVOLUTION OF SOCIAL MEDIA

This chapter discusses the evolution of social media and situates social media within today's global environment.

## What Is Social Media?

Why are we asking "What is social media?" when everybody already knows what social media is?

We're asking this because each and every day companies fail at social media for numerous reasons; the most common of these is that they simply do not understand the premise behind social media. Another common reason is that they are trying to fit marketing or advertising principles to social media because they don't understand the fundamental ideals behind social media. Additionally, many organizations tend to seek outside assistance within this area and hire one of the many self-proclaimed "gurus" to manage their social strategies—but often the so-called guru isn't really an expert at all. Most companies tend to overlook how smart their consumers really are. A company cannot use the same old marketing techniques and tactics to spam consumers. Consumers know the difference between true engagements with a company or brand versus simply being sold to.

To gain a deeper level of understanding of social media so that you don't repeat this common mistake, let us break down the two words separately and explore their meanings as they relate to social media.

Social: so-cial *adjective* \'sō-shəl\[1]

a. marked by or passed in pleasant companionship with friends or associates
b. of or relating to human society, the interaction of the individual and the group, or the welfare of human beings as members of society
c. tending to form cooperative and interdependent relationships with others.

As you can see, *social* is the need that we, as human beings, have to connect with others through companionship via relationships with others in society, either individually or in groups. Think about your own relationships. We want to be around people who make us most comfortable and have similar interests, ideas, ideals, and experiences.[2] This also holds true for consumers who desire to interact with companies they relate to, connect with, and feel comfortable aligning themselves with.

Media: me-di-a *noun* \mee-dee-uh\[3]

a. Communication channels through which news, entertainment, education, data, or promotional messages are disseminated. Media includes every broadcasting and narrowcasting medium such as newspapers, magazines, TV, radio, billboards, direct mail, telephone, fax, and Internet. *Media* is the plural of *medium* and can take a plural or singular verb, depending on the sense intended.

The word *media* relates to the channels through which we make connections with others. The sampling provided in the definition is narrow in scope. Today, we connect through pictures, email, texting, websites, and a myriad of mobile and handheld devices.

By bringing the two words together, we can begin to understand how this book applies the term *social media*, and how you should interpret the term going forward. A commonly accepted definition of the term *social media* refers to the "activities, practices, and behavior among communities of people who gather online to share information, knowledge and opinions using conversational media. Conversational media are web-based applications that make it possible to create and easily transmit content in the form of words, pictures, video, and audio."[4] Social platforms, including Facebook, Twitter, Instagram, Pinterest, WordPress, and LinkedIn, among others, are forms of social media. They represent conversational media since each application allows users to gather online and easily exchange photos, videos, audio files, and content while building and cultivating relationships. Social media should be viewed as how a company or brand effectively utilizes each of the aforementioned technologies to connect, interact, and cultivate trusting relationships with *people*.

As we begin to situate social media in a historical context, we must also understand the innate connection between social media and social networks. Social networks comprise a complex system of web-based services that allow for the self-organization of individuals to construct a public or semi-public profile with a set of users that they share a connection.[5] This connection is important in understanding not only the relationship between the two but also their principal differences and how they are commonly interpreted as being the same.

## Social Media's Rise

We can no longer argue that social media is on the rise or that it is in the early phases of adoption. Social media is here, and it is growing by leaps and bounds. At this point in the social revolution, social media is in the refinement stage wherein best practices and case studies are being shared. People are finding new ways to engage with the brands, people, and events that matter most to them and affect their lives on a regular basis. Think about these interesting statistics:

- Seventy percent of the Internet population use social networks in a multitude of ways, and this number grows daily.[6]
- People continue to spend more time on social networks than any other category of sites—20 percent of their time spent on personal computers and 30 percent through mobile applications.[7]
- Facebook reports one-billion-plus accounts.[8]
- Flickr has ninety-two million users, with a million photos shared per day.[9]
- Fifty-eight million Tweets are tweeted per day.[10]
- Foursquare boasts connecting thirty-three million users with 1.3 million businesses.[11]
- Instagram has one hundred million users and holds four billion photos.[12]
- Fifty percent of consumers say they interact with social media while watching TV.[13]

- Forty-four percent of US tablet owners use their device daily to access social media.[14]
- Thirty-eight percent of US smartphone owners use their devices daily to access social media.[15]
- There are 48.7 million Pinterest users.[16]
- Every minute, seventy-two hours of video is uploaded to YouTube.[17]

If we simply look at the numbers involved, now more than ever, public relations practitioners must understand how to create, cultivate, maintain, and grow successful social strategies by building strong social relationships.

In its current form, social media could still be considered relatively new. However, the roots of social media surprisingly began in 550 BCE with the introduction of the postal service. Historically speaking, much of what we currently define as social media occurred during the twenty-first century. To grasp a greater understanding of social media, it is essential to examine the early forms of social networking and how it evolved into its current form.

## Prehistory: Ancient Persia 600–490 BCE to 1800s

The post, as referred to during this period, was the first form of communication between people allowing correspondences beyond the confines of their village. It is argued that the original credible claim for the development of a true postal system has its roots in ancient Persia, attributing the invention of the postal system to King Cyrus the Great.[18] With the establishment of a postal system, people could communicate and converse with one another over larger geographical areas. These early forms of communication were not without issues. Letters could take hours, days, or even months to arrive at their final destinations.

It wasn't until 1792 that Claude Chappe, a French inventor, developed the first practical telecommunications system of the industrial age. He became a telecommunications mogul through what has been called the "mechanical internet."[19] The telegraph transmitted messages instantaneously, altering communication thereafter. The electronic telegraph was the first form of communication that transmitted and received messages over long distances. Rightfully so, the telegraph has earned its place in the historical landscape of social media.

## 1890s

The year 1890 brought about the telephone, and in 1891 society was introduced to the radio.[20] The telephone and radio both brought about a sense of community. People were connected across long distances in a more intimate way. Information moved between and among people from big cities to small rural communities.

## 1960s

The 1960s were rich with introductory technologies that have since become an integral part of our daily lives. In 1966, a crude form of email first came about. It was not the typical email as we understand it today. Early email was similar to a file directory. Users were able to place a message in another user's directory, where they would retrieve it upon logging into the system. The first email system of this type was MAILBOX, used by the Massachusetts Institute of Technology.[21] ARPANET, the Advanced Research Projects Agency Network (launched in 1969, along with CompuServe), served as the first major commercial online service in the United States.[22]

## 1970s

The year 1978 brought about two very important contributions to the history of social media. Multi-User Dungeon, or MUD, created by Roy Trubshaw, is the first and oldest virtual community in existence.[23] Additionally, BBS, a computer system, was also introduced, allowing users to log into a central location where they could connect with other users. Once logged in, users were able to exchange messages with others, upload or download software and data, read news, and even direct chat.[24]

## 1980s

In 1985 the WELL, Whole Earth 'Lectronic Link, was introduced; it is one of the oldest virtual communities that has been in continuous operation since its inception.[25] By 1988 Internet Relay Chat (IRC) was used for file sharing, link sharing, and keeping in touch.[26]

It was around this time that a real technological breakthrough was about to be introduced that would change how virtual communities formed and interacted going forward. Web 1.0 was initiated during the 1990s. This period of growth ushered in the introduction of the URL, or uniform resource locator, and the basic search functions. Internet technologies became accessible to the public on a larger scale. Web 2.0 was the platform on which new, innovative applications could be built. The web became easier to navigate and offered a more dynamic user experience. The result was a generation of tech-savvy individuals who were able to navigate through the ever-growing Internet. This initial foundation positioned technology to where it is today.

## 1990s

The year 1997 marked the first introduction of what we now have come to understand as a social networking site. Coined "SixDegrees," the site offered users the ability to create personal profiles, set up friend lists, and surf friend lists belonging to other users within their networks. They could send messages to one another, affiliate themselves with networks, and invite family and friends to become members. This quickly became popular due to its level of interactivity.[27] In the year 2000, SixDegrees was purchased for $125 million. One year later it was shut down. These options may not seem impressive by today's standards; however, in 1997 no other site offered a combination of these features.[28] The concept was well ahead of its time. Additionally, LiveJournal was one of the Internet's most popular early blogging and online communities built around the use of personal journals. This community was started by Brad Fitzpatrick in April 1999.[29] During 1998 and 1999 other well-known social sites were introduced, including MoveOn, Asian Avenue, BlackPlanet, Napster, Third Voice, Epinions, and Blogger.[30]

## 2000s

The twenty-first century has generated many of the most popular social networking sites, many of which are still in use today. In the early 2000s, some of the largest growth of social networking sites occurred. In 2001 Wikipedia was first launched, 2002 brought about Friendster to the Internet, and in 2003 we were introduced to both Myspace and LinkedIn.[31] Myspace was the first social networking site to allow users to completely customize their pages and upload music and video. LinkedIn was the first social networking site dedicated to business users. Other popular social networking sites that came into use in 2003 included last.fm, Photobucket, Second Life, and Delicious.[32] In 2004, Digg, a website wherein users share links and vote as to whether they "digg" the article or want to "bury" it, came into existence.

Flickr popped on the scene in 2004 as well, and now it boasts ninety-two million users who share approximately one million photos daily.[33] Ning, orkut, mixi, Piczo, Hyves, Care2, Multiply, and Harvard Facebook were established in 2004. YouTube, the first massive video-sharing site, launched in 2005, along with high school Facebook, Bebo, Yahoo! 360, and reddit. In 2006 Twitter and Facebook emerged and gained use and popularity quickly. Twitter's status sprung out of use at the South by Southwest (SXSW) conference.[34] Tweets increased from twenty thousand per day to sixty thousand per day. Today, more than fifty million Tweets are sent daily. When Facebook originally launched, users signed up at an unprecedented rate. Currently, Facebook is the sixth most visited social networking site in the United States, with a user base that would independently rank as the third largest country in the world.[35] In 2007 Tumblr and FriendFeed materialized. In 2008, we were introduced to Spotify, Ping, Groupon, and Kontain, and in 2009, the ever-popular location-based social networking Foursquare launched with great popularity. More recently, the photo-sharing site Instagram rose to mass appeal in 2010, along with Google Buzz and Pinterest. Continuing with this trend, in 2011 Google introduced Google+, and Pheed was unveiled in 2012, a unified platform whereby users can share photos and videos, text, create voice notes, and live broadcast. Finally, this brings us to 2013, in which Vine was launched by Twitter.[36] Vine is a mobile service that allows users to capture and share short looping videos. Similar to Tweets, the brevity of videos on Vine is six seconds or less.[37]

Through this chronological history of the advancement of social media, encompassing both social networking sites and social media tools, we have seen brilliant developers, coders, gamers, idea generators, and early adopters. None of the technological achievements seen in the social media community would have been possible without forward-thinking pioneers who developed the principles, values, ideals, and standards behind the social media movement.

Stewart Brand, Howard Rheingold, Kevin Kelly, Esther Dyson, and John Perry Barlow were early visionaries of the Internet and the emerging digital world in which we live today.[38] Rick Levine, Christopher Locke, Doc Searls, and David Weinberger developed the set standards by which we have come to understand and utilize today as social media engagement.

Let's examine these pioneers who made history by taking social media and making it an everyday occurrence both personally and within a business strategy.

## Pioneers of Social Media

### Stewart Brand (1938– ) @longnow

Writer Carole Cadwalladr defined Stewart Brand as "the heart of 60s counterculture" and a widely revered "tech visionary whose book anticipated the web."[39] Brand published *The Whole Earth Catalog*, which was described by Steve Jobs as "Google only on paper" in his Stanford commencement address. The catalog contained information on everything from deerskin jackets to the latest technological advances, including ideas about cybernetics from Norbert Wiener.[40] *New York Times* writer John Markoff said the catalog was "the Internet before the Internet. It was the book of the future. It was a web in newsprint."[41]

*Thinking the* Whole Earth Catalog *legacy was coming to an end, Stewart Brand issued* The Last Whole Earth Catalog *in 1971. (Courtesy of Regina Luttrell)*

Brand is credited with putting the two words *personal* and *computer* together, thus introducing the concept of owning your own *personal computer* to the world. He was a man before his time and "understood before almost anyone else, was that cyberspace was some sort of fourth dimension and the possibilities were both empowering and limitless."[42] He helped shape the public's understanding of computing. This revelation led to many early Internet technologies, virtual communities, and ideals. He led the way in co-founding the WELL, and later the Global Business Network, *CoEvolution Quarterly*, the Hackers Conference, and Long Now Foundation. All of these technologies were based on the concept of a social presence among users.

### Howard Rheingold (1947– ) @hrheingold

At a time when the idea of an online community could not yet be rationalized, and an emerging interest in the cultural and social implications of modern media was merely a thought, Howard Rheingold was building a foundation for these interactions. He was another pioneer who was ahead of his time. Described as a critic, writer, teacher, artist, designer, theorist, and community builder, Rheingold is "one of the driving minds behind our net-enabled, open, collaborative life-style today" and why he is considered a founding father of social media.[43]

*Howard Rheingold is one of the founding fathers of social media. He is credited with coining the term* virtual community. *(Photo courtesy of Howard Rheingold)*

Early in his career, Rheingold wrote about the history of the individuals behind the personal computer, which, in turn, fueled later research and ultimately his book *Tools for Thought*. In 1985 he began writing for the WELL, wherein he became an influential contributor on life inside virtual communities and the implication of this newly formed communications medium. It was during this experience when he coined the term *virtual community*, a term synonymous with social media today.[44] He became editor of *The Whole Earth* review in 1985 and then shortly thereafter editor in chief of *The Millennium Whole Earth Catalog*. By 1994 he founded and became the executive editor of HotWired, one of the first commercial content websites published by *WIRED* magazine.[45] After leaving HotWired, he founded Electric Minds in 1996, where he chronicled the growth of online communities. In 1998, he created Brainstorms, a private web conferencing virtual community that caters to those who want to have conversations about "technology, the future, life online, culture, society, family, history, books, health, home, mind, phun, money, spirituality, media, and academiaville."[46]

Still an ever-present voice in the social community, Rheingold presents at conferences throughout the world, writes, researches, and teaches. A nonresident fellow of the Annenberg School for Communication at Stanford University, students now learn about the virtual community and social media from him. UC Berkeley students learn about digital journalism. In 2008, he was the recipient of the MacArthur Foundation's Digital Media and Learning Competition. With this award, he developed and created Social Media Classroom and Collaboratory (http://socialmediaclassroom.com/). Spreading the idea of open education, he founded Rheingold University (http://www.rheingold.com/university/), a completely online learning community where participants can take courses in everything from "Introduction to Mind Amplifiers" to "Social Media for Educators."

## An Interview with Howard Rheingold

During my PhD studies, I was fortunate enough to have Howard Rheingold as a professor, and he has since filled the role of mentor as well. His writings, insights, and teachings have inspired and challenged me to think critically about the Internet and social media and how I currently view and understand them. Howard was gracious enough to chat with me on a number of topics related to this book and also share some thoughts on his time at the WELL, the beginnings of social media, where social media is today, and the future of social media.

*In the book, you are featured as one of the pioneers of social media. Can you tell me what social media was like before we, meaning society, even knew what it was? When you were part of the WELL it was a groundbreaking time that many of us were not part of.*

Well, you know, I think that you have to go back about three prehistoric eras to talk about that. There have been an awful lot of people who think it started with Facebook. I had a company called Electric Minds in 1996 in which I talked about the social web; about the web becoming a social medium. So that was 1996. To, I think, a lot of people that was pretty prehistoric. The article I wrote—well, let's see, the book, *The Virtual Community*, was 1993. That was the year of the famous *New Yorker* cartoon on the Internet, "Nobody Knows You Are a Dog." That was when the Internet sort of broke into the public consciousness for the early adopters. My article that coined the term *virtual community* was 1987 and so that came from the WELL which I joined in 1985. And we felt, we being the people on the WELL at that point, felt that this was going to be big. We didn't really have an idea of what the shape of the web would turn out to be but we knew that people would want to communicate in this way in the future. When I set out to write *The Virtual Community*, it was very clear that there was a much longer history than that. There were the BBSs. At one point in the US there were about 50,000 BBSs around the time of the WELL. And these were mostly inexpensive PCs with a modem and usually a teenage boy's bedroom and like only one person could log on at a time. There was also UseNet, which started in 1980, which was worldwide and pretty large. There were, I would say tens of thousands of people if not hundreds of thousands of people on UseNet. Most of them, what we would now call "geeks," but weren't called geeks then, you know, electrical engineers, people, computer science professors, researchers, and before that it, of course, was the ARPANET and that went back to 1969–1970. And before that even was Plato, the system that controlled data, created in Minneapolis. So for some, you know it's the old William Gibson quote, "The future is already here. It's not evenly

*(continued)*

31

### An Interview with Howard Rheingold (*continued*)

distributed." There were people online in the 1960s, 1970s, and 1980s. It really took off with the web. If you think about it, it's a little bit strange that the Internet was worthy of a *New Yorker* cartoon in 1993. The web really didn't exist yet. It was all text and you had to give arcane commands on your keyboard. It was mostly email that attracted people. So there's a long, long history here that most people don't really know about.

*I agree with you. I don't think that people realized where social media was going to go at that time, but I believe technology was on the brink of something "big." Did you expect people to use the technology the way that we are using it now?*

Well, there were things called MUDS then—Multi-User Dungeons—where people had fantasy worlds that were totally based on text. And the pretty widespread fantasy among MUDDERS was that someday we would have graphical MUDS. You would have kind of cartoony computer graphics worlds. The idea that people would be streaming video to each other from their phones in their pockets was totally out of the question. Nobody even imagined that. I participated in some of the first experiments with video. There was something called See-You-See-Me that the Mac had way back in the late 1980s. And the frame—well, it was black and white. It was postage-stamp sized. The frame rate was very, very low so it was kind of jerky. That we would do what we are doing right now for free, full color, real-time, pretty good detail video—that was not really something that people foresaw. But we did—you know, I think the social affordances were foreseen. The fact that you could communicate with someone you had never met, on the other side of the world, but you shared a particular interest, I think was very important. Again, the social side of it—connecting with people around shared interests, even if you did not know them, that was—that is, radical.

*I suppose that's what many businesses mistake. Businesses use social media to connect with their audiences, but they fail to understand the notion that people are on the other side of this network. I find that to be very interesting.*

Well, let me say a couple of things about that. First of all, when I was out talking about electric minds in 1996, I pointed out that social communication had driven the growth of the Internet from the very beginning and as soon as the tools were there, it was going to drive the web as well. And I think that that is essential. I think that people wanting to communicate with people has not been something that has been added on recently. It has been a driving force.

*We have seen how Twitter has changed the landscape for companies, reporters, and civil uprisings. In your opinion, what is the most important quality or impact social media possesses? For example, when the tsunamis hit, there were donations that came from all over.*

Well, it is an instantaneous, global way for ordinary citizens to participate in everything from news gathering to disaster relief to political organizing. That is a radical change. The police and the army have always been able to communicate with each other wherever they were. An illustration of many-to-many communications. That has never existed before. You have the alphabet and the printing press broadly expanding the number of people who are able to receive broadcast communication—read the newspaper, tune in on the radio, watch the television. Of course, there were only a small number of people who were able to create the content—to tell them what the news was. Now, anybody with a smartphone with a camera is a reporter. You see these massive demonstrations; the difference between the massive demonstrations today and the massive demonstrations of the past is that everybody there knows where their friends are. They are talking on the phone, they are tweeting, and they are sending SMS messages. The ability to organize collective actions—whether that is political demonstrations or organizing disaster relief or fact checking a news report; the ability to organize with people you were not able to organize with before in places and at speeds that you were not able to organize before. Now that is radical. It's not only many to many; it's everywhere now because of mobile communications.

*To build off that answer, do you think that our communication or content is going to become more abbreviated? For example, today, we have Vine, which is six-second videos, and Instagram and Pinterest and all of these other sites that compress communication. Blogs allow us to expand upon our thoughts and link out to other places, but some of the newer technologies are quite short.*

You know, I just think that there is a rich ecology of communication media and cannot imagine that there are going to be too many people that are going to communicate in tiny bursts. But I think that all of us are adding that to our vocabulary.

*What do you think the future of social media looks like?*

The future of social media. Well, you know I wrote a book called *Net Smarts* and the premise behind that book is that we have all of this power at our fingertips, but the critical uncertainty about whether the web is going to end up being any good for us in the long run. Because there is a lot of bad stuff, I am not an unpredictable enthusiast. There is a lot of spam and porn and porn-spam and bad information, misinformation, deceptive information, bad people, crimes—will it just descend into a mass of garbage? I think the answer is that it depends on how many of the people that have access to the media also have some know-how about

*(continued)*

### An Interview with Howard Rheingold (*continued*)

it. So I wrote about attention and training attention—a huge distraction issue. I don't think that distraction issue means that your smartphone or laptop is going to magnetically suck your attention away, I think that it means that you need to exercise some control over your attention. Which nobody has time and you have not practiced. The next one is "crap" detection. You know, if you are talking about Googling your symptoms, or you are talking about rumors about political figures, bad information has real consequences. And we live in a world where you can now ask any question, any questions, and get an answer, get a lot of answers, anywhere in the world within a second. It is up to you to determine whether the answers are accurate or inaccurate. That's a big, big change. People need to learn how to do that. It is not rocket science—certainly at the elementary level. And [we need to learn] how to participate. Unless we want Facebook and Google and Apple to dictate how we communicate online, we need to continue to blog and create new media like Twitter. Individuals need to put up websites and link to others. Don't leave it to the big guys. Collaboration [is also important]. [There are] so many different genres of collaboration. Virtual communities, smart mobs, crowdsourcing, collective intelligence, social production. If you know how to do it, you can wield a lot of power with others collaboratively. And then finally, some network literacy. Understanding how things work in a networked world. So, again, I wrote *Net Smart* to try to do something about it. There are some strong critiques of social media, and those are important. But a critique can only tell you that something is broken. It does not tell you how to fix it. I think how to fix it is education and more people learning how to use these media productively, effectively, mindfully.

*I certainly appreciate your time and consideration for this interview. Do you have any closing thoughts that you would like to share with us?*

Technology is moving faster than our social institutions. If we are going to do this kind of learning that is going to improve the commons, we have to teach each other.

## Kevin Kelly (1952– ) @kevin2kelly

For more than twenty years, innovator, writer, and technology guru Kevin Kelly has been viewed as one of the most significant information technology revolutionists of our time. As a member of Brand's original group of visionary technologists, Kelly acted as publisher and editor from 1984 to 1990 of the *Catalog*, where he authored articles on topics that leveraged power to individuals. He took an active role in helping to launch the WELL, and he cofounded the ongoing Hackers Conference.[47] In 1993 he launch *WIRED* magazine and served as executive editor for six years, during which time the magazine was the recipient of the National Magazine Award for General Excellence twice.[48]

Today he holds the title of Senior Maverick at *WIRED* and is the publisher and editor of the Cool Tools website. His most recent book, *What Technology Wants*, builds upon his book *Out of Control: The New Biology of Machines, Social Systems, and the Economic World*. In this book Kelly included an in-depth look at the connections between computer science, biology, systems theory, cybernetics, and artificial intelligence. Kelly introduced us to "vivisystems" or lifelike, complex, engineered systems capable of growing in complexity. He wrote about a new era in which machines and systems that drive our economy are as complex and autonomous as to be indistinguishable from living entities.[49] *What Technology Wants* takes Kelly's initial theories and expounds upon them, arguing that technology is alive much like each of us and has evolved in the same way human beings have evolved.[50]

### John Perry Barlow (1947– ) @JPBarlow

A contributor to *WIRED* magazine, John Perry Barlow's manifesto, "A Declaration of the Independence of Cyberspace," could be considered his most influential early paper. In a response to the government of the United States passing of the Telecommunications Act of 1996, Barlow wrote that the United States did not have the right to apply laws to the Internet because it was outside any country's borders. Barlow suggested that the Internet could develop its own social contracts to determine how to deal with its problems based on the golden rule "do unto others as you'd have done to you."[51] This was the first time in US history that laws governing the Internet were enacted.

Barlow founded the Electronic Frontier Foundation (EFF), an international nonprofit digital rights group protecting free speech, fair use, privacy, international rights as they pertain to the Internet, and transparency problems that threaten digital freedoms (EFF 2013).

### Esther Dyson (1951– ) @edyson

One of the world's preeminent visionaries of the digital age, Esther Dyson has written about how the Internet affects an individual's life. She was the first person to expand upon the notion of the "humanization" of the Internet and to introduce this concept to a wide audience. "Everything that happens on the Net will happen to human beings . . . the Net is not going to push us into some antiseptic digital landscape."[52] Her predictions from 1998 have become today's reality. Social media allows for us to extend our emotional and intellectual selves through the use of social networking sites. We develop relationships, conduct business, share ideas, and even connect globally. Her publications on technology include *Release 1.0*, her monthly technology-industry newsletter; her 1998 book *Release 2.0: A Design for Living in the Digital Age*, about how the Internet affects us individual beings; *Release 3.0*, a bimonthly column for the *New York Times*; and *Release 4.0*, her blog.[53]

## The Forward-Thinking Four

Rick Levine @ricklevine, Christopher Locke @clockerb, Doc Searls @dsearls, and David Weinberger @dweinberger teamed up to write the *Cluetrain Manifesto: The End of Business as Usual*. The book revolutionized concepts and perceptions of how business is conducted under the impact of the Internet. Through a series of ninety-five theses, they explain that businesses are fundamentally human: "Markets consist of human beings, not demographic sectors. Conversations among human beings sound human. They are conducted in a human voice. Whether delivering information, opinions, perspectives, dissenting arguments or humorous asides, the human voice is typically open, natural, uncontrived."[54] The central message of the book is that the marketplace is a conversation and that the web gives people a voice. Locke, Levine, Searls, and Weinberger agree that too often conversations by

The Forward-Thinking Four: Rick Levine, Christopher Locke, Davis "Doc" Searls, and David Weinberger. (Photo courtesy of Rick Levine Creative Commons License)

individuals are ignored by large corporations because these corporations see the Internet as another vehicle to broadcast marketing messages. Consumers, employees, and stakeholders yearn for genuine dialogue on the Internet.

For the first time, the ideals and basis of all interaction via social media was summarized in the *Cluetrain*. The fundamentals of this new marketplace and how to converse effectively are illustrated through three simple decrees as outlined within the book:

1. Be authentic to stakeholders: talk like people and eliminate buzz words and overly technical terms.
2. Have fun and laugh: people drive the Internet; they drive interactions, so be real with them, and cultivate authentic conversations.
3. Above all, listen: the marketplace is where conversations are happening. Without careful attention, businesses can miss out on important exchanges.

I had the opportunity to ask David Weinberger where the inspiration for *Cluetrain* sprung. He responded with the following:

> *Cluetrain* grew out of a set of conversations among the four of us about just how wrong the media and most businesses were about the Web. They were viewing the Web primarily as a business opportunity, whereas we thought it was obvious to the people on the Web that we were there because we finally got to talk about what mattered to us with the people we wanted to talk with, and to do so in our own voice. That is, the Web was and is social more than anything else.

Modern visionaries like Brian Solis (@briansolis), Deirdre Breakenridge (@dbreakenridge), Guy Kawasaki (@GuyKawasaki), Philip Sheldrake (@sheldrake), Scott Monty (@ScottMonty), Becky McMichael (@bmcmichael), Stuart Bruce (@stuartbruce), Adam Parker (@AdParker), Rachel Miller (@AllthingsIC), and Don Tapscott (@dtapscott) understand that "authenticity, honesty, and personal voice underlie much of what's successful on the Web."[55]

## Global Perspectives

Social media can be viewed as a catalyst for global transformation. The world is changing before our eyes, day by day, minute by minute. With every change begins a metamorphosis. Philip Slater's *The Chrysalis Effect* outlines the process of change that the world is experiencing and compares these shifts to that of the caterpillar's metamorphosis into a butterfly.[56] Our global world, through social media, is in the midst of one of the largest transformations we have ever seen.

As a result, we are connecting with one another through social networking sites, online and virtual communities, chat rooms, instant messaging platforms, newsgroups, multiplayer games, wikis, blogs, microblogs, and video-sharing sites. People are establishing and maintaining social relationships and even organizing collective action. In recent years, we have started to see a shift toward a more inclusive global community. The Internet, cyberspace, and virtual and online communities are part of this global evolution. The "Internet has created a generation of people accustomed to finding their own answers, creating their own systems, forming their own new communities."[57] The impact that social networking sites have on society has only just begun to surface.

When people took the streets to protest fraudulent conduct of the presidential election in Iran in June 2009, they had a new tool at their disposal: Twitter. Massive street protests in Egypt spread virally as the tech-savvy demonstrators used TwitPic, Facebook, and YouTube to disseminate videos and photographs. An earthquake in the United Kingdom, the Boston Marathon bombings, the US Airways plane crash into the Hudson River, the Mumbai massacre, and, yes, even Michael Jackson's death are all examples of breaking news via social networking sites. Haiti, a small country located in the Caribbean, was struck by a massive catastrophic earthquake in 2010 with a magnitude of 7.0 and at least fifty-two aftershocks measuring 4.5 or greater on the Richter scale. An estimated three million people were affected by the earthquake, and the Haitian government reported that roughly 230,000 people had died, 300,000 had been injured, and 1,000,000 made homeless. Experts also estimated that at least 250,000 homes and 30,000 commercial business buildings had collapsed or were severely damaged. The global social community came together to support a country in need through the new age communication tools making up social media. US mobile users donated more than $8 million just a day after the earthquake struck via the Haiti earthquake relief text message appeal.[58] The donations were pledged in $10 increments to the Red Cross for Haiti disaster relief, by far the largest outpouring of support via mobile devices in history.[59]

The widespread enthusiasm generated by the status updates on Facebook raised $100,000 and unprecedented awareness. Even more impressive, the donations to the American Red Cross exceeded the total amounts "received in the first 48 hours of both Hurricane Katrina and the 2004 Indian Ocean Tsunami."[60] Today, through the use of Facebook, Twitter, and text messaging, organizations that want to have an effect globally can accomplish this very efficiently. Through retweeting information using Twitter and Facebook "likes," organizations are able to get the word out and drive people to their websites. Instances of global catastrophes can now be supported by any organization simply by posting a series of short videos on a website and setting up a PayPal donation system. These steps allow an organization's consumer base to easily contribute and support the cause at hand. All told, the heart of social media employs an integrative global culture.

More recently, the F5 tornado that struck Moore, Oklahoma, in May 2013 illustrated just how much social media has become integrated within society. An outpouring of support for all who were affected via Twitter came in the form of hashtag identifiers that included "#Oklahoma," "#OKC," and "#PrayforOklahoma."[61] Facebook communities were set up that provided weather alerts, information about resources, and options for the global community to donate time and money. Google helped confirm the safety of tornado survivors, while the Oklahoma Humane Society and reddit users worked together to inform the public of the whereabouts of missing pets.[62] Entire communities of people within the social sphere, ranging from everyday citizens to news anchors, shared powerful images of the catastrophic damage on Instagram.

These events highlight just how important these new communication channels between communities have become. The acceptance of social media as a primary mode of communication is significant because it speaks to the extensive integration of social media into everyday communication. This phenomenon is even apparent from outer space—or, for you social media junkies, "Google Earth"—for all 6.8 billion people who inhabit the earth share one world. The convergence of the Internet allows us to become a single global community by putting everyone online. Our ability to unite together universally has exploded. We work in partnership with people all over the world, from big cities to little villages, from small companies to large corporations—everyone doing their part to enact change. Social media technologies offer a way to direct this massive interconnectivity of networks into real, sound solutions for a number of global concerns including feasible drinking water, improved sanitation, food production, public health, energy challenges, and nearly every other area of need. Whether we are trying to bring an end to racism, educate others on the hazards occurring to the environment, protect our children, or give selflessly amid devastation from an act of nature, the power of social media is greater than all of us.

People connect and technology facilitates these relationships. With these two concepts in mind, we can now look at the numerous tools that permeate the social media landscape.

## Components of Social Media

As you will learn in part III of this book, understanding the primary role for the various avenues of communication via the social web is critical when evaluating when, where, and how to communicate with your consumers.

The landscape of social media is a complex bionetwork of overlapping platforms that vary in use and support communication through networking sites, publishing applications, discussion boards, and mobile applications. In his book *The Social Media Bible*, Lon Safko introduces the idea that the social web has been organized into fifteen categories.[63] Brian Solis pegs this number at twenty-eight categories, which are represented through his graphic pictorial "The Conversation Prism."[64] Both present a thorough explanation of the various tools, communities, and social sites that a company can use to interact with consumers.

Commonalities exist between the categories presented by Safko and Solis. Although it may not seem obvious, a social media model can be extracted from these categories allowing for the development of an organizational social strategy. I would like to introduce such a model for social media planning: the Circular Model of SoMe for Social Communication—*Share, optimize, Manage, engage.* Up to this point, there has yet to be a widely accepted model for social media planning. In keeping with a more simplistic approach to understanding the application of social media planning, the Circular Model of SoMe for Social Communication is based on the fundamentals supporting the *Cluetrain Manifesto* and Grunig's two-way symmetrical model of communication.

The Circular Model of SoMe for Social Communication—Share, optimize, Manage, engage (courtesy of Regina Luttrell)

## Share

Social media through social networks help people connect with others who share similar interests, passions, and beliefs. Organizations that use specific networking strategies wherein their consumers are participating in conversations are able to socialize online together with their targeted populations. Within each of these networking sites a degree of trust is formed between users. These are the users that can become consumer influencers.[65] With 53 percent of the people on Twitter recommending companies or products in their Tweets, and 48 percent of people delivering on their intention to buy the product, sharing the right information within the right category of the social web is extremely important.[66] Astonishingly, 90 percent of online consumers trust recommendations from people they know, and a whopping 70 percent trust opinions of unknown users.[67] Why would a company *not* want to get to know its consumers and influencers?

A sampling of social networking sites considered "sharing" sites include:

- Facebook
- Instagram
- Pinterest
- Myspace
- LinkedIn
- YouTube
- Vimeo
- Flickr
- orkut
- Kaboodle
- Bebo
- hi5

This is certainly not intended to be a comprehensive list of all sharing sites on the social web, but rather to provide an understanding of the types of sites that would be categorized under "share." This list could be further broken into subcategories such as business networking (LinkedIn), photo sharing (Instagram), video (YouTube), or even collaborative consumption (Kaboodle).

## Optimize

To optimize its message, an organization must listen to what is being said and learn from the conversations being shared. Your stakeholders will talk about your brand with or without you. However, the conversations that they have will be much richer if you, as a practitioner, are part of them. Public relations practitioners operate in a new world where people have come to expect transparent communication. It is our job to give them that. Meaningful exchanges filled with substance lead to mutual fulfillment. Tools such as Social Mention allow organizations to track and measure in real time the conversations that are being said about you, your company, products that you offer, and just about any topic being discussed across the web's social media landscape. Social Mention monitors more than one hundred social media sites directly, including Twitter, Facebook, FriendFeed, YouTube, Digg, and Google. There are numerous listening and targeting tools available that allow organizations to collect important metrics: Sprout Social, Meltwater, Sysomos, Radian6, Linkfluence, Spiral16, Klout, and Collective Intellect are a few examples. By simply being informed about what is being said about your organization and on what social networks the conversations are taking place, it will be easier to participate in authentic exchanges between your consumers and your business.

## Manage

Conversations occurring on social sites happen quickly, in a matter of seconds in fact. Consumers have come to expect quick responses and answers from public relations practitioners and social media strategists who manage online presence. Surprisingly, many companies are not prepared for the quick response consumers have come to expect. Responses to consumers are limited by availability of time on any given day, other job responsibilities, and simply the ability to manage the volume of interactions that emanate from a company's various social streams. Many times it is the case that a company simply may not have enough resources to monitor and manage its social presence. All of these factors contribute to slowed responses with consumers.

In 2008, we saw for the first time the term *attention dashboard*. This is described as a tool that pulls in content from various sources across multiple networks into one place in an effort to monitor and manage what is being mentioned on the social web.[68] Today these are better known as *social media dashboards*. TweetDeck and HootSuite are among the most popular and widely used social media monitoring systems on the market. By incorporating these tools within its communications arsenal, a company can stay current with conversations, respond to consumers in real time, send private messages, share links to company news and recently published blog posts, and monitor trending conversations. Tools such as these allow a company to easily engage with consumers, stakeholders, and influencers.

## Engage

Engaging in conversations with your consumers and influencers is the most critical component to a social strategy. The more challenging question to answer might be "Where to engage?"

I equate social strategies to the rush to create websites in the late 1990s. During this period of advancement, nearly every manager approached their public relations practitioner and laid down the decree: "Build us a website!" Naturally, our responses as public relations practitioners were to ask, "What is the purpose of the website? What shall we have on it?" Not surprisingly, without a blink of an eye this nebulous manager would spout back, "I don't know! But everyone else is getting one, so we need one too!"

This exact occurrence is happening again today as it relates to social strategies. In today's workplace, public relations practitioners hear, "Everyone is on Facebook, so go create us a Facebook page!" We have learned that this response simply is not the answer. An organization needs to be where its consumers are. If your consumers are not on Facebook, it does not make sense to waste precious resources targeting an area that will yield very little. With that in mind, it should be obvious that no two social strategies will look the same. Social strategies are unique to each company and each brand. Coca-Cola, for example, does not employ the same strategies and tactics for Coke that it uses for Sprite. The social strategies that work for Panera Bread will not necessarily work for Gerber.

An important takeaway here is that conducting research analysis allows you to understand how to properly measure your company's current presence within the social sphere. These results will make it easier to determine the level of effort put forth and dialogue being discussed regarding your organization or brand on social media platforms. Are your consumers on Twitter? Is Instagram or Pinterest a place where you see your influencers engaging in activity? Does the demographic of your stakeholder base sway toward sites like LinkedIn or Plaxo? Only a thorough analysis will reveal the direction your company should be headed.

There are many tools that assist companies in conducting a social media audit. Public relations professionals can use the chief marketing officer's (CMO) guide to the social media landscape to help break down some of the available social media channels and their impact on specific areas. The document uses a color-coded scale ranking of "good," "OK," and "bad" to assess the effectiveness of customer engagement, search engine optimization (SEO), brand exposure, and web traffic.[69] In the 2013 version the CMO Council focused on Facebook, Google+, Twitter, Pinterest, LinkedIn, and YouTube. Earlier versions include a more comprehensive breakdown of available social networking sites that can be used to conduct a more complete social media audit. The Social Marketing Compass is also useful in helping companies identify where to engage.[70] To use the Social Compass, a company must imagine the brand is at the center and from there all layers radiate outward. The model presents multiple options and directions to help guide companies when assessing brand, players, platform, channels, and emotions.

*The Social Marketing Compass (courtesy of Brian Solis and JESS3)*

## Where Do We Go from Here?

From the humble beginning of a simple email to our robust bionetwork of social platforms, social media has caused a revolution and altered modern public relations. Today, organizations are beginning to understand that on the other side of the web, behind that personal computer, there are *real people*, and they can gain insights into the thoughts, views, and opinions of these *people* in real time simply by listening intently, engaging authentically, and having fun.

---

**#LRNSMPR**

Learn More about the History of Social Media

Quick Links

- What the WELL's Rise and Fall Tell Us about Online Community, http://bit.ly/ZodVjU
- Passages from *The Cluetrain Manifesto*, http://bit.ly/10NVeYb
- A Declaration of the Independence of Cyberspace, http://bit.ly/14sH0co
- History of the Internet, http://bit.ly/16HpgBm
- The Conversation Prism, http://bit.ly/11YNF26
- The Big Brand Theory: Nissan Builds a Car and Its Social Community, http://bit.ly/14HGURS

---

## Theory into Practice

The Truth Campaign[71]

As you read this case study, here are some questions to keep in mind:

1. Can you identify the Circular Model of SoMe for Social Communication?
2. Can you further identify the tactics of SoMe within this campaign?
3. Are there specific social media tools that are used in the truth Campaign that could be beneficial to use in your own organization? How might you best identify which tools would work best?
4. Can you recommend a strategy that the truth Campaign could follow to better understand the user-based metrics for this campaign?

The truth Campaign, an antismoking campaign dedicated to decreasing the use of any tobacco products by young adults and children, is active in all forms of social media as well as the Internet. Tactics include a presence on Twitter, Myspace, Xanga, hi5, and Bebo. The truth website incorporates interactive elements wherein teens can play games, download screensavers and desktop themes, view mini-sites and television advertisements, and have the ability to access fact-based messaging on tobacco use, health hazards, and the prevention of smoking.[72] All of the information provided within these websites is intended to be shared. The organization is creating a global community for youth to feel connected. The utilization of these social networking sites allow teens to access and spread the campaign's messages quickly, thus coming together to take a stand against smoking and tobacco. According to its website, these social networking sites receive a combined total of around sixty thousand visits each week.[73]

The truth Campaign has also successfully integrated Facebook as an additional approach to reaching its target audience. Facebook seems the most comprehensive of all the social networking sites used within this campaign. Visitors to the truth Facebook page have access to numerous features including original television ads, musical remixes of songs from truth commercials, facts regarding tobacco-related issues, and the ability to post comments on "The Wall"—a comment space provided by the site. Visitors are also able to view the truth Campaign pictures, participate in polls about tobacco issues, have access to links and other truth specific Facebook pages and sites, and view a list of upcoming truth events and appearances. Additionally, Facebook users can illustrate their support for truth by adding it as a "cause" on their individual Facebook profiles in the form of a "Twibbon." The truth Facebook application also includes a "Truth or Dare" application loosely based on the party game of the same name. This application allows truth Facebook users the option to challenge their friends to either answer a question about themselves or work some slight mischief on the social networking site.[74] Each challenge completed carries with it a wager amount, giving users the chance to earn points and move up on the "Truth or Dare" leaderboard. This feature tracks scores among the user's friends within any social networks that they are a part of, including all Facebook users.

# Notes

1. Merriam-Webster, *Merriam-Webster's Collegiate Dictionary*, 11th ed. Merriam-Webster, 2013.

2. L. Safko, *The Social Media Bible Tactics, Tools and Strategies for Business Success* (New York: Wiley, 2010); J. Wood, *Interpersonal Communication: Everyday Encounters*, 7th ed. (Boston: Wadsworth Cengage Learning, 2013).

3. Merriam-Webster, *Merriam-Webster's Collegiate Dictionary*.

4. Safko, *The Social Media Bible Tactics*.

5. D. Boyd and N. Ellison, "Social Network Sites: Definition, History, and Scholarship," *Journal of Computer-Mediated Communication*, no. 13 (2008): 210–30. doi:10.1111/j.1083 -6101.2007.00393.x (accessed May 30, 2013); J. Scott and P. Carrington, *The SAGE Handbook of Social Network Analysis* (Thousand Oaks, CA: Sage, 2011).

6. K. Howell, *Share This: The Social Media Handbook for PR Professionals* (West Sussex: Wiley, 2012).

7. Nielson, "State of Social Media: The Social Media Report 2012," accessed May 28, 2013, http://www.nielsen.com/us/en/reports/2012/state-of-the-media-the-social-media -report-2012.html.

8. C. Smith, "DMR Digital Marketing Ramblings," last modified May 26, 2013, accessed May 28, 2013, http://expandedramblings.com/index.php/resource-how-many-people -use-the-top-social-media/.

9. D. Etherington, "Flickr at 10: 1M Photos Shared Per Day, 170% Increase Since Making 1TB Free," *TechCrunch* (2014), retrieved May 2, 2014, from http://techcrunch .com/2014/02/10/flickr-at-10-1m-photos-shared-per-day-170-increase-since-making -1tb-free/.

10. "Twitter Statistics," last modified May 5, 2013, accessed May 29, 2013, http://www .statisticbrain.com/twitter-statistics/.

11. Nielson, "State of Social Media."

12. Nielson, "State of Social Media."

13. Howell, *Share This*.

14. Howell, *Share This*.

15. Howell, *Share This*.

16. Smith, "DMR Digital Marketing Ramblings."

17. E. Qualman, Socialnomics World of Mouth, "Social Media Video 2013," last modified 2013, accessed May 31, 2013, http://www.socialnomics.net/2013/01/01/social-media -video-2013/.

18. "History of Iran: Cyrus the Great," *Iran Chamber Society* (blog), http://www.iran chamber.com/history/cyrus/cyrus.php (accessed May 30, 2013); D. Mink, "The Complete History of Social Media," *Avalaunch Media* (blog), April 15, 2013. http://avalaunchmedia .com/infographics/the-complete-history-of-social-media (accessed May 31, 2013).

19. R. Beyer, *The Greatest Stories Never Told: 100 Tales from History to Astonish, Bewilder, and Stupefy* (New York: HarperCollins, 2003).

20. M. Bellis, About.com, "The Invention of Radio," last modified 2013, accessed May 30, 2013, http://inventors.about.com/od/rstartinventions/a/radio.htm; M. Bellis, About.com, "The History of the Telephone," last modified 2013, accessed May 30, 2013, http://inventors .about.com/od/bstartinventors/a/telephone.htm.

21. I. Peter, "The History of Email," last modified 2004, accessed May 30, 2013, http:// www.nethistory.info/History of the Internet/email.html.

22. Qualman, "Social Media Video 2013."

23. K. Kelly and H. Rheingold, "The Dragon Ate My Homework," *Wired 1*(3).

24. M. Sippey, "Vine: A New Way to Share Video," *Twitter Blog* (blog), January 24, 2013, https://blog.twitter.com/2013/vine-new-way-share-video (accessed May 31, 2013).

25. H. Rheingold, "Howard Rheingold's Story," last modified 2012, accessed June 3, 2013, http://www.rheingold.com/howard/.

26. M. Lucas, A. Singh, and C. Cantrell, "Defining a Firewall," in *Firewall Policies and VPN Configurations*, edited by Anne Henmi (Rockland, MA: Syngress Publishing, 2006).

27. Wood, *Interpersonal Communication*.

28. Qualman, "Social Media Video 2013"; L. Prall, "Sixdegrees.com—Social Networking in Its Infancy," *Afridesignad* (blog), September 15, 2010, http://blog.afridesign.com/2010/09/sixdegrees-com-social-networking-in-its-infancy/ (accessed May 31, 2013).

29. LiveJournal, "Our Heritage," last modified 2012, accessed May 30, 2013, http://www.livejournalinc.com/aboutus.php.

30. Qualman, "Social Media Video 2013."

31. Qualman, "Social Media Video 2013."

32. Qualman, "Social Media Video 2013."

33. Etherington, "Flickr at 10."

34. Qualman, "Social Media Video 2013."

35. "Twitter Statistics."

36. Qualman, "Social Media Video 2013."

37. M. Sippey, "Vine: A New Way to Share Video," *Twitter Blog* (blog), January 24, 2013, https://blog.twitter.com/2013/vine-new-way-share-video (accessed May 31, 2013).

38. F. Turner, *From Counterculture to Cyberculture: Stewart Brand, the Whole Earth Network, and the Rise of Digital Utopianism* (Chicago: University of Chicago Press, 2006).

39. C. Cadwalladr, "Stewart Brand's Whole Earth Catalog, the Book That Changed the World," *The Guardian*, last modified May 4, 2013, accessed June 4, 2013, http://www.guardian.co.uk/books/2013/may/05/stewart-brand-whole-earth-catalog.

40. Prall, "Sixdegrees.com—Social Networking in Its Infancy."

41. LiveJournal, "Our Heritage," last modified 2012, accessed May 30, 2013, http://www.livejournalinc.com/aboutus.php.

42. LiveJournal, "Our Heritage."

43. TED Ideas Worth Spreading, "Howard Rheingold: Digital Community Builder," accessed June 3, 2013, https://www.ted.com/speakers/howard_rheingold.html.

44. Kelly and Rheingold, "The Dragon Ate My Homework."

45. Kelly and Rheingold, "The Dragon Ate My Homework."

46. S. Lee, "BBSDocumentary, An Overview of BBS Programs," last modified 2002, accessed June 6, 2013.

47. K. Kelly, KK*, "Biography," accessed June 4, 2013, http://www.kk.org/biography.php.

48. Cadwalladr, "Stewart Brand's Whole Earth Catalog."

49. R. Luttrell, "Reflections on What Technology Wants," manuscript, California Institute of Integral Studies, 2010.

50. TED Ideas Worth Spreading, "Howard Rheingold: Digital Community Builder."

51. J. P. Barlow, "A Declaration of the Independence of Cyberspace," last modified 1996, accessed June 4, 2013, https://projects.eff.org/~barlow/Declaration-Final.html; Business Dictionary, "Media," accessed May 23, 2013.

52. Edge, "Esther Dyson," accessed June 4, 2013, http://www.edge.org/memberbio/esther_dyson; Electronic Frontier Foundation, last modified 2013, accessed June 4, 2013, https://www.eff.org/press/mentions.

53. Kelly, "Biography."

54. Rick Levine, Christopher Locke, Doc Searls, and David Weinberger, *The Cluetrain Manifesto: The End of Business as Usual* (New York: Basic Books, 2009).

55. Luttrell, "Reflections on What Technology Wants."

56. Philip Slater, *The Chrysalis Effect: The Metamorphosis of Global Culture* (Eastbourne: Sussex Academic Press, 2009).

57. Barlow, "A Declaration of the Independence of Cyberspace."

58. Fox News, "Haiti Text Donations to Red Cross Exceed $8 Million," last modified January 15, 2010, accessed June 4, 2013, http://www.foxnews.com/us/2010/01/15/haiti-text-donations-red-cross-exceed-million/.

59. Associated Press, "Haiti Text Donations to Red Cross Exceed $8 million," published January 15, 2010, retrieved from http://www.foxnews.com/us/2010/01/15/haiti-text-donations-red-cross-exceed-million/; http://www.businessdictionary.com/definition/media.html; Inside Facebook, "Haiti Earthquake Aid Gets Big on Facebook," last modified January 13, 2010, accessed June 4, 2013, http://www.insideFacebook.com/2010/01/13/haiti-earthquake-aid-gets-big-on-Facebook/.

60. Edge, "Esther Dyson."

61. P. Gloviczki, "Social Media's Uses Expanding, as Seen after Oklahoma Tornado," MinnPost, last modified May 13, 2013, accessed June 10, 2013, http://www.minnpost.com/community-voices/2013/05/social-medias-uses-expanding-seen-after-oklahoma-tornado.

62. R. Golijan, "Oklahoma Tornado: How to Find People, Pets," *U.S. News*, last modified May 21, 2013, accessed June 10, 2013.

63. Safko, *The Social Media Bible Tactics*.

64. B. Solis, *Engage: The Complete Guide for Brands and Businesses to Build, Cultivate, and Measure Success in the New Web* (New York: Wiley, 2011).

65. Safko, *The Social Media Bible Tactics*.

66. "Twitter Statistics."

67. "Twitter Statistics."

68. Inside Facebook, "Haiti Earthquake Aid Gets Big on Facebook."

69. Social Media Audit, http://bit.ly/1cl8uJR.

70. Inside Facebook, "Haiti Earthquake Aid Gets Big on Facebook."

71. truth, last modified 2013, accessed June 4, 2013, http://www.thetruth.com/faq/.

72. Solis, *Engage*.

73. Solis, *Engage*.

74. Solis, *Engage*.

## CHAPTER THREE

# STATUS: "IT'S COMPLICATED"

> The relationships between public relations, marketing, and advertising have changed dramatically over the past five years and are increasingly becoming more complicated. This chapter examines the present-day public relations industry and focuses on the relationship between public relations and social media, as well as how social media works with advertising and marketing departments.

## The Field of Public Relations Today

The field of public relations is experiencing its most dramatic paradigm shift to date. Mainstream Internet acceptance has ushered in virtual communities, and with that, the vision of a global village with unprecedented expectations for public relations practitioners to service a new, global audience.[1] As we learned in chapter 1, public relations practitioners in today's digital environment possess a multitude of skills.

The mounting convergence of traditional media platforms in conjunction with new media technologies has created a rich mixed-media environment, promoting communication and even collaboration with an audience through the web.[2] As professionals, we cannot deny that this emerging and evolving form of communication and promotion is advantageous for the professional communicators as well as the consumers we serve.

The roles and relationships between public relations, social media, advertising, and marketing are evolving.

public relations + SoMe = harmony

## The Courtship of Social Media

The field of public relations and the idea of fostering meaningful relationships with stakeholders are synonymous. In fact, the Public Relations Society of America (PRSA) defined public relations as follows: "Public relations is a strategic communication process that builds mutually beneficial relationships between organizations and their publics."[3] Social media is built upon the premise of creating authentic relationships. It is no wonder that the two disciplines integrate so well and are harmonious in nature.

With this in mind, we need to work to better understand why companies are failing at social media. There are certainly numerous reasons for this, but one major contributor to such failure focuses on when an organization attempts to mock or rush the process of developing relationships. Too often the offenders are the advertising and marketing departments. The primary function of advertising is to sell goods and services while the goal of marketing is to achieve the economic objectives of an organization through the processes of promotion, sales, and distribution of products or services.[4] Neither of these two individual disciplines is necessarily designed to foster authentic relationships with their customers.

For example, imagine it is your first day at a new job. You have been shown to your office and completed the initial "walk around" making introductions with your coworkers. You have even attended the Monday Mojo meeting, and now it is lunch time. One of your new coworkers, Jamie, invites you to join her, including others from your department, to go off site for lunch. It is close to the Fourth of July holiday, and everyone is talking about their plans for the long weekend. Jamie begins to talk about the barbeque that she is hosting with family and friends at her home. All of a sudden, you speak up and say, "That sounds like so much fun, Jamie. Do you mind if my family and I come too? I'm happy to bring a side dish."

Placing etiquette aside, can you identify what is wrong with what you just said?

Everything! To begin with, you just met Jamie earlier in the morning. It might even be a stretch to say that you have known Jamie for a total of four hours, and yet you just invited yourself to her family picnic. Socially speaking, this would be considered unacceptable. You have not yet had the time to develop any kind of relationship with Jamie or gained her trust enough to be a part of her barbeque. Additionally, Jamie has not invited you (or your family, for that matter) to the barbeque.

This example parallels the same type of mistakes that various companies make by rolling out poorly thought-out social strategies. It is easy to see why their social media campaigns fail miserably. The organization is essentially barging in on someone's picnic and inviting its family to the table when nobody has even thought of including them.

Users of social media *invite* you into their lives once they feel they have been courted. When a company wishes to connect with its customer base, it should consider the connection as a personal invitation into each of their individual lives. Remember, your customers are human beings. Their reach is greater than your grasp. Listening and conversing over time is how meaningful relationships are built and trust is earned.

### It's All about "Me, Me, Me" in This Relationship

Listening does not mean talking about you all the time. Companies must abandon the "me, me, me" and "I, I, I" philosophy of chatter for a more balanced "you-we" approach. Too often, a company will create a Facebook page or Twitter account to broadcast information about its company and any relevant achievements. There are countless feeds on social networking sites covering information related to new hires, products or services, employee promotions, and long, drawn-out bios on the C-suite executives. This type of information equates to being on a date with a person who is guilty of never listening and continually boasts about their lives and accomplishments. With this in mind, we can all do well to learn a lesson from Red Bull. This company consistently connects with its stakeholders in unique ways. With more than thirty-six million fans on Facebook alone, Red Bull understands the value of establishing a connection. The company's main Facebook page typically posts new material once or twice daily; yet you would be hard pressed to find any posts that include an image of its product. Rather, Red Bull's Facebook page focuses on images and videos of extreme sport athletes that it sponsors.

To take steps toward becoming more successful on a social level, organizations must break the habit of self-promotion. Although this sounds simple, this task can be quite difficult to execute correctly. In part, this is due to the fact that many executives are eager to promote all of the great successes happening within the company. Naturally, these same executives view the company social networking platforms as the place to announce such content to their customer base. This is only partially true. Company social networking sites are established to engage with consumers, not bombard them with how great the company is. If your consumer has followed your business on Twitter, liked the company Facebook page, commented on your blog, or posted a photo of themselves interacting in some way with your brand, they already know how great the company is. It is your job to keep them there by contributing to meaningful conversations. It is the job of the public relations professional and social strategist to understand the role that social plays and to educate executives how to engage with consumers using social sites. Public relations professionals have traditionally been considered a function of management, advising on strategies and coaching about tactics. This perception can now also be applied to social media.

### Mindful Listening in Social Media

Within the social media arena, the basic principles of interpersonal communication come into play. As humans, we "communicate to develop identities, establish and build relationships, coordinate efforts with others, have impact on issues that matter to us, and work out problems and possibilities."[5] Conversing, engaging, and developing relationships with consumers online through a company social site highlight some of the roles that practitioners assume, as well as the channels through which a company or brand can connect with its intended audience.

The concept of listening to stakeholders has been part of the public relations industry for years.[6] Through mindful listening, public relations practitioners build formidable relationships with external stakeholders. To be successful today, we need to continue to listen to these stakeholders for a variety of reasons, all the while mastering the many available assorted tools to glean distinct information.

## SoMe Drives Engagement

The Circular Model of SoMe for Social Communication promotes listening. Companies benefit from real-time insights from consumers because they establish a window into their thoughts, views, feelings, and reactions regarding your brand. Gathering these unaltered opinions that manifest via social networking sites would have been near impossible to obtain prior to the mainstreaming of social media. Because consumers feel comfortable enough to praise or prosecute brands on social networking sites, their opinions can be interpreted as pure. Contributing to the conversation is how a company becomes part of their community. The moment that a company embarks on a social strategy, it is no longer a logo or a tagline or a nebulous presence—it has become human. Users of social media expect genuine, authentic connections; therefore, the responsibility shifts to the brand to deliver.

Social media strategies should not be implemented in seclusion. Social media should be ingrained throughout an organization on every level and deep within every department. This is an important point in that one can see that it makes sense that the marketing and advertising departments need to be part of the social strategy planning process.

> "Many years ago, we recognized the changing communications environment and increasingly heard client demands for integrated solutions." —Dave Senay, FleishmanHillard president and CEO

## Can't We All Just Get Along? The Integration of Public Relations, Social Media, Marketing, and Advertising

Companies are investing time, money, and energy in their social media strategies and are beginning to see the value—therefore, everyone wants to "own" it. The marketing team believes it should lead the strategy, while advertising considers itself as the proper proprietor. Neither is correct. Today, the public relations department should drive social media strategies, aligning synergies between the three. Because of the inherent connection public relations and social media share, it makes sense for public relations departments to lead the social strategy. We, as public relations professionals, are the ones developing the relationships with the consumer base. With that in mind, one might argue that in the not-so-distant future social media will be a department unto itself working harmoniously with public relations, marketing, *and* advertising. Until then, the bulk of the responsibility of social media strategies should be led by public relations.

Distinct differences between public relations, social media, marketing, and advertising have been defined. However, the need to integrate and send a single, clear message via various channels is evident. The 1990s gave rise to terms like *integrated marketing communications, convergent communications,* and *integrated communications.*[7] More recently, we have seen IMPR—integrated marketing public relations.[8] IMPR includes social media strategies and tactics. The idea of integration creates a consistent message. Success can be seen when each field recognizes they complement one another. Each field has strengths, and together these strengths complement and reinforce a comprehensive strategic plan.[9] Choosing the best attributes from each field based on their strengths and weaknesses will result in a synergy throughout the campaign. When all pieces work together, the whole is greater than the sum.

## Market without Selling and Still Be Profitable

By using integrated efforts, a brand can successfully build an online presence that can resonate with the intended consumers. However, this can be tricky to execute, since the social web is made up of people, and a very large group at that, many of whom *don't* want to be sold to. Companies can use social media marketing strategies or content marketing to help strike a balance between the human social networks, while also remembering that it is running a business intended to be profitable. Social media marketing and content marketing are two successful methods being used today.

When implementing a social media marketing strategy, the individual campaigns are managed directly within the social networking sites. Whether Twitter, Pinterest, Facebook, Google+, or whichever social networking site is right for its consumer base, these sites produce content about the brand and run its campaigns there.[10] Content marketing occurs directly on a brand website or a microsite created by the company itself.[11] Social media marketing and content marketing can be implemented simultaneously. The outcomes of each campaign can be quite different based on the specific goals and objectives.

The key principle within both of these strategies is not to sell. According to the 2012 Social Media Report nearly one-third of social media users find ads on social networking sites more annoying than other types of Internet advertisements.[12] Businesses tend to use spokespeople or feature their products and services on their websites or throughout their social networking sites to drive sales. This type of an old-school, outdated advertising/marketing mix will not resonate with the social user.[13] Products and services come second to sharing information, connecting with your online community, and telling your story through genuine interactions with consumers. Creating content that is not about your brand, but rather about the topics your audience is interested in, is the quintessential idea inherent within successful social media marketing and content marketing campaigns. Social media marketing strategies give you the opportunity to "genuinely connect with people in ways and in places where their attention is focused and impressionable, using a human voice."[14]

The Content Marketing Institute compiled more than one hundred successful social media marketing campaigns that can be read in full at http://bit.ly/1c7A7S7. A sampling of some creative campaigns, including some favorites, are highlighted below.

### The Waffle Shop: http://bit.ly/11UpQE0

A restaurant in Pittsburgh, Pennsylvania, broadcasts live-streaming talk shows with its customers. "Open Talk," "CookSpeak," and "Waffle Wopp" each have their own format and are filmed within the restaurant. The Open Talk show invites customers to step up to the stage and talk about anything that is on their minds. Tom Totin, a local Pittsburgh cook, hosts Cook-Speak, on which he delivers an "out-of-the-box" culinary commentary. The Waffle Wopp show is promoted as a teen magazine talk show hosted and produced by Pittsburgh teenagers. While the restaurant does sell waffles, you won't see it selling the waffles on any of its live broadcasts.

### Indium Corp.: http://bit.ly/19e7pTB

A group of sixteen engineers from Indium Corp. developed a blog series titled "From One Engineer to Another." By participating in interactive conversations with their audience, the engineers produce valuable content and videos that resonate with their consumer base. Community members can ask questions on just about any engineering topic—from the Limits of Mixing: A Chocolate Chip Example to The Magic of Engineered Solders.

## Procter & Gamble: http://bit.ly/12UzI5K

BeingGirl.com, a microsite developed by Procter & Gamble (P&G), delivers targeted content to its preteen and teen female audience. Using a colorful and engaging microsite, girls learn about what it is like to be a girl and are provided with a platform for asking questions to experts on any number of topics, from premenstrual syndrome to beauty to their changing bodies. The site even addresses serious topics like confidence and self-esteem, substance abuse, cybersafety, sex and intimacy, and eating disorders. In addition to the microsite, P&G has a fan page on Facebook wherein community users can interact in a more public forum if they wish. But on both the microsite and the Facebook fan page you might be hard pressed to find any overt ads. The conversations may indeed discuss products that P&G sells, but not in the traditional marketing or adverting manner. In a study performed by Forrester Research, P&G found that a microsite like BeingGirl.com was four times more effective than a traditional marketing campaign (see http://bit.ly/1862Gls).

## General Mills: http://bit.ly/1aCEois

The Tablespoon Cooking Community is an interactive website for people passionate about food and entertaining. The site itself gathers first-class content on topics that matter most to its audience and delivers it straight to them, including topics related to Quick Dishes, Taste for Adventure, and Rock UR Party. These categories help community members find content effortlessly in a much more innovative way than traditional websites. Community members can subscribe to the newsletter and even participate in "Table Talk"—a forum that brings members together with General Mills to connect and share recipes, ideas, and learn about the latest trends within the food industry. The Tablespoon Cooking Community also has a presence on Facebook, Pinterest, YouTube, and Twitter to connect in more ways.

In each of these examples, none of the parent companies directly sold their products utilizing these forums. You do not see blatant product pitches, demonstrations, or spokespeople spewing claims. However, what you do see are brands establishing themselves as trusted, friendly resources that are available and accessible via a variety of avenues.

## Why "Or"? Why Not "And"?

The lines of responsibility in the public relations, marketing, and advertising departments across the country have most certainly blurred over the last decade. Social media has thrown a wrench into the neatly assembled silos the communications industry had developed over time. Research has shown us that, generally speaking, in addition to traditional public relations activities, public relations departments oversee blogging, podcast recordings, video creation, social networking site management, mobile marketing, and website development, while marketing departments tend to supervise direct mail marketing, email marketing, advertising efforts, and SEO optimization.[15]

James Collins and Jerry Porras, authors of *Built to Last: Successful Habits of Visionary Companies*, proposed that rather than using an *either/or* philosophy, companies should adopt a *both/and* approach: "A truly visionary company embraces both ends of a continuum: continuity *and* change, conservatism *and* progressiveness, stability *and* revolution, predictability *and* chaos, heritage *and* renewal, fundamentals *and* craziness. *And, and, and.*"[16]

Using the logic behind Collins and Porras's philosophy, a company may ask itself: Why not have *both* the public relations department *and* the marketing department blog? Each department has a great deal of knowledge to share with the social community. Why must a company choose the public relations department *or* the marketing department? They simply do not have to, and that is the point. Sharing resources, coordinating efforts, and offering a consistent and effective message can result in a smoother, more highly integrated effort spanning multiple departments.

I cannot claim that these departments will instantly embrace the ideas presented here, nor can I assert a synchronized effort all the time, but what I can say is that public relations, social media, marketing, and advertising have begun to see the benefits of working together on a single message to achieve corporate objectives.

## Theory into Practice

### Integrating Efforts

In May 2013, Dave Senay, president and CEO of FleishmanHillard, unveiled a newly refreshed corporate brand. The company press release noted,

The new branding reflects the evolution of the leading public relations firm into a fully integrated communications company that provides clients with the world's most complete communications solutions. FleishmanHillard has redefined the boundaries of traditional public relations by becoming channel agnostic, able to solve client business problems by working across paid, earned, shared and owned (PESO) media channels.

Richard Edelman, of Edelman Public Relations, responded to the announcement by commenting,

I agree with Senay's assessment of the convergence of media. I also agree with his recruitment of non-traditional talent. Where we part company is his strategy for becoming a one-stop shop that is as much an ad agency as PR firm. At Edelman, we are going to evolve and expand the remit of the public relations business. The world is moving in our direction. We are not selling to an audience; we are trying to build relationships across the community of stakeholders.

Use the following links to read the full articles, and then assess whether you agree with the views held by FleishmanHillard or Edelman Public Relations.

- Is the communications industry moving toward a "one-stop shop"?
- Should agencies focus on targeted efforts within a specific field?
- How does a company integrate efforts and yet maintain the strengths of each field?
- What are the pros and cons of each approach?

FleishmanHillard Unveils Newly Refreshed Brand, FleishmanHillard, http://bit.ly/19kEZUs

Edelman Public Relations: The New Look of Public Relations—A Dissenting View, http://bit.ly/14kl9Ep

#### #LRNSMPR

Learn More about Social Media Campaigns

Quick Links

Major car companies seem to understand the idea of integrating public relations and social media efforts resulting in successful communication strategies. Watch the following videos and read the trailing article highlighting separate campaigns from Ford, Mercedes, and Nissan.

1. What is common among the three examples?
2. Utilizing the Circular Model of SoMe for Social Communication (**S**hare, **o**ptimize, **M**anage, **e**ngage), identify each stage from the examples provided.
3. Explain how success was achieved as highlighted within each example.

- How Mercedes Benz Successfully Uses Social Media to Engage, http://bit.ly/10AIsiy
- Ford's Jim Farley on the Importance of Putting Your Brand in the Hands of Customers, http://bit.ly/19UTIrY
- The Big Brand Theory: Nissan Builds a Car and Its Social Community, http://bit.ly/14HGURS

## Notes

1. H. Rheingold, *Smart Mobs: The Next Social Revolution* (Cambridge, MA: Basic Books, 2002); S. Fitzgerald and N. Spagnolia, "Four Predictions for PR Practitioners in the New Millennium," *Public Relations Quarterly*, no. 3 (1999): 12–14.

2. J. Pavlik, "Mapping the Consequences of Technology on Public Relations," *Institute of Public Relations* (2009): 2–17; C. A. Platt, "Writing in Public: Pedagogical Uses of Blogging in the Communication Course," *Electronic Journal of Communication*, no. 1 (2010): 1–16.

3. The Public Relations Society of America, "What Is Public Relations? PRSA's Widely Accepted Definition," last modified April 11, 2012, accessed June 19, 2013, http://www.prsa.org/AboutPRSA/PublicRelationsDefined.

4. D. Wilcox, G. Cameron, B. Reber, et al., *THINK Public Relations* (Upper Saddle River, NJ: Pearson Education, 2013).

5. J. Wood, *Interpersonal Communication: Everyday Encounters*, 7th ed. (Boston: Wadsworth Cengage Learning, 2013).

6. Wilcox, Cameron, Reber, et al., *THINK Public Relations*; F. Seitel, *The Practice of Public Relations* (Upper Saddle River, NJ: Pearson Education, 2014).

7. Wilcox, Cameron, Reber, et al., *THINK Public Relations*.

8. G. Giannini, *Marketing Public Relations: A Marketer's Approach to Public Relations and Social Media* (Upper Saddle River, NJ: Prentice Hall, 2009).

9. Wilcox, Cameron, Reber, et al., *THINK Public Relations*.

10. T. Murdock, Content Marketing Institute, "Content Marketing vs. Social Media Marketing: What's the Difference?" last modified February 27, 2012, accessed June 22, 2013, http://contentmarketinginstitute.com/2012/02/content-marketing-vs-social-media -marketing/.

11. Murdock, "Content Marketing vs. Social Media Marketing."

12. Nielson, "State of Social Media: The Social Media Report 2012," accessed May 28, 2013, http://www.nielsen.com/us/en/reports/2012/state-of-the-media-the-social-media -report-2012.html.

13. B. Solis, *Engage: The Complete Guide for Brands and Businesses to Build, Cultivate, and Measure Success in the New Web* (New York: Wiley, 2011).

14. Solis, *Engage*.

15. D. Guth and C. Marsh, *Public Relations: A Values Driven Approach*, 5th ed. (Boston, MA: Pearson Education, 2012).

16. J. Collins and J. Porras, *Built to Last: Successful Habits of Visionary Companies* (New York: HarperCollins, 2004).

**Part II**
# FORMULATING A STRATEGY: SOCIAL MEDIA TOOLS USED BY PUBLIC RELATIONS PRACTITIONERS

# SOCIAL PRESS

Today's practitioner moves in a fast-paced, real-time environment, but that doesn't mean "getting ink" isn't important anymore. It is now even more important to gain journalists' attention between all the media-rich messages they receive on a daily basis. This chapter explores how to break through the clutter and get your message heard by today's journalists, bloggers, and online influencers.

## Ushering a Wave of New(s) Consumers

Gone are the days when the paperboy diligently delivered the morning newspaper before sun-up, and we eagerly read it page by page. No longer do we gather at five in the evening to watch the day's top news stories or turn on the radio to catch a noteworthy broadcast. Today, there are a great number of outlets for Americans to acquire their daily news fix. Online platforms play a pivotal role in how we consume news.

Research indicates that 36 percent of Americans turn to the Internet as a regular source for news. When we include social networking sites, email, mobile devices, and tablets, that number increases to 44 percent.[1] Even more staggering is the recent increase from 9 percent to 19 percent in the number of Americans reporting that they consume news *only* via social networking sites.[2] Traditional media platforms including television, radio, and print have been edging downward over the past decade; however, these media avenues cannot be altogether discounted.[3] This is an important point of distinction.

Despite all the talk about the death of journalism, we do see that journalism is not dying at all. Publishers and journalists are adapting just like the public relations professionals are. News outlets are striving to ensure that the content they produce is relevant for today's audiences.[4] Americans are integrating technology into how they consume news, using both digital and traditional sources at a much faster pace than imagined.[5]

The methods in which Americans interact with news have also morphed. There is large number of people on the Internet at any given moment that we engage in conversations with and talk about what is happening around us. A two-minute advertisement by *The Guardian*, a British newspaper, illustrates just how much of an active role viewers and periodical readers play in responding to news coverage, or, as some may argue, even contribute to the news. The video (http://bit.ly/17dTVlQ) "reimagines the Three Little Pigs as a modern news story, beginning with the Big Bad Wolf's death in a boiling pot and a SWAT team descending on the home of the porcine suspects. *Throughout the video*, reporters chase every twist and turn with help from readers across social media."[6] The commercial brilliantly illustrates the intimate relationship consumers have with news and with those that report the news.

Practitioners should also learn to recognize that anyone can be a publisher or editor. When blogs initially began popping up on the Internet, they changed everything and signaled a paradigm shift. Anyone with access to the Internet could have a voice—and today, millions of people do. Readers regularly publish comments on journalists' articles, tweet views and opinions and debate with one another (and journalists alike) about the coverage, facts, and details of the story. Social media spreads word of mouth at broadband speeds with instantaneous diffusion.

Reporters today must have the capacity to write, be on the air, and both shoot and edit video while interacting and maintaining an online presence. The new reporter, along with consumer-generated news and online influencers, have altered the landscape of media relations. There was a time when public relations practitioners knew, and I mean *really knew*, the reporter who covered their beat—knew they could count on a truth-seeking editor and understood that an honest, unbiased story would run.[7] Americans could rely on three television networks and a handful of dependable, honorable newspapers to deliver the top stories.[8] Today, conglomerates, fragmented media, breaking news in a twenty-four/seven cycle, and the ever-present online platforms dominate media relations protocol.

This unparalleled shift in news reporting, including how Americans obtain news, has had a direct impact on media relations and birthed what has come to be known as "social press." Traditional media relations and social press have become standard job duties for today's public relations practitioner. To penetrate news outlets and reach our audience, we must now build relationships with traditional journalists as well as bloggers, online reporters, administrators, citizen journalists, and new influencers. By following the Circular Model of SoMe for Social Communication (*Share, optimize, Manage, engage*), today's public relations practitioner can thrive in a world inundated with new influencers.

## Community of New Influencers

In today's modernized societies, public relations practitioners are engaging with a different type of media professional. In addition to traditional journalists, practitioners are building formidable and fruitful relationships online at the same time. Not that long ago, public relations pros asked journalists for a "desk-side" meeting or networked at a local after-hours gathering. Today, professionals have the opportunity to instantly engage with a wealth of online influencers through mediums including Twitter, Facebook, LinkedIn, and other powerful blogs and forums. Social networking sites are seen as a way to complement traditional media relations by bringing the relationship between the public relations professional and their contact to life online.

### Influencer Relations

Public relations professionals have been criticized over the years for attempting to apply traditional media relations tactics to online relations. Simply put—these tactics are different. A new set of tools is required in an online world above and beyond the previously accepted conventional tactics and press releases. When we correctly **S**hare, **o**ptimize, **M**onitor, and **e**ngage with an online influencer such as a blogger, or a contact on Twitter, or a forum administrator, we are opening the door to building a successful relationship in the social press world.

### Blogger Relations

It is a predominant opinion in the online community that the blogosphere is fueled by *people*—people who are part of the human network of connections we make on a regular basis.[9] They could be journalists, analysts, experts, or simply writers who are passionate about sharing their views. Similar in nature to pitching traditional journalists, it is critical to get to know bloggers as well. It is extremely important to understand the blogger's focus and point of view, their writing style, how long the person has been blogging, the audience, and even how the blogger prefers to be contacted. These questions are not unlike the ones that you might already utilize when getting to know a traditional journalist. To send a press release to everyone in the newsroom is inappropriate. The same rule of logic is implied in blogger relations: Don't spam bloggers with irrelevant information that has little or nothing to do with their area of expertise.

In 2007 Chris Anderson, editor of Wired Blog Network and the Long Tail, wrote a blog post (http://bit.ly/1bRpBRy) that sent shockwaves throughout the public relations professions, so much so that it still resonates today. He publicly published hundreds of public relations professionals' email addresses after one too many "lazy flacks" bombarded his inbox with irrelevant news.[10] You read that correctly—he *published their email addresses for the world to read.* His post came out of frustration, but it was indeed a strong one. Bloggers are people who want public relations professionals to tell a story that is engaging to their readers and one they want to tell, just like journalists. Engaging genuinely and effectively takes a good deal of practice. Effective blogger relations can be boiled down to two simple rules: Rule No. 1: Follow, listen, interact. Rule No. 2: Be a good storyteller.

*Rule No. 1: Follow, Listen, Interact*

According to Nielsen, bloggers are active across many social media platforms. They are two times more likely to post and comment on consumer-generated video sites like YouTube, and nearly three times more likely to post in message boards and on forums.[11] Finding the right blogger will become critical to a company's overall plan to gain social press, earned media, and awareness. As a rule, "big" does not always mean better in the blogosphere. Search for blogs that are relevant to your company or area of expertise. Find out where your customers are on the web, who they read, and who influences them. If you do not know where to begin searching for this information, use tools like Technorati, Alltop, or Gorkana and search their databases.[12]

Once you identify a list of bloggers who are influential within your company's sector, become knowledgeable, transparent, and trustworthy to them. In essence, begin establishing a relationship with them. This is done through careful exploration of their blogrolls.[13] That means public relations practitioners need to read the blog frequently and comment regularly. The only way to form a solid relationship with a blogger is by understanding him or her. Make sure you link to the blog, even tag the blog in your own company blog, tweet important articles the blogger writes, and participate in their community without the anticipation of being covered.[14] Ultimately, you want to immerse yourself within their blog world. This takes time and patience, but the rewards are bountiful.

### Rule No. 2: Be a Good Storyteller

You must first establish a solid relationship with a blogger before you can tell your story.[15] Public relations professionals have always been storytellers. To effectively tell your story to a blogger, you need to make sure that it is interesting and compelling. Creating videos and offering ebooks, interviews, podcasts, images, or a Pinterest board can help tell your story and grab the blogger's attention.[16] Your content should be genuinely useful and exciting. A "one-size-fits-all" approach will not work with bloggers.

### The Perfect Pitch

Once you have established yourself and your company as part of the blogger's community, pitching your news to them will become easier and easier. Keep in mind, just as in traditional media relations, there are rules. In fact, the rules are similar.

***Personalization*** When pitching to a blogger, address the blogger by name and demonstrate that you've read their blog by injecting a reference to it in your opening sentence.[17] This illustrates that you are interested in what they are writing about, and are taking part in their community because you know them, understand them, value their likes/dislikes, and have a keen appreciation of what types of articles their readers want to hear more about.

***Create an Impact—Softly and with Value*** Bloggers aren't into press releases that include quotes from CEOs, nor are they inclined to respond when asked to write a blog post or beg for a retweet (RT) of a recently published article.[18] What a blogger wants is a compelling story that is truly interesting and connects back to the purpose of the blog.[19] *A story is not worth covering simply because the company we work for thinks it is.* This is a valuable takeaway.

*Brevity*   A whopping 6.7 million people publish blogs on blogging websites, and another twelve million write blogs using their social networks.[20] On average, bloggers write between three to five blog posts each week. Their time is precious, and so the better written and honed your pitch is, the better your chances for a response.

Online influencers permeate the Internet. Twitter, Facebook, and niche forums have become havens of influence within the media world—both online and behind the desk.

## Twitter Relations

Public relations professionals should get in the habit of using Twitter to engage with online influencers rather than simply using it as a network to connect with peers.[21] More than half of all journalists worldwide use Twitter to follow trusted sources and find stories.[22] Twitter has come to play a vital role in how journalists gather and break news, as well as how they locate credible sources that become critical contacts as they are putting a story together. Prior to the social media revolution, journalists relied on wire services to garner important information. Today, they examine their Twitter feeds daily or organize their feeds through tools like HootSuite, allowing an individual to create lists according to topics or people that they follow.[23] With the creation and availability of HootSuite, journalists can essentially create their own newswire services.

Journalists also use the service Twitterfall because it reveals topics that are currently most popular and most discussed at any given moment.[24] One of the most famous Tweets in the United States came from Keith Urbahn, a former chief of staff to Defense Secretary Donald Rumsfeld, when he tweeted, "So I am told by a reputable person they have killed Osama bin Laden. Hot damn." Simply due to the fact that Urbahn is a credible source in this instance, this tweet went viral quickly.[25]

At the end of the day, as public relations practitioners, we need to better understand how to leverage services like Twitter in shaping our news sources and information channels. By referencing the Circular Model of SoMe for Social Communication, identifying influencers can become much more straightforward and simplified than first thought.

- **Share**: Become part of the Twitterverse. Being active in conversations with journalists, bloggers, online influencers, and editors can help you discover who is most relevant in your personal learning network (PLN).

- **o**ptimize: Use your time wisely and refer to your existing media contacts. Look through your media lists, contacts, and stacks of business cards—then take those names and find those professionals on Twitter and other social networking platforms.
- **M**anage: To locate new influencers, use tools like Social Mention or Twitter Search to find influencers who are apropos to you. You can also use lists like those found on Listorious or PeerIndex to help as well.
- **e**ngage: Once you have identified influencers who are pertinent to you or your business, build your relationship beyond Twitter. Refer to their blogs, newspapers, or media that they work for and take part in discussion forums, offer up items you see that may be of interest to them, and connect them with sources. Since a pitch is not generally going to happen over Twitter, but rather through more conventional avenues like email, it is important that you gain their attention. Just because you follow them does not mean they will follow you, so you need to put in twice the effort to make them notice you and for you to become a trusted resource.

### Forum Administrator Relations

Forums, which can also be referred to as message boards, are fertile with audiences that provide quality insights and engagement in conversations specific to that niche group. They are intended to be a place for discussions relevant to a specific topic or industry. These focused conversations are central to the success of an organization's online media relations initiatives plan and should not be overlooked. As with all types of outreach via the Internet, blogosphere, or Twitterverse, persistent engagement within targeted forums is essential prior to a public relations professional pitching an administrator.[26]

Developing a strong online presence with influencers will carry over into traditional media relations. The two are a bridge to one another and are not mutually exclusive. Media relations are still considered a top skill that all public relations practitioners must hone and cultivate.[27]

## Progressive Media Relations

The role of the public relations practitioners is to regularly manage the relationship between their organization and the media, regardless of the medium.[28] The evolution of media communicated through the Internet has led to a compression in publication times and a greater focus on breaking news, neither of which diminishes the job of the reporter or the job of the public relations professional. Each profession still has distinct roles and responsibilities.

(Insights on working with professionals in today's media environment can be seen in an interview available to readers of the print book at http://ginaluttrellphd.com/videos/; electronic readers can use the link embedded in the ebook.)

### *Reporters' Job*

Reporters are tasked with a relatively short list of duties compared with public relations professionals. They must:

- Generate reader interest.
- Objectively tell *all* sides of the story, *not just your company's.*
- Gather information from multiple sources: customers, competitors, analysts.
- Obtain timely, useful information.
- Work under deadline pressure—twenty-four/seven news cycle and second-to-second Tweets.
- Report on a variety of news, which may or may not include your area of expertise, industry, or company.

## Your Job, the Public Relations Practitioner

The responsibility of a public relations practitioner is a bit more complex, but the fruits of building a healthy relationship with journalists, bloggers, or online influencers most often realized through the generation of news coverage, fair reporting, and an enhanced receptivity to pitched stories. We are the middleman, the connector between an organization and the public. Once you establish yourself and your area of expertise, you can become a valuable resource for journalists.

Try to keep the following principles in mind when working with traditional media or hybrid media (indicative of media in their original medium—newspaper, radio, TV), as well as online media formats including websites, blogs, and social networking sites:

- Establish Credibility
  - Get as much information as possible prior to meeting or pitching to journalists.
    - Understand the journalist's interests, and yes, even biases.
    - Become familiar with the journalist's knowledge of the industry. So often, journalists have multiple beats to report on. Your industry may be one of three or four that they cover, and so understanding the depth to which they are familiar with your topic will be important as you build up your relationship with them.
    - Distinguish the media outlet and its audience.
      - Tailor your message to the audience and the journalist. This means you need to do your homework and know the readership and the reporting style of the person you are pitching.
      - Time your message to publication or the journalist's deadlines.
      - Initiate contact if and when appropriate.
    - Distinguish pitches between online influencers and traditional media.
    - Know and respect the journalist's deadline.
  - Determine your agenda.
    - Analyze your audience.
    - Identify your objectives.
    - Identify the key points or messages that you want to promote.
  - Do not wing it!
    - Set time aside prior to meeting any reporter or taking part in an interview to relax and collect your thoughts.
    - Rehearse your key messages. Be sure to support your points with colorful anecdotes and compelling statistics. Keep your responses as jargon free as possible. Your

company may have an acronym for every day of the week, but it does not mean that anyone outside your company understands the meaning. For example, in the telecommunications industry a frequent acronym used is "COW." To the average person, this is an animal, but to a well-versed telecomm person it is a "cell-site on wheels." See how easily one could misinterpret the meaning?

- Do not forget to provide the most important information first!

- Tell the truth: Do not lie, because the truth will eventually reveal itself.[29] You risk ruining your credibility and relationship that you have worked so hard to foster. Public relations practitioners should never withhold bad or negative-leaning information because it can turn into a damaging, negative story quite easily.

- Do not pick a fight: Journalists are neither friends nor enemies; they are professional colleagues. They never forget how to work with public relations professionals, but if you make an interview difficult, they will remember you and may opt not to call on your expert.[30] You need them just as much as they need you.

- Fatal Flaws—Do not succumb!
  o Off the record: There is no such thing! Public relations practitioners and journalists develop healthy, professional relationships over time, but make no mistake, regardless of how friendly you become with the journalist, anything that you say is fair game and can be reported in a story. Take it from Barbara Morgan, the communications director for New York City mayoral candidate, Anthony Weiner. Her comments to a reporter landed her in hot water all over the news and social sphere by calling intern Olivia Nuzzi a myriad of less-than-flattering adjectives. Read the full article: http://nydn.us/16k56uq.
  o "No comment": Makes it look as if the company has something to hide.
  o "Off the cuff": When you speak from the hip, you risk saying an outrageous verbal faux pas. Any person who works with the media must remember that they "are" the company. Regardless of personal feelings, this person represents the

company at all times. Speaking "off the cuff" can get your media representative in quite a bit of hot water and possibly damage the organization's image and brand. It is a good idea to develop a media relations policy for working with the media to ensure that all representatives understand the company's etiquette.[31]

o Do not repeat false statements. Each spoken word during an interview is a sound bite or quote. If the reporter phrases a question negatively or uses undesirable language, and you then repeat the negative wording when responding, your overall message could be interpreted adversely.

o Just the facts: It is okay if you don't have an answer, but get back to the journalist as soon as possible with the information. It is quite common to respond with something like "I don't have those numbers in front of me, but let me find out and I'll get back to you."

o Do not over-answer: Once you have made your point, stop talking. Too often, we are afraid of silence. Avoid filling the silence. Over-answering can lead to "off the cuff" responses, and we all know where those can lead!

o Missing a deadline: The news cycle moves quickly. It is our job to help the journalist meet their deadlines. Your company can easily be looked over when a journalist is on deadline and they cannot reach you for a comment. More often than not, this is becoming common practice in our digital-driven news cycle.

• Devour news! Whether you get your information online, in print, over the airwaves, or on the run via mobile devices, you must always be informed as to what is going on in the world, what stories are trending, and which stories journalists in your industry are reporting on.[32]

• Say "Thank you!" Too often, public relations professionals neglect to send a quick note of appreciation for the reporter's time and the ensuing article.

"I carry my Blackberry and, like an addiction, must check it every few minutes; not to do so can mean missed media opportunities, or worse, a newswire quote which reads, 'couldn't be reached for comment'—which occurred recently when I didn't call a reporter back within an hour. The journalist also expected instant gratification, and when I finally did call back, it had already appeared on more than 80 websites. Is this indeed life today?" —Ronn Torossian, CEO, 5W Public Relations, in Bulldog Reporter (photo courtesy of Ronn Torossian)

## New Tools of the Trade

Connecting with reporters has never been easier. In addition to using social networking sites, there are a number of online tools that public relations professionals have available to help connect them directly with journalists, bloggers, and online influencers.

As an example, HARO (Help a Reporter Out)[33] is a free service that connects reporters looking for sources on articles they are covering. Those who sign up for the service receive three emails daily that include queries from independent writers, freelancers, and mommy bloggers to big media outlets, including the *New York Times* and ABC News. In addition to simply responding to inquiries, the emails can also be used to observe and jump on stories that are currently trending. For example, when gas prices began to rise and people across the United States were seeing $3–$4 per gallon prices for the first time, nearly every query on HARO was seeking experts to comment. I viewed this trend as an opportunity to pitch my local Associated Press (AP) reporter. At the time this was occurring, I happened to be working in the home care industry as a public relations manager. Home care workers were quitting their jobs in droves because their pay did not cover the rising cost of gas prices. The higher cost of gas was specifically impacting their ability to complete their daily tasks. I knew this was not exclusive to my area, so I wrote a pitch email about the fact that this was an issue affecting the home care industry in general. When I called to follow up, the reporter loved the pitch and ran with it. The story appeared in almost every newspaper across the United States. What was even more astonishing was that from this single AP article, the story catapulted to a featured segment on *The Evening News* with Katie Couric. Every public relations professional should have an account with HARO.

Another example of a tool to help connect public relations professionals directly with journalists is Muck Rack.[34] However, this service does have a cost associated with it. Muck Rack is quite popular with journalists and bloggers because the pitches that they receive are short and concise— only three hundred characters long, relevant, and personal based on the reporter's interest and beat.[35] Public relations professionals also travel to this website because they can use it to monitor, pitch, and further develop relationships with journalists and bloggers. Muck Rack does allow users to search by topic, publication, and beat. Additionally, by allowing the user to personalize their account with a set of keywords, the website allows alerts to be set up based on when a story runs regarding its company, industry, or even its competitors.

Subject Line: High Gas Prices Compromise Health Care for Elderly

Mr. Stevens,

I think I may have a story idea with wide appeal that I want to share with you. Everyone is feeling the crunch at the gas station—that's not news. However, fuel prices are having a severe impact on providing home care services to the elderly, disabled, and chronically ill.

The rising cost of fuel is greatly impacting services provided by home care agencies. We have found that agencies are having a difficult time recruiting and retaining workers due to the cost of fuel. To alleviate some of this pressure, a few agencies lease cars, some provide a set reimbursement, some give gas cards or bus passes, but it's not enough to make up for the cost of fuel. Some agencies have received calls from aides that they are stuck on the side of the road—out of gas!

In addition, agencies providing Medicaid took a 35 percent cut in this year's state budget while fuel prices have increased 100 percent in the past couple of years.

Simply put, high fuel prices are affecting access to cost-efficient and patient-preferred home care. Plus, agencies have a difficult time finding aides for referrals in rural areas.

While we are a local association, home care providers across the nation are experiencing the same problems, which is why I feel this story has such wide appeal.

I will be following up in the next day, but please feel free to contact me should you have questions before then.

Sincerely,

Regina Luttrell
Assistant Director, Public Relations and Marketing

## Where Do We Go from Here?

In today's fast-moving business environment wherein breaking news is often tweeted before major news outlets can even broadcast the story, many of the key conversations that we participate in happen in our online communities. It is here that our media influencers reside and where their messages carry an elevated level of importance. For this reason, public relations practitioners must make every effort to ensure they have identified and cultivated a relationship with the correct media influencers in support of their organizational business strategies and objectives. Employers of public relations professionals have already come to expect that they have hired an individual who is bringing substantial knowledge related to these relation management skills, as well as a mastery of the available online tools, in order to effectively communicate and engage within established online communities.

Those public relations professionals that follow the influencer relations guidelines for cultivating relationships will become an invaluable, interactive addition to their organization and open new possibilities and communication channels that were previously unavailable. By choosing not to take place in these conversations, an organization misses out on opportunities to broaden its exposure and promote its brand.

## Theory into Practice

Pitching Journalists via Social Media

*Eight Tips for Successfully Using Social Media in Pitching Journalists from Airfoil Group*

Social networks provide a valuable avenue for pitching journalists, and those who master social techniques often can engage with reporters earlier and more deeply. The communications professionals of Airfoil, based in Detroit and Silicon Valley, have been exceptionally successful in establishing such relationships with journalists and offer their own personal recommendations for ways to incorporate social media into the pitching matrix:

1. Do your homework. Never pitch to a reporter on Twitter unless you are 100 percent sure they would be interested in the story. No public relations professional wants to risk being called out on Twitter for pitching something irrelevant or being annoying.

2. Use social media as a way to easily see whether reporters are writing about topics similar to the one you're pitching. Then offer a fresh perspective or source for a story: "Saw you're into robots, this might be up your alley: Sphero, robotic ball controlled with a swipe #kidsloveit."

3. If you're pitching a reporter via email or phone, mention that you follow them on Twitter, Instagram, or other channels and comment on something they recently posted. Encourage reporters to follow you as well by putting your social channels (as appropriate) in your signature and business cards.

4. Because Twitter can be personal, check to see how the reporter uses it. Most often, reporters are tweeting with the world, but it's good to check on whether they write something like "Personal Twitter" in their bio. Tweet directly to them, rather than using direct messages, because you can only direct message (DM) people who follow you back.

5. Use Twitter sparingly to avoid looking like a spammer. Recommended use is two or three times monthly for pitches, usually only after a reporter is unresponsive via phone or email.

6. Keep pitches short and to the point. For example, "Hey (@reporter)—Have new national consumer survey results on social media behavior/trends + infographic. Interested in an advance?" If they respond that they are interested and provide an email address, email them with the full pitch and a subject line of "Per Twitter" or "Per our Twitter Convo" to better stand out in their inbox. Afterward, respond to their tweet with something like "Great—just sent you an email" to remind them to look.

7. When you already have a relationship with a reporter through email or phone, use social media as a way to maintain and grow your relationship. Talk about anything other than your clients, so the relationship becomes increasingly authentic; this also builds trust. That way, when it comes time to pitch them via social media, it's not so nerve-wracking and doesn't come off transactional.

8. It's a good idea to follow reporters on Twitter for a number of reasons. Reporters tweet a lot about pitches they receive, so it's just useful to see their feedback. They may also call for sources via Twitter. Additionally, Twitter is a good source for discovering what reporters care about in their own lives. Finally, always retweet or tweet about a story that you've worked on with a reporter.

Airfoil maintains offices in Silicon Valley, Detroit, London, and Hong Kong. It is an independent firm specializing in marketing communications and public relations for both emerging and leading technology companies. Connect with Airfoil at www.airfoilgroup.com; Twitter, @airfoilpr; YouTube, http://www.youtube.com/user/airfoilpr; Facebook, https://www.facebook.com/AirfoilPR; and LinkedIn, http://www.linkedin.com/company/20238?trk=tyah.

#### #LRNSMPR

Learn More about Social Press

Quick Links

- Effective Blogger Relations, http://bit.ly/13YJhIZ
- Anatomy of a Great PR Pitch, http://bit.ly/1aDVpYM
- Samsung's Blogger Relations Failure, http://bit.ly/19dlRKK
- Nine Tips for Awesome Blogger Relations, http://bit.ly/1370blN
- Pitching the Perfect Pitch to Bloggers, http://bit.ly/1bgXili
- Using HARO to Create Fresh, Compelling Content, http://bit.ly/15fJ8rr

## Notes

1. T. Rosenstiel, ed., Pew Research Center, "Ideological News Sources: Who Watches and Why. Americans Spending More Time Following the News," 2010, http://www.people-press.org/files/legacy-pdf/652.pdf (accessed July 22, 2013); K. Hampton, L. S. Goulet, L. Rainie, et al., ed., Pew Research Center, "Social Networking Sites and Our Lives: How People's Trust, Personal Relationships, and Civic and Political Involvement Are Connected to Their Use of Social Networking Sites and Other Technologies," 2012, http://www.pewinternet.org/files/old-media/Files/Reports/2011/PIP%20-%20Social%20networking%20sites%20and%20our%20lives.pdf (accessed July 22, 2013).

2. Hampton, Goulet, Rainie, et al., "Social Networking Sites and Our Lives."

3. Rosenstiel, "Ideological News Sources"; Hampton, Goulet, Rainie, et al., "Social Networking Sites and Our Lives."

4. J. Romo, *Share This: The Social Media Handbook for PR Professionals* (West Sussex: Wiley, 2012), chap. 16.

5. Rosenstiel, "Ideological News Sources"; Hampton, Goulet, Rainie, et al., "Social Networking Sites and Our Lives."

6. T. Nudd, "The 10 Best Commercials of 2012," *Adweek*, November 26, 2012, http://www.adweek.com/news/advertising-branding/10-best-commercials-2012-145324?page=1 (accessed July 14, 2013).

7. F. Seitel, *The Practice of Public Relations* (Upper Saddle River, NJ: Pearson Education, 2014).

8. Seitel, *The Practice of Public Relations*.

9. B. Solis, *Engage: The Complete Guide for Brands and Businesses to Build, Cultivate, and Measure Success in the New Web* (New York: Wiley, 2011).

10. C. Anderson, *Sorry PR People: You're Blocked* (blog), October 29, 2007, http://bit .ly/1bRpBRy.

11. Nielsen, "Buzz in the Blogosphere: Millions More Bloggers and Blog Readers," last modified March 8, 2010, accessed July 26, 2013, http://bit.ly/16i9ZC1.

12. Romo, *Share This*.

13. Solis, *Engage*.

14. Solis, *Engage*.

15. A. Parker, *Share This: The Social Media Handbook for PR Professionals* (West Sussex: Wiley, 2012), chap. 15.

16. Solis, *Engage*.

17. R. Johnson, "Pitching the Perfect Pitch to Bloggers," *Hoosier PRSA Blog* (blog), July 12, 2010, http://bit.ly/1bgXi1i.

18. G. Livingston, "Anatomy of a Great PR Pitch," *Geoff Livingston* (blog), September 9, 2010, http://bit.ly/1aDVpYM.

19. Livingston, "Anatomy of a Great PR Pitch"; Johnson, "Pitching the Perfect Pitch to Bloggers"; H. Whaling, "Effective Blogger Relations," *prTini* (blog), September 15, 2010, http://bit.ly/13YJhlZ.

20. Nielsen, "Buzz in the Blogosphere."

21. Parker, *Share This*.

22. G. Macmillan, "How Twitter Won the Social Media Battle for Journalism," *The Wall Social, Marketing, Media: Blogged* (blog), March 5, 2013.

23. H. Hahn, ed., Eurovision, "What Is Good Twitter? The Value of Social Media to Public Service Journalism," 2013, http://bit.ly/15kr5An (accessed July 26, 2013).

24. http://www.twitterfall.com

25. Hahn, "What Is Good Twitter?"; N. Newman, ed., *Reuters Institute for the Study of Journalism* (Oxford: University of Oxford, 2011), s.v. "Mainstream Media and the Distribution of News in the Age of Social Discovery," http://bit.ly/15Qgo7B (accessed July 26, 2013).

26. Romo, *Share This*.

27. Seitel, *The Practice of Public Relations*; D. Wilcox, G. Cameron, B. Reber, and J. Shin, *THINK Public Relations* (Upper Saddle River, NJ: Pearson Education, 2013).

28. Seitel, *The Practice of Public Relations*.

29. Seitel, *The Practice of Public Relations*.

30. Seitel, *The Practice of Public Relations*.

31. Seitel, *The Practice of Public Relations*.

32. Seitel, *The Practice of Public Relations*.

33. http://www.helpareporter.com/.

34. http://www.muckrack.com.

35. http://www.twitterfall.com.

# SHARING EXPERTISE

Corporations create and curate their own content using multiple media platforms. Doing this takes time; doing it effectively takes knowledge, skill, and the right tools. In this chapter, you will learn how to successfully use self-publishing tools to connect with consumers and disseminate your company's message, while concurrently selecting and organizing content.

## Content Reigns Supreme

Journal articles, trade magazines, conferences, and blogs all repeatedly preach the mantra "content is king, content is king, content is king." Bill Gates was the first to introduce this premise to readers in his article titled (appropriately enough) "Content Is King." Gates talks about the impact that the Internet would have on the creation and curation of content and wrote, "One of the exciting things about the Internet is that anyone with a PC and a modem can publish whatever content they can create."[1] This statement foreshadowed today's world: the Internet ushered in a revolution of self-publishing tools and leveled the playing field.

Social media strategies are essential because they provide channels that connect audiences with similar interests, thus enabling dialogue where meaningful relationships can be forged. Information is the key to holding any customer's attention. By developing a solid social strategy and focusing efforts on superior content creation, a business can:

- build long-lasting relationships
- increase a company's social influence
- improve SEO efforts

## Blogs

The general population uses blogs more frequently than any other self-publishing tool. Worldwide, 6.7 million people have more than 181 million blogs. WordPress, Blogger, and Typepad are the most popular blogging platforms because they have easy-to-use, easy-to-understand interfaces that facilitate growth from a novice blogger to pro blogger.[2] Most blogs concentrate on one area of interest, industry, or particular topic. The blogosphere contains everything from "foodie" blogs to "techie" blogs. Maintenance of a blog is generally the responsibility of an individual, a group of individuals, or a corporation. The intent of a blog is to encourage communication by establishing conversations within a community of like-minded people. Interactive in nature, blogs incorporate text with photos, links, and videos allowing the author to paint a complete picture of the topic at hand.[3] Public relations professionals can utilize blogs as a platform to create branded content.

### Corporate Blogging

Corporate blogs can be a blessing and a curse.[4] As with other forms of communication via the social web, corporate blogs provide information about a company through open, two-way communication. They establish a channel that can demonstrate expertise, communicate insights, listen, engage and respond to customers, and promote meaningful conversations about the company and the company principles, values, and vision.[5] Often corporate bloggers become industry experts on the subjects that they support regarding a particular company's services and products. By positioning the blog content properly, corporate bloggers can provide valuable information to all interested parties on a consistent basis. Companies that possess blogs or participate in blogging communities effectively deal with a myriad of issues, including crisis situations, often in the very medium where these topics are first discussed. By participating in these conversations, corporate blogs allow a company to react quickly. If properly executed, blogs are a platform where a company can determine the direction of content.

However, corporate blogs often miss the mark. Only 16 percent of on-line consumers who read corporate blogs trust them.[6] This statistic does not mean that companies should throw in the towel and give up on corporate blogging; rather, it highlights the fact that corporate blogs need to evolve and rethink their strategy.[7] One challenge for a large number of corporate blogs is that, frequently, the content is better suited for a marketing piece. Blogs should place a minimal focus on a company's products, CEO highlights, or boast about the company accomplishments. Generally speaking, corporate blogs that resonate stick to the eighty/twenty rule.[8] That is, they contain content that is relevant to their audience at least 80 percent of the time to increase engagement. The remaining 20 percent is dedicated to content about the company or company products. Blogs that establish a purpose and encompass the larger online community make sense.[9] With that in mind, some disadvantages of corporate blogs do exist and pertain directly to the messenger, messages, and content. A number of discussions focus on who, within the organization, holds the responsibility for blogging.[10] Originally, corporate blogs acted as personal journals. This, in theory, would empower executives to become effective bloggers by allowing their personal voices and important concepts to benefit from personalization.[11] If a company chooses a poor corporate blogger, it could have a negative effect on the blog. That is why there are so few examples of good corporate blogs. Notwithstanding, Southwest Airlines and Dell are two companies that consistently provide excellent corporate blogs.[12]

Nuts about Southwest, the corporate blog maintained by Southwest Airlines, is successful because it has everything to do with its customers and nothing to do with the marketing of the company.[13] The blog is separate from the company website and is maintained by a myriad of bloggers—thirty in all—including employees, customers, and partners. This variety is exactly what makes it unique and effective. The blog embraces the "FunLUVing" attitude of the company, and connects Southwest employees with its community of flyers in a fun, engaging way.[14] Nuts about Southwest provides information ranging from blog posts, videos, social updates, photos, Pinterest boards, and podcasts—all with the user in mind. This simple-to-use platform also incorporated the use of tags that allow users to quickly find the content they want to read or see.

Direct2Dell, the official Dell corporate blog, was launched in 2006 and is one of the oldest business blogs that thrives in its market segment.[15] The intent of the blog is to open the lines of communication between the customers and the company—*to participate in the conversation*. With regular updates, the blog provides a balance of commentary on new products, product releases, consumer services, customer tips, and issues that are relevant to its customers. If we apply the eighty/twenty rule to this blog, it is easy to see why the Direct2Dell blog is effective in promoting conversations with its customer base.

Additional examples of effective corporate blogs include:

- Starbucks: This company embraces the true concepts behind social media, and its blog only tangentially relates to coffee. Rather, Starbucks uses its blog as a worldwide think tank. Customers can submit ideas for new drinks, different food items, and product packaging though the blog. The company then blogs about the proposals put forth by Starbucks customers and allows the readers to grow them through comments and ratings. Some of your favorite items may have come from this consumer-generated blog. In 2013, the company also used its blog to address allegations regarding the treatment of deaf customers in two of its New York City stores.[16]

- Fiskars: Yes, Fiskars scissors has one of the most engaging and loyal blogging communities on the social web. In 2005 the company examined how to connect and communicate with the crafters who used its products. A four-city casting call was issued for crafters possessing big personalities and a passion for crafting. From this search, four outstanding ladies—Stephenie Hamen, Holly Harris, Cheryl Waters, and May Flaum—now lead the corporate blog and are genuine craft ambassadors both online and off. Today they are known as "The Fiskateers." The blog encourages its participants to share crafting ideas and, of course, to use Fiskars products.[17]

- GE Reports: General Electric's corporate blog is a place where community users can immerse themselves in viewing beautiful photography, poetic storytelling, videos, and graphics, all of which illustrate a point. The company describes its blog as a "no-frills way of communicating what's happening" at GE, with the goal of becoming a resource for people who are interested in learning more about the company. Of all the corporate blogs, GE Reports will not only surprise you but possibly educate you as well.[18]

There are many attributes, features, and elements that contribute to the success of corporate blogs. Because blogs provide an opportunity for organizations to talk directly to more than 180 million people at any given moment, ensuring proper maintenance of a company blog is paramount.[19]

**Five Helpful Blogging Tips**

1. Keep blog posts between 250 and 600 words.
2. Brevity counts! Short headlines are key. This allows others to RT important posts. Plus, titles with eight words received a 21 percent higher click-through rate as compared to the average.
3. Take part and encourage conversations. Negative comments can be seen as an opportunity to develop good customer relations.
4. Become part of the blogging community by participating on other blogs.
5. Be authentic. Your online community will see through marketing strategies.

### Getting Started

The decision to initiate a corporate blog should not be taken lightly. It is a long-term communication strategy. It takes time and resources to start a blog, develop the voice of the blog, and build an active community.[20] Many companies are thrilled to launch a blog, but after the initial excitement fades, the corporate blogs often die off. The standard life cycle of a blog is quite dim to begin with. It takes off in the initial week with a flurry of two or three posts, which then decreases to once a week, and then to once a month before being abandoned altogether.[21] When a company decides to embark upon blogging, there are ten simple steps that it needs to first consider.

1. Determine the Blog Team: A blog cannot be sustained by one person alone. It requires a team of people to support the efforts of the blog.[22]
2. Determine the Blog's Purpose: Blogs can be used in a variety of ways, but a company should focus on a short list of purposes for the blog—otherwise the intent can be diminished or confusing. Decide what messages you would like the readers to take

away from your blog. These messages can help build brand awareness, expand reach, encourage loyalty, foster customer satisfaction, increase sales, assist in times of crisis, and cultivate thought leadership.[23]

3. Determine the Blog's Target Audience: The blog's overarching goal will help you establish the target audience. Research the habits of the target audience; do they comment and participate in the online community, or are they lurkers?[24]

4. Determine the Persona and Voice of the Blog: Every blog has a persona and voice. Blogs are not traditional marketing pieces. They are less formal in nature, project a personality, have a distinct point of view, and contain no corporate-speak. Although less formal by nature, blogs need to be well written. The best blogs engage us and make us want to participate in them. It may take time to find a company persona and voice. When starting a blog, ask multiple people at the company to try their hands— human resources, engineers, customer service, product development, customers, and vendors. The individuals that are good bloggers will gravitate to the top, while the others should cease blogging for the company. Every now and then try to incorporate a blog post from a C-suite executive. Their voice should round out the corporate blog.[25]

5. Develop the Meaning for the Blog: Determine the type of content the blog will contain.[26] Create categories that will be covered on a consistent basis. For example, NYC PR Girls has eleven categories that it routinely blogs about, including PRofiles, events, public relations, and life in New York City.[27] How-tos, narratives, lists, and video posts are also often found in successful blogs.

6. Develop an Editorial Calendar for the Blog: Develop an editorial calendar to keep the blog on track, and maintain consistency within the blog.[28] As a rule of thumb, new blogs should post two to three times per week. Adhering to this schedule is partially why many corporate blogs are abandoned. Know what is coming up over the next week, month, and year to help bloggers stay on top of their posts. Michele Linn has created a great tip sheet for establishing editorial calendars: http://bit.ly/13frm4H.

7. Develop a Publication Schedule for the Blog: Editorial calendars are useless without publication schedules. Publication schedules clearly assign deadlines for the final publication date.[29]

8. Develop the Rules for the Blog: All blogs should have rules.[30] These outline the social media guidelines, the types of acceptable posts, as well as the consequences for rule breakers. Provide prospective bloggers clear guidelines from the outset. This will help eliminate confusion for your bloggers and your blog community.

9. Develop a Content Curation Plan for Your Blog: Content curation is one of the hottest buzz phrases in the industry.[31] Beth Kanter defines it best as "the process of sorting through the vast amounts of content on the web and presenting it in a meaningful and organized way around a specific theme."[32] A curator's duties include determining the best content and selecting the most relevant content to share with the online community.

10. Develop a Promotional Plan for Your Blog: Once you push "post," only the people on your team actually know that there is new content available. To grow your blog, you will need to promote it.[33] Keyword searches, RSS feeds, URL shorteners, and status updates on other company social networking sites are some of the most common elements in a promotional plan. Additionally, you can promote your new posts in your email signature or send them out directly to your customer list.

Blogging is an easy channel of communication with your customers, prospects, employees, and general stakeholders, and creation of a blog account is free and simple. Blogs are one of the few platforms whereby you own, create, and curate company- and product-related content. The goal of a blog is in the creation of conversation between the writer and the intended audience via comments. With this in mind, to set aside twenty to thirty minutes each week to promote these conversations is not asking much.[34] Keep in mind that companies can grow their presence on the social web over time through *interaction* and *engagement* with their larger community.

## Evaluate Your Company Blog

Is your company blog effective? You can assess this by taking the time to evaluate it.

Answer the questions below *before* participating in your online community. Save your initial answers to refer to after you have completed your analysis.

Then, objectively, observe and participate in your own company blog for one full week to determine its effectiveness and purpose.

Using the following criteria to addressing the following:*

- What is the blog's title and purpose? Is this clear to an outside audience? It may be clear to insiders, but as a community member this may not be obvious.
- Who are the bloggers? What are their credentials? Are bios on the bloggers evident? Since many company blogs have several bloggers, it is important that the readers know who is writing the blog posts. For example, when Starbucks posts on its blog, the byline reads "Starbucks." However, when the vast majority of bloggers post, readers tend to see something like this: "Posted by Paige D., Digital Community Manager."
- Is there an email or contact section? Community members may want to contact the blog host. Is this information clearly visible?
- How often is the blog updated? What is the regularity of updates?
- Are comments from the blogging community answered? If so, how quickly? If not, why not? This may be an area to address.
- How well is the blog organized? Is the template effective?
- Are the "Blog Policies" clearly stated? Are they easy to find? Are they followed?
- How effective are some of the blog's features (i.e., availability of an RSS feed, available podcasts, external links, photos, videos, social networking sites)?
- Is the language used in the blog appropriate to the forum?
- Does an easily retrievable archive section exist?
- Is the content accurate and appropriate for the blog?

Now that you've examined your own company blog, how did it perform? Compare your original answers with the answers you now have after your week of participation. You may see that changes need to be made, areas need to be enhanced, and issues addressed. This simple task should be performed at least three to four times per year. This will help keep the company blog on task and on message.

---

* K. McGrath and R. Luttrell, "Blog Analysis" (unpublished lecture, College of Saint Rose and Eastern Michigan University, 2013).

## Podcasting

Companies tend to forget the versatility of podcasts when planning their over-all social strategy. Similar to blogs, podcasts are based on content that you own. This means that you have complete control over what you create and share. As with blogs, users should create podcasts with the audience in mind and steer clear of direct marketing of your products. Podcasts allow companies to record seminars, conferences, spotlight customer success anecdotes, invite cohosts, create a monthly talk show, MC roundtable discussions, or feature a panelist of subject-matter experts.[35] With podcasts, the content options are limitless, with creativity as the main driver of valuable content.

To create, edit, and publish podcasts is a straightforward and simple endeavor. The infrastructure necessary to record a podcast is a computer or tablet, a microphone, and great content. Today's computers are pre-assembled with the necessary tools that make creation of a podcast very easy to complete. Podcasts are versatile in format (.m4a, .mp3, .mp4, .mov, .pdf, and .epub), which means that anyone can listen anywhere. The potential reach of a podcast is vast.[36] If your audience is at the gym, walking the dog, or driving to work, they can listen to a podcast. The key to this social chan-nel is that it provides a platform for uninterrupted, quality time with your listeners. As a bonus, subscribing listeners are notified each time that you post new content.[37] Since each podcast has its own distinct RSS feed, many are connected to podcatchers. The intent of podcatchers is to read the RSS feeds and automatically download media files for users to review at their

### Podcasting Statistics*

- More than half of podcast consumers use social networks nearly every day.
- Forty percent of podcast consumers have a household income of at least $75,000 annually.
- Roughly one in five smartphone owners are podcast consumers.
- Approximately one in six Americans listens to podcasts regularly.

* T. Webster, T. Edison Research, "The Podcast Consumer 2012," last modified May 29, 2012, accessed August 7, 2013, http://www.edisonresearch.com/home/archives/2012/05/the-podcast-consumer-2012.php.

convenience.[38] Podcatchers can download audio files in MP3 format, video, newsfeeds, text, and photos. Some podcatchers even move the files to a user's MP3 player automatically, while others download each file to a separate folder. Either way, the delivery of messaging and material directly to each individual listener is a huge benefit of podcasts.

By developing a voice for your company, podcasts can help further develop relationships with your customer base. The key to all social media is the ability to be authentic. The audible word has a much stronger connection with people than the written word. Podcasts allow for an audience to hear the speaker's emotion and connect with their personality.[39] Genuine connections build loyalty. The host must engage the audience and entice them to return. Diction, sincerity, and attitude play a significant role in the creation of a podcast.[40]

Additionally, take time to reward and acknowledge loyal listeners. Often listeners email the host or post their opinions in comment sections. It is important to incorporate these insights into your podcasts on a regular basis. By doing so, trust will be established with the online community and positively affect the company's social presence.[41] Listeners feel a heightened sense of validation when they believe that their contributions matter.

The ability to share a podcast has also never been easier. Their format is embeddable and easy to share within websites and blogs and can be incorporated across all social platforms that the company utilizes.[42] Also, do not forget to upload all completed podcasts onto iTunes. Millions of people search iTunes daily seeking new content, so it is important that your podcast is available to be searched by the larger audience.[43]

## Public Relations and Social Media Podcasts That Resonate

For Immediate Release (FIR),[44] hosted by Neville Hobson and Shel Holtz, is a series of podcasts that focus on topics within communication and public relations. Subscribers can listen to the biweekly podcast "The Hobson and Holtz Report" and learn about the current happenings in the online communication and public relations circles. Hobson and Holtz also interview experts in the technology and organizational communication arena, review popular books on public relations and communication, and offer podcasts from public relations meetings and conferences.

The Public Relations Society of America (PRSA) broadcasts "Voices of Public Relations," a series of podcasts from guest bloggers. Podcast topics include advocacy, media relations, "On the Record . . . Online," and even some case studies. The intent of the PRSA podcast format is to connect public relations professionals with experts in the field.[45]

Business Wire broadcasts the "All Things Press Release" podcast.[46] This is a series of three-minute-or-less podcasts that address FAQs posed to Business Wire editors and account staff. Tips, how-tos, and guidance based on industry experience are discussed courtesy of the Business Wire staff and outside counsel. Many popular podcasts include "How to Write a Good Headline," "Getting Your Press Release into Google News," and "When's the Best Time to Send a Press Release."

The Social Media Marketing podcast, with the Social Media Examiner's Michael Stelzner, is a show that targets marketers and business owners.[47] Each episode reveals effective uses of social media marketing. Example podcasts contain Stelzner's interview with Mari Smith on the latest features Facebook has to offer, as well as an interview with author Jonah Berger on his latest book, *Contagious: Why Things Catch On*.

The Social Pros Podcast: Real People Doing Real Work in Social Media,[48] with creators and hosts Jay Baer, Jeffrey Rohrs, and guest contributor Zena Weist, broadcast thirty- to sixty-minute podcasts that highlight various preeminent social media strategists, FAQ sessions, and specialized "four your information" segments, wherein guests share their insights and thoughts on four questions asked by the host.

The connection that makes these five podcasts unique is that, while the hosts are all experts in their fields, they also all own businesses. Take notice—none of these hosts hawk their wares to their listeners. Through genuine conversations, they produce interesting messages whereby listeners can learn and share with others.

## Internet Radio

Companies can also use an alternate social channel, Internet radio, to promote their brands, and reach audiences with original content. BlogTalkRadio is one such platform that fuses telephones with the Internet.[49] This web-based utility allows users to host live call-in shows similar to traditional radio shows. The only difference is that everything is online. Like most social networking services, Internet radio is free. Users do not require special equipment, and hosting a show is simple. Users access the radio show by logging on to a web portal using a given password. The host reserves a time for the show to air, and via any telephone—land based or mobile—a listener calls a BlogTalkRadio assigned telephone number.[50] Once the show is "live," the listener's phone numbers populate the computer screen, and the host fields the calls with just a click of a mouse.[51] Listeners may also download a podcast version of the show if they are not able to join the live session.

In a business sense, BlogTalkRadio is a tool to connect with customers by answering their questions or seeking their advice in a live format. For example, if you own a cleaning service business, it could benefit the company to produce a weekly live call-in show wherein consumers can have their toughest questions answered. Topics might range from guidance on cleaning to questions to ask when interviewing and hiring a cleaning service. Companies can use the live call-in format as an opportunity for customers to directly connect with the CEO or other C-suite executives. A format such as this provides customers the opportunity to connect more intimately with your brand, thereby further solidifying their relationship with the company. Moreover, a BlogTalkRadio show should complement other social media channels, including the corporate blog. A series of blogs on ethics in public relations would lend itself well to a live call-in show on the same topic. Ultimately, the public relations practitioner and supporting team is responsible to cross promote all social media efforts so that customers can see, hear, and interact on as many platforms as possible.

Hosting live call-in shows have the ability to promote straightforward, genuine dialogue with consumers, employees, venders, the media, and just about every external stakeholder. BlogTalkRadio is a great accompaniment to any social strategy.

## Wikis

Wikis are an exceptionally useful tool for further involving internal and external audiences with your company. Because wikis are so dynamic in nature, they offer users an unprecedented ability to connect with a company. The most widely known wiki is the online encyclopedia Wikipedia; however, a large number of companies already use wikis in conversing with their online communities.

As an example, Ford of Europe sponsors the wiki "Where Are the Joneses?"—a fictional interactive comedy that chronicles the adventures of

Dawn and Ian Jones. The ingenious aspect of this wiki is that the public participates in shaping the storyline and decides what happens to the couple as they travel on their Ford-sponsored European road trip.[52] Episodes of the couple are available on YouTube and are supported by a blog featuring videos from viewers, images, and diary entries written by both the characters and the audience by means of comments. This wiki has been a huge success. The supporting blog logged 141,455 overall visits, with the wiki totaling 15,367 visits during Dawn and Ian's adventures, with an average of fifteen minutes spent on the website per visitor.[53]

Ford is renowned for engagement with its consumer base through the use of original, unique, and innovative methods. The company is adept at establishing close connections between its audience and its brand. The success for "Where Are the Joneses?" stems from this innovative mind-set and approach. Other companies are also taking fresh and original approaches to their wikis. In addition, wikis can be a platform to gather uncensored customer feedback, provide customer service, extend the brand through user-generated experiences, and work to create and sustain knowledge.[54]

## Socializing Business

As organizations move toward a social, integrated way of conducting business, public relations professionals and social media strategists must rethink a customer's journey and relationship with a brand. Blogs, podcasts, and wikis allow customers to engage and interact with brands that they know and trust in ways that move them from passive to active interaction with companies. It is time for a sweeping change, a reorganization of how companies share what they know with their consumers. Adoption of an increased social, integrated customer experience using an evolved communication process will drive companies to better position themselves as being part of the customer's experience with their brands.[55]

**#LRNSMPR**

Learn More about Sharing Expertise

Quick Links

- 40 of the Best Corporate Blogs to Inspire You, http://bit.ly/1c318LO
- Blog Lingo, http://bit.ly/12VxSCB
- Become a Content Curation King, http://www.clickz.com/clickz/column/2104954/content-curation-king
- Throw Out Your Social Media Policies, http://bit.ly/13U8iYl
- Top 10 Social Media Podcast Shows 2013 for Business Owners and Entrepreneurs, http://bit.ly/15bFw68
- PodioBooks give listeners the ability to hear free audiobooks distributed via RSS, much like a podcast, http://podiobooks.com/
- Podcatcher Rundown: A Look at the Top 4 Podcast Apps for iOS, http://bit.ly/1beKV2m

## Theory into Practice

Role Mommy

*Meet Beth Feldman from RoleMommy.com*

Role Mommy is an online community established to inspire, entertain, and inform today's busy moms. Beth Feldman, president and Role Mommy herself, has built her online community from the idea that women do not have to give up their hopes and dreams simply because they decide to have children.

*About Role Mommy*[56]

Beth oversees all of the online content—from movie, television, and book reviews to witty articles and podcasts. She even produces events that feature women who are raising a family while continuing their careers at the top of their fields—from entrepreneurs to authors to fitness gurus and television anchors.

*Social Channels*

Beth maintains a full spectrum of social networking sites, including Twitter, Facebook, and YouTube, which allows her to connect with her audience in meaningful and engaging ways. She complements her communications strategy by incorporating both BlogTalkRadio and a blog that she maintains on her website.

**BlogTalkRadio (http://www.blogtalkradio.com/rolemommy)** Beth's talk radio show provides listeners with the most up-to-date, significant information on popular and effective parenting strategies that one should consider in today's often hectic world. She employs many successful strategies that resonate with her listeners when utilizing a social platform such as this. For example, experts join her on her radio show on a regular basis to discuss topics that interest her listeners, including healthy eating, parenting techniques, and being a mommy on the go. Her listeners also get a peek into the lives of some very famous Role Mommys, like Sandra Lee from the Food Network. Every so often she invites listeners to catch up with her by asking questions and becoming more involved in the Role Mommy community. She keeps the format focused, which keeps her listeners coming back.

**Blog (http://www.thegotomom.tv/)** Beth's blog also complements the needs of her audience by addressing many of the topics important to parents. This allows for a well-rounded experience for the online community. By incorporating multiple social channels within her repertoire, Beth also recognizes that she does not have to do it all by herself. Role Mommy also features four talented contributors to the blog, including Alma Schneider, Susan Hirshman, Lorraine Brock, and Danielle Feigenbaum. Alma addresses healthy habits in the kitchen, Susan focuses on money-related topics, Lorraine teaches other Role Mommys how to get organized, and Danielle is the editor of Role Mommy's deals and giveaway sections.

Individuals who sign up for Beth's social community can do so through an RSS feed, allowing them to receive the most recent blog posts and radio shows. This technique empowers her audience to stay connected to her topics even when they are on the go.

As our society becomes more mobile, consumers now gravitate and desire on-demand content. Blogs, podcasts, and Internet radio shows are excellent social tools that allow businesses to connect with consumers and promote a business. These tools can also go a long way to establish you as a thought leader within your respective industry. Hosting an Internet radio show can nicely complement other social tools due to its relative simplicity and low cost. The right choice of topics can nicely harmonize with the strengths of your company, as well as promote thoughts and ideas that you and your target audience are passionate about. That passion, and the time committed to establishing a deeper connection with your customers, will shine through and provide ample content to share as the use of these tools evolve within your business.

# Notes

1. B. Gates, "Content Is King," *Internet Archive Wayback Machine* (blog), All rights reserved Microsoft Corporation, January 3, 1996, http://www.microsoft.com/billgates/columns/1996essay/essay960103.asp.

2. Nielsen, "Buzz in the Blogosphere: Millions More Bloggers and Blog Readers," last modified March 8, 2010, accessed July 26, 2013, http://bit.ly/16i9ZC1; www.wordpress.com; www.blogger.com; www.typepad.com.

3. L. Safko, *The Social Media Bible: Tactics, Tools and Strategies for Business Success* (New York: Wiley, 2010), chap. 7; E. Terra, "What Is a Podiobook?" *Podiobooker* (blog), September 21, 2012, http://blog.podiobooks.com/frequently-asked-questions/.

4. P. Smudde, "Blogging Ethics and Public Relations: A Proactive and Dialogic Approach," *Public Relations Quarterly* (2005): 34.

5. B. Solis, *Engage: The Complete Guide for Brands and Businesses to Build, Cultivate, and Measure Success in the New Web* (New York: Wiley, 2011).

6. J. Bernoff, ed., Forrester Research, "Time to Rethink Your Corporate Blogging Ideas," 2008, www.forrester.com/marketing/campaign2.1,6538,1946,00.html (accessed August 2, 2013).

7. Solis, *Engage*.

8. E. Robertson, "The 80/20 Rule for Social Media Success," *Marketing of a Different Color* (blog), August 2012, http://www.marketingofadifferentcolor.com/2012/08/the-8020-rule-for-social-media-success/.

9. P. Smudde, "Blogging Ethics and Public Relations: A Proactive and Dialogic Approach," *Public Relations Quarterly* (2005): 34.

10. W. Waddington, *Share This: The Social Media Handbook for PR Professionals* (West Sussex: Wiley, 2012), chap. 11; K. Hanson, "Should the Boss Be Blogging?" *Melcrum Publishing Ltd.* (2006): 6–7.

11. Robertson, "The 80/20 Rule for Social Media Success."

12. Solis, *Engage*; Robertson, "The 80/20 Rule for Social Media Success"; N. Harbison and L. Fisher, "40 of the Best Corporate Blogs to Inspire You," *Ragan's PR Daily* (blog), September 13, 2012, http://www.prdaily.com/Main/Articles/40_of_the_best.

13. www.blogsouthwest.com.

14. Solis, *Engage*.

15. http://dell.to/14dfqUo; Robertson, "The 80/20 Rule for Social Media Success."

16. Starbucks Blog, "Starbucks on Inclusion of Deaf Community," *Starbucks* (blog), July 15, 2013, http://www.starbucks.com/blog/starbucks-on-inclusion-of-deaf-community/1262.

17. http://www.fiskateers.com/.

18. General Electric, "About," last modified 2013, accessed August 5, 2013, http://www.gereports.com/about/.

19. Nielsen, "Buzz in the Blogosphere: Millions More Bloggers and Blog Readers," last modified March 8, 2010, accessed July 26, 2013, http://bit.ly/16i9ZC1.

20. Nielsen, "Buzz in the Blogosphere."

21. Nielsen, "Buzz in the Blogosphere."

22. H. Cohen, "9 Must-Have Elements for Company Blogs," *Content Marketing Institute* (blog), November 24, 2010, http://contentmarketinginstitute.com/2010/11/company-blog -elements/.

23. Solis, *Engage.*

24. W. Waddington, *Share This: The Social Media Handbook for PR Professionals* (West Sussex: Wiley, 2012), chap. 11.

25. Solis, *Engage*; Robertson, "The 80/20 Rule for Social Media Success"; General Electric, "About," last modified 2013, accessed August 5, 2013, http://www.gereports.com/about/.

26. Smudde, "Blogging Ethics and Public Relations."

27. http://nycprgirls.com/.

28. General Electric, "About."

29. General Electric, "About."

30. R. Luttrell, "Throw Out Your Social Media Policies!" *Gina Luttrell PhD* (blog), July 26, 2013, http://ginaluttrellphd.com/2013/07/26/throw-out-your-social-media-policies/.

31. Luttrell, "Throw Out Your Social Media Policies!"

32. B. Kanter, "Content Curation Primer," *Beth's Blog* (blog), October 4, 2011, http://www.bethkanter.org/content-curation-101/.

33. Solis, *Engage*; General Electric, "About."

34. Safko, *The Social Media Bible.*

35. J. Van Orden, "How to Podcast Tutorial IS," last modified 2013, accessed August 7, 2013, http://www.howtopodcasttutorial.com/seven-reasons-to-create-your-own-podcast.htm.

36. C. King, "6 Podcasting Tips from the Pros," *Social Media Examiner* (blog), September 8, 2012, http://www.socialmediaexaminer.com/6-podcasting-tips-from-the-pros/.

37. Safko, *The Social Media Bible.*

38. Terra, "What Is a Podiobook?"

39. Safko, *The Social Media Bible.*

40. Van Orden, "How to Podcast Tutorial IS."

41. Van Orden, "How to Podcast Tutorial IS."

42. Solis, *Engage.*

43. Safko, *The Social Media Bible*, chap. 10.

44. http://forimmediaterelease.biz/index.php.

45. http://podcast.prsa.org/podcast.

46. http://blog.businesswire.com/2009/07/15/all-things-press-release-how-long-does-it -take-to-write-a-press-release/.

47. http://www.socialmediaexaminer.com/category/podcast-episodes/.

48. http://www.convinceandconvert.com/social-pros-podcast/.

49. Staff Writer, "Howard Kurtz—With BlogTalkRadio, the Commentary Universe Expands," *Washington Post*, accessed June 23, 2014, http://www.washingtonpost.com/wp-dyn/content/article/2008/03/23/AR2008032301719.html.

50. www.blogger.com.

51. http://www.imagination.com.

52. http://www.imagination.com/en/our-work/where-are-joneses-ford.

53. http://www.imagination.com/en/our-work/where-are-joneses-ford.

54. K. Colley, *Using Wikis in Marketing and Media Relations* (lecture, Texas Wesleyan University, 2009), http://www.slideshare.net/klcolley/Using-Wikis-in-Marketing-and-Media -Relations.

55. M. Fidelman and D. Hinchliffe, "Rethinking the Customer Journey in a Social World," *Forbes*, November 26, 2012, http://www.forbes.com/sites/markfidelman/2012/11/26/re thinking-the-customer-journey-in-a-social-world/ (accessed August 8, 2013).

56. B. Feldman, "About Role Mommy," *Role Mommy*, last modified 2013, accessed August 1, 2013, http://www.rolemommy.com/about.php.

## CHAPTER SIX

# SOCIAL NETWORKS

In today's digital age, the frequency of individuals using social networking sites to connect with brands they love increases daily. Influencers initiate conversations with other influencers about what's trending, what's hot, what's new, who's who, and where to go for the best sushi. These conversations allow some brands to excel at connecting and resonating with their social users, while other brands flounder in the social web of confusion. This chapter will focus on the top five social networking sites and companies who understand their audience.

## Setting the Stage

On a daily basis, it seems as though we are being introduced to a new social networking site or tool within the social web. Some have staying power, some linger a bit, and some simply fizzle out as quickly as a new one gains traction. Currently, there are hundreds of social networking sites on the social web. This chapter focuses on what we will refer to as the "Big 5"—Facebook, Google+, Twitter, LinkedIn, and Pinterest.

With so many ways to approach and design a brand strategy, it is always beneficial to the success of the strategy to plan ahead. Social media strategies should be synergistic with the overall corporate communications, public relations, and marketing plans. Successful social strategies include elements from every department within the company. A few elements to keep in mind as you begin to design your social media strategy include the following:

- Goal Plan: When companies decide to embark upon a social strategy, including setting up a Facebook fan page, creating a Pinterest board, or initiating a Twitter account, they must first define what they want to achieve. Set clear goals and be sure to consider how this activity fits within the overall communications strategy. You also need to take the time to determine whether your customers utilize the particular social networking site that you plan to launch.

- Content Plan: Formulate a plan for maintenance of your content. Social sites must be maintained or consumers will leave. Your social strategy should outline the frequency that devised content will be uploaded—hourly, daily, weekly, or monthly. Consistency is key; however, posting relevant content is equally important.

- Conversation Plan: Companies must determine the types of conversations that they are seeking to engage with their consumers. It is also helpful to consider any anticipated responses that will materialize. Is an "RT" good enough, or is the expectation to converse back and forth between customers and your brand? Is liking a post on Facebook okay, or does the company want consumers to share the information with their audiences too?

- Operation Plan: Who is going to manage the social site? Planning is always fun, but once the planning is over someone must curate content and maintain the site. Creating protocols, reputation management guidelines, and rules for conduct are all essential.

- Evaluation Plan: As with all public relations planning, the "evaluate" stage is critical. One method of measurement is to record the number of conversation starters. For example, you can track the number of status updates, videos, or links that a company shares to generate conversations. Companies can also track the number of fans, increased fans, likes, and posts generated by fans. Measuring outcomes that correlate with corporate goals and communication goals are also a good way to evaluate the success of a social strategy.

As noted, social strategies should support the overarching goals of the communications plan and those of the company. Any metrics collected should be weighed against those goals to understand the level of success that each initiative has achieved.

## Facebook

With more than one billion people using Facebook and more than 665 million active users daily spending 700 billion minutes on the website each month, Facebook is considered one of the most influential social networking sites in the world.[1] Facebook provides users with the ability to share information and communicate with family and friends, and it promotes openness and connectivity throughout the world. More than seventy billion pieces of content from web links, news stories, blog posts, status updates, photos, and other sources are shared through this platform.[2] Facebook provides a place to not only share information but also interact with it. News organizations, for example, allow people to send their stories directly to their Facebook walls to share with friends. Brands use Facebook to build communities and engage with their consumers in a more personal and meaningful manner. Facebook is also accessible through mobile phones, iPads, and other tablet devices. It makes sense to consider including Facebook in a company's social strategy considering that the average Facebook user is connected to eighty pages, groups, and events.[3]

### Back to Basics

Understanding the fundamentals will go a long way in establishing a strong presence on Facebook. Certain terminology is used frequently, and therefore it is important for public relations professionals and social media strategists to have a firm grasp on the language used and its meaning. A list of the most frequent terms used when referring to Facebook is provided below:[4]

> **Brand Page/Profile**: the official presence of a business, artist, political official, brand, cause, or product where the owner shares information and interacts with fans on Facebook. Pages create a culture that allows businesses to interact and engage with their fans one-on-one.
>
> **EdgeRank**: an algorithm used to determine the content that appears in a person's newsfeed.

**Fan**: a Facebook user who "likes" a corporation's business page.

**Friend**: (v) to add a person as a connection to your personal profile; (n) a personal connection on Facebook.

**Friend List**: an ordered sorting of friends.

**Group**: an organized group of users with a common connection or similar interests—for example, "coworkers" or "family." Groups can be public or private.

**Insights**: the metrics used to analyze the performance of demographic data about the user's audience. Insights also highlight how people see, discover, and respond to posts.

**Like/s**: (v) to become a fan and "like" a business's page or to "like" a comment posted by a friend or business; (n) the number of users who "like" your page.

**Network**: a collection of Facebook users that could be related to a school, location, place of employment, or category such as "engineer," "nurse," or "educator."

**News Feed**: the center column of a user's home page. The news feed is continually updated with status updates, photos, videos, links, likes, and app activity from friends and pages that users follow. This section can be broken down by "top news" or "recent news."

**Personal Profile**: individuals, not businesses, who have an account in which they are able to share information and interact with brands.

**Timeline**: a collection of the photos, stories, and experiences that users or brands post.

## Constructing Your Brand Page on Facebook

Setting up a brand page on Facebook is fairly straightforward and easy to construct. Facebook has very simple and straightforward instructions for novices, which can be found at http://on.fb.me/1c9gVFr. Brand pages offer "Insights" that include statistical data that can be useful in measuring growth. As a company's social strategy develops and matures over time, analytics will become ever more important. Understanding which promotions work, which may need tweaks, and promotional "reach" can be evaluated through Insights.

A brand page also affords a company an additional opportunity to highlight important information that the customers might find important. The company address, telephone number, URL, email address, or other social networking sites that the company is on are all excellent pieces of information that a company should include. The company logo should be the profile photo for your brand page. Purina Dog Chow, Maybelline New York, Adidas, Mattel, and even television shows such as *Downton Abbey* and *Modern Family* are examples of brands that incorporate their logos as their profile photos. This helps reinforce the company brand. A company may also elect to set up customized Facebook landing pages that require users to "Like" the company page before they are able to access certain features. Pier One Imports and Victoria's Secret require users to like their pages before they can receive a coupon during certain promotions.

### Attractive, Interactive, and Fresh

Brand pages should be attractive to your audience and provide enough information to generate interest in your products, services, and company. One of the benefits of a brand page is that it allows for mutual interaction. Set up a photo gallery, update the company status regularly, post videos, share links, and invite consumers to events. Facebook events can be used to promote anything from product demos to Internet shows, community events, and open houses. Invite users to the event so that they can then share it with their friends. This is an excellent technique to generate buzz about upcoming special occasions. Keep content fresh. Write fun, creative posts daily that employ the eighty/twenty rule—also known as the Pareto Rule. Businesses should post content that is relevant to their audience at least 80 percent of the time and content explicitly about the company or products no more than 20 percent of the time.[5] Companies understandably want to make fans aware of their products and services, but it is important to make use of customer stories, photos, video, and other interesting and informative responses when establishing the community.

### Customized URL Address

Custom URLs make it easy to direct people to your brand page. Facebook allows brands to choose a specific URL address. For example, *The Ellen DeGeneres Show* uses https://www.facebook.com/ellentv. Illustrated here, you can see that "ellentv" is the customized portion of the television show's Facebook URL. Companies should use the same username, or a very similar username, on all social networks to reinforce consistency within the brand. Keep it short so that consumers are able to remember it.

## Badges, Widgets, and Apps

Once a user likes a company brand page, a company then has access to that fan on a consistent basis. Badges, widgets, and apps are excellent techniques to connect on a more in-depth level. There are four types of badges for sharing different information. "Profile" badges are used to share profile information, a "Like" badge showcases pages that users have liked, a "Photo" badge shares Facebook photos, and a "Page" badge advertises a company page on Facebook.

Brands will often want to expand the audiences that their Facebook pages reach. Adding third-party widgets from Facebook's App Center allows companies to run contests on their pages, collect data with forms, import external feeds, and customize content through HTML coding.[6] Facebook apps allow for a deeper incorporation into the core Facebook experience and even tap into Facebook algorithms to help reveal the best content for users.[7] Apps fully integrate with Facebook.com, the News Feed, and the notifications—all of which drive traffic and engage users.

## Top Fan Brand Pages

Generating buzz through creative incentives such as "liking" a page or reaching a certain number of "shares" allows fans to become brand advocates. Fans naturally want to engage with brands that resonate with them. By sharing a post or liking a company status update, a fan is promoting your business.

The first priority of a public relations or social media practitioner is to listen to customers and communicate by engaging in conversations with them. Unlike traditional advertising or marketing, employing a Facebook strategy requires a deeper and more meaningful level of interaction. Here are some brands that are building formidable relationships on Facebook:

1. TOMS Shoes: The brand has tapped into its core belief system of the one-to-one principle. It follows the eighty/twenty rule by balancing fan responses and interactions with promoting its products.
2. Domino's Pizza: The brand has created a "Fancentric" experience. Rarely does the company overtly promote its products; rather, it engages its fans with humorous posts that promote

interactivity. Here are two posts that generated hundreds of responses and thousands of likes: "1,2,3,4 I declare a last slice war. #GameOn," and "When has the power of pizza helped you the most? #poweredbypizza."

3. Burberry: A brand that excels at hitting its target market with content that its users want. Elegant, simple, and stylish images present everything fans love about the brand. The company also connects with fans by showcasing past campaigns from previous years.

4. Starbucks: This Facebook brand page includes photos and updates from local stores. The company connects with fans by illuminating the intimacy of friends enjoying the coffee experience together.

5. Ford: The brand excels at having meaningful conversations with fans. The company promotes content that highlights the history of the Model T to Ford enthusiasts of today. Fans can download wallpaper or earn badges to declare their allegiance to their favorite Ford car—the Mondeo, Mustang, and even the Escort.

Facebook may currently dominate the social connectivity market in terms of popularity and familiarity, but Google+ is making headway in establishing its own sizeable global audience as well. In the two years since Google+ was introduced, it has surpassed both YouTube and Twitter in becoming the second largest social platform that hosts active users.[8]

## Google+

What is becoming quite apparent to public relations practitioners is that Google+'s network is far reaching and incredibly valuable. This growing social networking site currently has 359 million monthly active users and reported 33 percent overall growth from June 2012 to March 2013.[9] It should be noted that during this time of immense growth, Google+ did incorporate a number of exceptional features that aided in further distinguishing the user experience from that of Facebook.

### The Venn Connections

Among the many distinguishable features, Google+ boasts the ability to separate friends from "friends." Facebook does not truly allow a user to separate their personal life from their professional life, nor the brands that they connect with online. One may argue that the Facebook "lists" feature accomplishes this, but it simply is not so. Mothers, brothers, sisters, and cousins are "friends" and comingle with coworkers, bosses, neighbors, the book club, and the brands that one follows and enjoys. Ultimately, the major differences between Facebook and Google+ boil down to these two principles:

1. **Facebook** centers on connecting a user with existing "friends" and the user's relationships with them, lumping all people into a single group.
2. **Google+** helps users build new connections, find interesting people, and discover personalized content, while at the same time keeping connections separate yet equal.

A key differentiator for Google+ is the introduction of "circles" as a way to revolutionize online connections. Google+ empowers users to create their own customizable circles of connections, and group them depending on the specific relationship that the user has with the particular person, group, or entity. For example, a user could create a circle of family members, a circle of friends, coworkers, other public relations professionals, journalists, or even cupcake enthusiasts. This feature becomes an excellent asset when promoting a brand. Not all brands have the same type of consumer. A company can now create various circles based on its consumers' buying habits, needs, and affinity with the brand. Brands can post content to one circle or to all of the circles that they manage. Google has even introduced the "+1" button. This feature is based on the premise that consumers turn to friends and family when making decisions.

### The Power of +1 and Search

The +1 button combines the power of personal recommendations with the influence that Google offers. Recommendations with +1 appear on websites, display ads, search ads, Google Search results, and now Google+ pages. This facilitates easy integration across all of Google's platforms and services, including Google Search, Gmail, and YouTube.

Since Google was built on the power of search, it should not be a surprise that Google+ also has a built-in search feature and ranking ability. Google can more easily monitor who has a real profile versus one that may be representing a spammer. For public relations professionals and social media strategists, the ability to pull data and analytics from these rankings provides a brand with the power to create strong and formidable Google+ campaign.

### Let's All Hang Out!

Another inventive feature within Google+, Google Hangout, allows brands to essentially "hang out" with users in real time. This is a function that has not easily been available on any platform. Facebook currently offers video chat functionality through a partnership with Skype, but this is only available for one-on-one calls. In comparison, Google Hangouts allows up to fifteen people to converse at once and opens the viewing for as many people as the host allows. Connecting with consumers is simple since downloads are not necessary to use the Hangout feature. It can be launched directly from a user's Gmail account as well as from a Google+ page. Hangouts can be aired in real time or saved to a company YouTube channel for viewing at a later date. A Los Angeles–based digital publishing platform for cooking enthusiasts, BakeSpace, is an example of a Google+ success story. The company has more than 360,000 people in its circles on Google+ and has hosted approximately forty Hangouts with topics varying from tutorials on cupcake decorating to conversations with the founders of Chameleon Cold-Brew Coffee.[10]

### Google+ Pages with Power

As with any social media platform or tool, some brands have adopted Google+ with a greater degree of success. Connecting to customers using Google+'s features tends to humanize the brand, make it more accessible to consumers, and have long-lasting effects. Here are two stellar examples:[11]

- **H&M**: Heralded as the "poster child" for Google+, the clothing store responds to and shares posts from followers to build an ongoing dialogue that keeps its customer base engaged. The company consistently posts content that focuses on inspirational fashion motifs that include videos and images. It invites followers to share their personal experiences and truly values their feedback and opinions. On average, H&M achieves seventy-two +1s per post, eleven reshares, and twenty-two comments. The most popular posts to date involve the brand's top collections by

Victoria Beckham, Versace, and Marni. Google reported that H&M's AdWords campaigns increased by 22 percent due in part to its Google+ social extensions.

- **Cadbury**: The company has made social central to its overall promotions strategy. On Google+, daily updates are posted that keep fans engaged by asking questions and sending teasers about new products. Cadbury uses Google Hangouts regularly for celebrating events, including the milestone of reaching five hundred thousand followers and hanging out with Cadbury's Olympic brand ambassador Rebecca Adlington.

Google+ empowers both the company and the consumer to share their interests through their stories, recommendations, opinions, and relationships, all of which contribute to make the social sphere better.

Another social tool, Twitter, is often incorporated into a social strategy because it is a great way to start a conversation with your target market and build and manage connections with customers, prospects, bloggers, and a myriad of other influencers.

## Twitter

Launched in 2006, Twitter is a powerhouse in the social sphere. People clamor to connect with one another, update their status, learn about new products, share ideas, and create connections on Twitter. Since 42 percent of Twitter users follow various brands or companies using this social tool, it is certainly time for brands to take action.[12] With more than five hundred million active users sending more than four hundred million tweets per day, Twitter has become a crucial social media tool.[13] Businesses, both big and small, use Twitter for a variety of reasons, including lead generation, customer service, and even competitive intelligence. The rationale for introducing Twitter within the social strategy will vary based on individual company goals and outcomes.

Twitter is known as a "microblogging" service, meaning users can post short updates constrained to 140 or fewer characters. Originally intended to be compatible with mobile phones and texting, the creators of Twitter limited how much an individual could write. Today, the 140-character limit is a signature feature allowing for concise information to be shared.

## ABCs and 123s of Twitter

Paralleling other social networks, Twitter also uses a set of common terms, symbols, and language—often dictating how users behave. There are ten key terms that all Twitter users should know:[14]

**Twitter Handle** is an individual's or entity's username. This is the name used to represent an individual or a company on Twitter. For example, Edelman, the world's largest public relations firm, tweets from the Twitter handle @EdelmanPR.

**The @ symbol** is probably the most common symbol used on Twitter. This signifies that you are commenting or conversing with another Twitter user directly. For example, "@McLean_ Don @RGA gotta say @HVSVN was pretty clever! Not surprised if we see more moves like this" indicates that the Twitter user is speaking directly with the people who tweet under the Twitter handles @McLean_Don, @RGA, and @HVSVN. Messages that are tweeted to other users will show up in their Twitter feed and in their "@" connections.

**RT** stands for "retweet." When a user RTs a fellow user's tweet, it is essentially like forwarding that tweet to all of the people in their Twitter stream. In business, RTs spread the information that a company wants to share with others, including links to articles, blogs, newspapers, websites, journals, contests, and coupons. When retweeting, a user should always credit the original user. For example, that would look like "RT via @eharrisondotorg Check out the Peer-to-Peer Learning Handbook by @**hrhein gold** & self-organizers with the #**Peeragogy**.org project http:// peeragogy.org." If you simply click the retweet button, this will happen instantly. Users can also "favor" tweets, which is similar to "liking" a Facebook status update.

**The # hashtag** is one of the most valuable assets that a Twitter user possesses. Twitter uses hashtags to aggregate a conversation surrounding an event, topic, or theme. For example, this book uses #LRNSMPR to share links about social media and public relations. Hashtags are created by combining the "#" with a word, phrase, or acronym. When a tweet is sent using a hashtag, it then becomes searchable.

**DM** stands for "direct message." These are private messages from one Twitter user to another. A DM can only be sent if both Twitter users follow one another.

**Status Update** is a Tweet.

**Twitter Stream** is a list of a user's real-time Twitter updates.

**Twitter Chat** is an event that is held entirely online and is intended as a forum for people to exchange ideas and discuss a specific topic. Twitter users connect with other like-minded Twitter users. Twitter chats are casual events that do not need a registration and are generally organized by an individual or small group, an organization, or company. The intention of any Twitter chat is to be educational and informative. Twitter chats are not forums to promote products or sell your wares. A popular Twitter chat among public relations professionals and public relations students is #PRStudChat. This event is designed to bring together public relations students, professionals, and educators for energetic conversations surrounding the public relations industry and to provide opportunities for learning, networking, and mentoring relationships. Monthly charts are organized by cofounders Deirdre Breakenridge (@dbreakenridge) and Valerie Simon (@valeriesimon).

**Twitter Lists** is a curated group of Twitter users that is organized by the commonalities among its participants. Lists help individuals and companies organize their followers into categories or groups. This allows a user to easily view tweets from a specific group without having to scan your entire feed.

**URL Shorteners** are used by Twitter users who need to shorten links and share them due to the 140-character limit. The most frequently used shorteners include Bitly (www.bitly.com), Google URL shortener (http://goo.gl/), and TinyURL (www.tinyurl.com).

## The Business of Twitter

There are numerous lists available that iterate the ways in which businesses are using Twitter to connect, and yes, even monetize their strategies. Just when we thought the Top Twenty-One Twitter Tips from *Forbes* could not be outdone, the experts at MonetizePros came up with 101 Ways to

Monetize Twitter.[15] Whether a company pulls ideas from the top five tips or the top one hundred, public relations practitioners should encourage their companies to share their expertise by tweeting useful resources, insightful ideas, and helpful tips that will ultimately benefit their followers. Establishing company representatives as leaders within an industry is common in public relations. Tweeting company resources, including white papers, blogs, or ebooks, is an excellent way to illustrate that a company representative is a thought leader. It is important to understand that following social media strategies and connecting with others on the social web is not just about your company. Take the time and commit the effort in making sure to link other resources within communications to your consumer base beyond those only written by the company.

Within the business realm, it is important to remember that using Twitter is more than merely tweeting content. A company Twitter page is like any other piece of collateral. It must be branded. The first thing a company should do when initiating a Twitter handle is to upload an image as the profile picture that represents the company and what the company has to say. Many companies opt to use a branded logo. Some small businesses or sole proprietors opt to use a photo of the person who maintains the Twitter account. Regardless of the image that is chosen, it should represent the professional image of the company. The profile background and header image should blend together well, since they also represent the brand. You want to make it easy for users to find what they are seeking when they search for you or your company on Twitter. It is important to detail your real name and location or the name of your company and where it is headquartered. Finally, write the best, most succinct bio that you possibly can. What captures your company attitude? Companies should have fun and be creative when writing the 160-character biography. Some companies include other Twitter handles managed by the company and even Twitter chats that the company hosts. The Coca-Cola Company, for example, has distinct accounts for specific products and independent channels. Twitter users who follow @CocaColaCo can learn about what's happening within the company itself. Those who follow @CocaColaZero can get the latest updates on their favorite soda, while users who follow @WorldofCocaCola can experience the story of the company, interact with the Coca-Cola polar bear, and learn more about the more than one hundred flavors the company offers throughout the globe.

Managing a company brand on Twitter is fairly straightforward and is accomplished by monitoring what is happening with your brand and what is going on within your industry. Staying abreast of the conversations on Twitter help brands connect more intimately with their customers, while at the same time eliminating surprises including disgruntled customers or faulty products. When a company appoints an individual to manage the Twitter account, that person should be knowledgeable, a good listener, and trustworthy.[16] Twitter is not an advertisement, marketing campaign, or fad. Any company that enacts a Twitter strategy would benefit from appointing individuals that it trusts completely with its brand reputation, since Twitter users expect to interact with a real person. Twitter accounts that are abandoned are not seen as credible in the eyes of the larger online community. Cheerios (@cheerios), for example, lacks sustainability. The company Twitter account goes days, even months, without sending a Tweet.

## Bonding with Followers

The value of any interaction on social media is the conversation and relationship that is cultivated with real people and real customers. Using Twitter, there are plenty of ways to interact with your customers and engage in meaningful conversations.

- Special offers and coupons are often used. Companies can easily tweet exclusive offers to their followers. A benefit of using Twitter to support this strategy is when the offer is compelling enough; the follower will not only redeem the offer but also share it with their followers. A good habit to get into is to link back to a company landing page where customers can download the coupon, ebook, or free code to the latest webinar the company has hosted. When companies steer customers back to a specified webpage, they create an opportunity to expose customers to the company website, where they may be inclined to look at other products or make purchases on other products.
- Customer service is often an avenue of connection on Twitter. When customers have questions for the company, they rely on Twitter. When customers have complaints, they rely on Twitter. Simply Measured conducted a study that showed that 99 percent of brands are on Twitter, and 30 percent of them have a dedicated customer service Twitter handle to where they respond to customer interactions.[17] One of the leading brands supporting

excellent customer service via Twitter is the team at Nike. They monitor the @NikeSupport Twitter handle, where their sole purpose is to respond to customers who need help. They boast a 73 percent response rate, which is three times higher than the closest brand.

- Team recruitment isn't saved for LinkedIn alone. Recruiting and hiring managers turn to Twitter to post open positions, leverage their network of followers, and view potential employee profiles.
- Philanthropic endeavors permeate the social sphere on Twitter. Twitter has been used to raise hundreds of thousands of dollars for charities and benevolent causes. In addition, Twitter has been a critical component to spread awareness about social issues. For example, the world came together to globally support the complex struggles of the Egyptian and Libyan populations using Twitter.

The key here is to take a look around the next time you wonder what you should tweet. Is there anything of note happening in the office that your customers may want to see? Maybe you could share a sneak peek at the latest photo shoot or the guest speaker who is spending a day at the office. Simply pull out that smartphone, snap a photo, and tweet it. Perhaps your company has an upcoming conference or webinar it is hosting—tweet the link to that event out. Tweet the latest blog post that the company wrote. You could also post a link to another industry leader's content that your customers may find relevant. Finally, and especially important in building brand awareness, just chat with your network. After all, Twitter is "a real-time information network that connects you to the latest information about what you find interesting."[18]

As consumers continue to flock to the social sphere in droves, so are businesses and brands, because it has been demonstrated time and again that these sites drive traffic, increase authentic engagement, and build brand loyalty. The changes LinkedIn implemented over the past year created more opportunities for businesses to launch a brand page, and the results are paying off.

## LinkedIn

An astonishing 225 million professionals are following more than 1.9 million companies on the professional social networking site LinkedIn.[19] This social network boasts 65.5 million unique monthly US visitors and 178.4 million visitors globally.[20] If you look a bit closer at these statistics, professionals are signing up on LinkedIn at a rate of approximately two new members per second.[21] This makes LinkedIn the world's largest professional social network. Creating a company profile with a company page on this network just makes sense.

Professionals come to LinkedIn for a variety of reasons. Some are looking for a new job, while others join groups to network with. The makeup of a LinkedIn member includes individuals spanning numerous sectors including employees, potential customers, purchasing managers, clients, and users who are simply interested in observing what is going on in industries in which they have an interest. LinkedIn members typically follow companies to keep abreast of new developments, compare products and services, track potential business opportunities, and keep a lookout for job openings. When members want to know more about a company, they seek out company pages and access specific profiles.

### Central to the Brand

Businesses should consider their company pages as anchors within LinkedIn. It is the first place a member lands to see company status updates, the latest blog post written by thought leaders within the business, Twitter updates, and special offers, and to network with other professionals. Company pages bring life to a brand, reveal the human side of a business, and reach millions of professionals through word-of-mouth recommendations. Businesses can manage and measure all facets of the company brand on LinkedIn, including product brands and the employment brands. There are four tabs on every company page on LinkedIn: overview, careers, products, and insights.

*Overview Tab*

The overview tab is akin to a front receptionist in a typical brick-and-mortar business. A receptionist will often greet visitors and make them feel welcome. A company page should accomplish the same goal. This is the first impression that a newcomer will have of your business. A high-level overview of the company should be included on the overview tab along with a cover image that represents the company and brand. Be mindful of how the company description is written and the images used to represent the company. Any written text and photography should be consistent with the company's brand position across multiple channels. Unilever (http://www

.linkedin.com/company/unilever) has a created a strong image that represents not only some of the brands that it sells but also its people, philanthropy efforts, and followers. The overview tab gives members the opportunity to connect with a company on various levels:

- Follow the company to stay abreast of significant developments, updates, employment opportunities, and landmark events.
- Access the latest news through the company Twitter feeds and blog posts.
- Connect with employees of the company.
- Access essential data on the company.
- View the "employee statistics" area to gain a better understanding of the company makeup. There is no better ambassador to a company than its own employees. Connecting with employees humanizes a company.

**Get Inspired**

Five Steps to a Successful Company Page on LinkedIn

1. *Creativity*: Be creative with how you present your company. Upload an image that welcomes visitors to the company page and reinforces the presence of the brand. Create and share videos that resonate with your target audience. Members are more likely to share information that they think their sphere of influence will appreciate.
2. *Conversation Starters*: Post regular updates that spark conversations with members.
3. *Share with Others*: Share all of your status updates and encourage members within your company to add the company page to their personal profiles. It should become common practice for employees to "like" and "share" the content published on the company page. Sharing drives traffic to the company page and increases the number of people who see your content updates.
4. *Show Off a Little*: Add your product or services so that LinkedIn members can see what you have to offer. Include recommendations to further highlight the reasons why your products and services are special.
5. *Extend Your Reach*: Feature relevant groups to reach a broader audience.

The feed on LinkedIn is a company's way of communicating important messages to its audience. Some businesses are more effective than others at using images to tell their stories, providing rich content, writing compelling status updates, and engaging in meaningful dialogue with their target audience. Walt Disney (http://lnkd.in/WaltDisney), Xactly (http://lnkd .in/xactly), IT Media Group (http://lnkd.in/ITMediaGroup), and Adobe (http://lnkd.in/adobe) are among the few that understand the best practices for creating an effective company page.

*Careers Tab*

Premium careers pages, a paid subscription section within LinkedIn, allow businesses to promote general job opportunities as well as post specific jobs that target candidates using an automated job matching system. It also allows a company to highlight awards, showcase the company's best employees, and even determine various career paths available within the company. Customized modules like this help complete the corporate story by providing a company with an opportunity to share the mission, vision, and goals.

*Products Tab*

The company products tab is particularly important because it accomplishes three goals: (1) the tab enables a business to showcase its best products and services to a highly targeted audience; (2) the tab creates a place to feature product recommendations; and (3) the tab facilitates meaningful conversations with current and prospective customers.

It would be prudent for a business to take advantage of the features provided within this tab. One such feature allows a company to capture the significant features of its products by incorporating powerful images and video clips that promote interactivity. Some businesses also include the contact details of the people behind the products in case members would like to connect directly with a designer or simply decide to learn more, buy a product, or contract with a company for work. Companies that understand how to connect with their members on LinkedIn create personalized content that is geared toward that specific target market. Using this technique, companies retain the ability to show different content to different members based on their preferences and needs. Currently, LinkedIn offers users up to thirty specific audience segments (based on date), including segmentation by industry, geography, company size, and more. Companies need to capitalize on the fact that recommendations from family, friends, and peers are greatly influential in our decision-making process.[22] By featuring recommendations from trusted third-party entities, organizations, or LinkedIn members, companies can potentially benefit from these influences related to specific products or brands.

*Insights Tab*

Analytics are invaluable to all social media strategies. Analytics are how most public relations professionals and social media strategists track the successes and failures of their campaigns. Each LinkedIn company page is outfitted with an insights tab that is only visible to administrators. Company administrators can analyze the number of visits to their company pages and the demographics of followers, and they track new followers, see which areas have the most hits, and monitor overall page growth. Using these analytics, administrators can easily populate graphs allowing insights regarding traffic, user-pattern page clicks, likes, comments, shares, and percentages related to a number of valuable metrics.

### LinkedIn Lingo

LinkedIn is a social networking site dedicated to professionals and businesses alike. The following glossary of commonly used terms is provided to help ground users with the LinkedIn lingo.

**1st Degree Connections:** These are users that you choose to connect with personally. In general, these are the individuals that you have established a personal relationship with prior to connecting on LinkedIn. These can be school-related connections, previous colleagues, or personal friends.

**2nd Degree Connections:** A contact of a 1st degree connection.

**3rd Degree Connections:** A contact of a 2nd degree connection.

**Activity Broadcasts:** Content that appears on the Activity Feed and that is visible for other users to see and comment on. This section can be edited.

**Activity Feed:** This feature of LinkedIn displays the current activity of any of your connections—generally other users or groups that you are a

*(continued)*

**LinkedIn Lingo (*continued*)**

part of. This would also include activities related to joining or starting groups, comments that you have made, changes to your profile, and application downloads.

**Anonymous Viewers:** A LinkedIn member who has chosen to keep part or all of their profile private.

**Applications:** Applications allow members to integrate other social media networks with their LinkedIn account, including Twitter, Facebook, and WordPress.

**Basic Account:** A free LinkedIn account.

**Connection:** LinkedIn members who have accepted an invitation to connect, network, and view each other's profiles and networks.

**Groups:** Allows professionals to develop their careers by sharing expertise, experience, and knowledge.

**InMail:** Private messages that allow a member to directly contact any LinkedIn user while protecting the recipient's privacy. This is a fee-based service.

**Invitations:** A request from an existing member or individual not on LinkedIn to join or make a professional connection.

**Job Seekers Account:** LinkedIn members can choose between three levels of fee-based job seeking accounts: basic, standard, or plus. The aim of this service is for the member to gain increased exposure to potential employers.

**LION:** An acronym that means "LinkedIn Open Networker." This is sometimes visible on a member's profile. It simply means that the particular member agrees to connect with anyone, regardless of industry or connection.

**Network:** A group of users that can contact you via connections up to three degrees away.

**Open Link Network:** Premium members can join this network, which allows any LinkedIn member to send them an InMail free of charge, regardless of relationship.

**Premium Accounts:** An upgraded LinkedIn account in which members can pay a monthly or annual subscription fee. Paid account benefits include InMail, better profile search results, expanded profiles, and larger storage space.

**Recommendations:** Similar to a letter of recommendation, recommendations are references that are written to recommend a colleague, business partner, or someone whom you have done business with.

## Proof Is in the Pudding

Successful companies lead by example (http://www.linkedin.com/company). LinkedIn is a great illustration of how a social networking platform can best utilize each offered feature to support business initiatives. On average, LinkedIn posts fresh, engaging content approximately 150 times each month to its members. Fresh videos, images, status updates, and blog posts keep members coming back for more and incidentally also promote increased sharing among members. From a social site whose original goal was to provide networking opportunities and recruit talent, LinkedIn has become a powerhouse in search, content, and influence.

Contrary to a veteran social networking site like LinkedIn, Pinterest, a relative newbie on the social web, has taken center stage in many public relations campaigns.

# Pinterest

Pinterest has quickly become one of the biggest social traffic referral sites, recording more traffic than YouTube, Google+, and LinkedIn combined.[23] The astonishing growth of Pinterest has led to widespread media coverage and an abundance of articles, blog posts, forum discussions, how-to podcasts, and videos about how this new social network is taking the social web by storm. Keenly adept at what other social networks have done so well, Pinterest connects people and triggers them to share and communicate, while at the same time facilitating *discovery*, rather than searching for what they want.

The fastest social site to garner ten million visitors per month in the short history of social media, Pinterest's rise to the top has communications professionals, tech junkies, and social media thought leaders amazed at the power it commands. Strictly speaking, Pinterest is a social network that allows users to visually share, curate, and uncover new interests by "pinning" videos or images to their own pinboards. Through pictorial representations, brands can connect with pinners who share similar interests and preferences that the brand represents. Pinterest is a social network meant to "collect and organize the things that inspire" its users.[24] With thirty-two categories of pinboards, brands have the ability to connect on many levels. There are five types of pinners:

> **The Influencing Pinner**—The influencer's activity affects the decisions of those who follow them. If an influencer pins or repins

an image from your brand, others are likely to follow suit. The influencing pinner recommends products, websites, contests, and social connections that they believe other Pinterest users will also enjoy. These individuals have the ability to sway the decision-making power of their followers.

**The Purchasing Pinner**—Pinners who express themselves through pictures and images relevant to items that they have purchased or plan to purchase.

**The *Almost* Purchasing Pinner**—Pinners who use Pinterest as a social bookmarking site or simply as a wish list fall into this category. These users pin images as a reminder of what they want to do, buy, plan, share, or come back to at a later date.

**The "In It for the Long Haul" Pinner**—Pinners in this category use Pinterest to explore and conduct research on products or projects that they know will eventually be purchased or implemented. Pinners who are "in it for the long haul" know what they want. For example, perhaps they are planning a wedding. These individuals know that they need invitations, but they do not quite know what type of invitation they like. They will create a board and save images that inspire what they are looking for. These users will keep collecting pins until they find the perfect pin.

**The Instantaneous Pinner**—Instantaneous pinners are precise in what they search for on Pinterest. For example, "hand-painted, classic, do-it-yourself wedding invitations" rather than "wedding invitations."

## Pinteresting Campaigns

Branded profiles allow businesses to develop promotions that encourage users to follow the profiles of individual brands and pin items from their websites. Whole Foods Market, an early adopter of Pinterest, has amassed close to 150,000 followers on this platform.[25] With fifty-four boards ranging in topics from organically grown foods—"How Does Your Garden Grow?"—to gift-giving ideas—"Great Gifts (. . . You May Not Think Of)"—the company presents itself to a variety of audiences. However, Whole Foods Market does not overly promote its products within these boards. Its pins relate to the core values of the company—being all natural, sustainable, and organic.

When defining a social strategy for Pinterest, brands should focus on creating genuine interactions that result in a community of dedicated and loyal followers. Think of pins in terms of "likes" and every comment and follow as a symbol between two people building a long-term friendship.[26] The social strategy for Whole Foods Market is to pull content from blogs and other online sites that align with its mission.

Other brands, including Bare Minerals and Lands' End Canvas, ran "Pin It to Win It" campaigns using Pinterest.[27] Fans of Bare Minerals were asked to follow the brand's pinboard, set up a themed board of their own following the company's set of directions, and then simply tag pins with #BareMinerals and #READYtowin. Lands' End asked followers to pin images from lands endcanvas.com for a chance to win one of the pinned items.

One of the most successful Pinterest campaigns was created by the brilliant minds at Honda. "You Deserve a Pintermission" promoted the CR-V's young, hip, live-life image by reaching out to five influential pinners and challenging them to a #Pintermission.[28] They were asked to take a twenty-four-hour break from Pinterest so they could bring something from their personal pinboards to life. To help the influential pinners complete the activity, Honda gave them each $500. Once the pinners were selected, Honda uploaded personalized posters to individual boards within the company's profile. Honda also had the pinners create their own Pintermission boards and add Honda as a collaborator. The results from this initiative were astounding primarily because these five "chosen" pinners were so influential within the target community. The #Pintermission boards attracted more than 4.6 million visitors resulting in more than five thousand repins and nearly two thousand likes. The campaign was so popular that it migrated to Twitter, resulting in hundreds of tweets and generating more than sixteen million media impressions.

Watch John Watts, Honda's head of digital marketing, discuss why the campaign was so successful: http://bit.ly/15jXPeD.

These types of campaigns illustrate that contests can be powerful draws using Pinterest if they are executed correctly. They create a more engaged fan base, broaden a brand's online reach, and foster longer-term relationships.

### Pinterest Patois

Although other social networking sites require mastery of a long list of essential definitions, Pinterest only has a few phrases that matter.

- *Follow*: Following means that a user wishes to pay attention to whatever another user is posting. Two levels of following exist:
    1. Following the overall user—any time that a particular user posts anything on Pinterest, it will show up on your newsfeed.
    2. Following an individual board—any time that something new is pinned to that specific board, it will show up on your newsfeed.
- *Pin*: An image added to Pinterest using the "Pin It" button. This is generally uploaded from your computer or from a URL. A pin can be an image or a video. Pins typically link back to the site that they originated from.
- *Pinboard (a.k.a. Board)*: A themed collection of pins. Pinners can create as many boards as they wish and as many categories as they can think of. Boards can be edited at any time.
- *Pinning*: The act of adding an image to a board.
- *Pinner*: A user who shares content on Pinterest.
- *Repin*: The act of reposting another Pinterest user's image to one of your own boards. (Similar to the RT.)

## Social Networks: The Platform— Social Networking Sites: The Channel

Loyalty is the foundation behind successful relationships in life. Relationships between a business and customers are no different. Customers who are loyal to a specific brand, product, or service tend to stay loyal throughout their lives. They even become brand champions and look for ways to share their love of a brand with others. The dynamics between a customer and a business have created an ever-evolving relationship that promotes and fosters loyalty.

People connect with brands on social networks using various social networking sites because they want to learn something about a brand, share valuable content with others, define who they are, grow and cultivate their online relationships, and support causes that resonate with them. Social media campaigns help businesses accomplish these goals while also building brand and company loyalties. Selecting the correct social platform to promote a business and incorporating the necessary elements that make sense is also core to building a successful social strategy or campaign. Analyzing these strategies and campaigns a bit more closely, one can see that businesses successful in building a community of brand advocates have incorporated many of the valuable principles highlighted within the Circular Model of SoMe for Social Communication—*Share, optimize, Manage, engage*—when interacting with their consumer base. Genuine, authentic interactions with consumers can be a company's best asset for enhancing relationships and expanding a brand. Social networking sites are easy, available channels for customers to reach out to a brand and, in turn, a company to respond.

**#LRNSMPR**

Learn More about Effective Uses of Social Networking Sites

Quick Links

- How to Create a Facebook Badge, http://bit.ly/1djdAl2
- You Need to Stop Ignoring Google+—Here Are 4 SEO Reasons Why, http://bit.ly/1oaYZ7g
- How to Use Twitter for Business, http://bit.ly/17OBYhw
- How to Use Twitter for Marketing and PR, http://bit.ly/19AQp6o
- 4 Reasons B2B Companies Should Use LinkedIn Company Pages, Plus 4 Examples and 4 Tips to Get Started, http://bit.ly/1dMDMKc
- Ballard Designs Email Marketing Goes Viral on Pinterest, http://ex.pn/1e9jgVn

# Notes

1. Associated Press, "Yahoo! News," last modified May 1, 2013, accessed August 22, 2013, http://news.yahoo.com/number-active-users-facebook-over-230449748.html; Browser Media, Socialnomics, MacWorld, "Social Networking Statistics," last modified November 12, 2012, accessed August 23, 2013, http://www.statisticbrain.com/social-networking-statistics/.

2. Browser Media, Socialnomics, "Social Networking Statistics," last modified November 12, 2012.

3. Statistic Brain, "Facebook Statistics," last modified June 23, 2013, accessed August 23, 2013.

4. R. Wilson, *Share This: The Social Media Handbook for PR Professionals* (West Sussex: Wiley, 2012), chap. 7; A. Sibley, Hubspot, "An Introduction to Facebook for Business," last modified 2013, accessed August 23, 2013, http://hubspot.uberflip.com/i/152427.

5. R. Luttrell, "Are You Abiding by the 80/20 Rule?" *Gina Luttrell PhD* (blog), August 9, 2013.

6. R. Menezes, "How to Add Widgets to Facebook," *eHow* (blog), 2013.

7. Facebook, "Games on Facebook Overview," last modified 2013, accessed August 26, 2013, https://developers.facebook.com/docs/guides/canvas/.

8. Wing Kosner, "Watch Out Facebook, With Google+ at #2 and YouTube at #3, Google, Inc. Could Catch Up," http://www.forbes.com/sites/anthonykosner/2013/01/26/watch-out-facebook-with-google-at-2-and-youtube-at-3-google-inc-could-catch-up/.

9. Kosner, "Watch Out Facebook."

10. T. Wasserman, "Should Your Business Use Google Hangouts?" *Mashable* (blog), May 19, 2013, http://mashable.com/2013/05/09/google-hangouts-business/.

11. D. Moth, "10 Brands with Great Google Pages," *Econsultancy* (blog), October 9, 2012, http://econsultancy.com/us/blog/10845-10-brands-with-great-google-pages.

12. M. Monahan, "Marketing Your Business with Twitter," *The Summing It Up Blog* (blog), February 7, 2013, http://www.sigmawebmarketing.com/blog/bid/171523/Marketing-Your-Business-With-Twitter.

13. C. Smith, "By the Numbers: 24 Amazing Twitter Stats," *DMR Digital Marketing Ramblings* (blog), August 18, 2013.

14. R. Luttrell, "Twitter Basics," *Gina Luttrell PhD* (blog), July 30, 2012, http://ginaluttrellphd.com/2012/07/30/twitter-basics/.

15. D. Adler, "Twenty-One Top Twitter Tips," *Forbes* (blog), July 31, 2009; M. Johnston, "101 Ways to Make Money with Twitter," *MP: Monitize Pros* (blog), July 13, 2013, http://monetizepros.com/blog/2013/101-ways-to-make-money-with-twitter/.

16. J. Duffy, "How to Use Twitter for Business," *PC: PCmag.com* (blog), April 16, 2013, http://www.pcmag.com/article2/0,2817,2383408,00.asp.

17. A. Stadd, "How Are Top Brands Doing with Twitter Customer Service?" *All Twitter* (blog), May 10, 2013, http://www.mediabistro.com/alltwitter/twitter-customer-service_b42180.

18. Twitter website: https://twitter.com/about.

19. http://www.linkedin.com.

20. QuantCast: https://www.quantcast.com/search?q=linkedin.

21. S. Rayson, "9 Ways to Improve Your LinkedIn Marketing," *Social Media Today* (blog), July 22, 2013, http://socialmediatoday.com/steve-rayson/1611011/improve-linkedin-marketing-9-ways.

22. B. Solis, *Engage: The Complete Guide for Brands and Businesses to Build, Cultivate, and Measure Success in the New Web* (New York: Wiley, 2011).

23. Eric Gilbert, Saeideh Bakhshi, Shuo Chang, and Loren Terveen. "I Need to Try This? A Statistical Overview of Pinterest," in *Proceedings of the SIGCHI Conference on Human Factors in Computing Systems*, 2427–36. ACM, 2013.

24. Pinterest: http://about.pinterest.com/.

25. S. Guneulis, "5 Brands Using Pinterest Brilliantly," *SproutInsights* (blog), February 13, 2012, http://sproutsocial.com/insights/2012/02/best-pinterest-brands/.

26. L. Indvik, "How Brands Are Using Promotions to Market on Pinterest," *Mashable* (blog), March 7, 2012, http://mashable.com/2012/03/07/pinterest-brand-marketing/.

27. S. Mallon, "5 Brands Using Pinterest Right and How to Learn from Them," *Online Marketing Insights* (blog), May 15, 2013, http://www.onlinemarketinginstitute.org/blog/2013/05/pinterest-marketing-examples/.

28. K. Piombino, "Honda's Shoestring Pinterest Campaign Attracts Millions," *Ragan's PR Daily* (blog), February 21, 2013, http://www.prdaily.com/Main/Articles/Hondas_shoestring_Pinterest_campaign_attracts_mill_13883.aspx.

## CHAPTER SEVEN
# PHOTO SHARING

> The overwhelming acceptance and widespread use of popular photo-sharing sites have inspired all types of brands to explore this new platform as a way to further connect with customers. Visual content is allowing companies to show, not tell, about their brands, business, and story.

## Before Instagram and Flickr

The use of images on Instagram, Flickr, and other mainstream social networking sites, including Facebook, Pinterest, Tumblr, and Twitter, is on the rise. It is quite common for public relations professionals to use images in promoting campaigns. Brochures, newsletters, annual reports, websites, and press kits include a bevy of images that complete a story, show off products, or highlight specific services. The evolution and mass acceptance of the digital camera has played an important role in how we share images online. The advent of the point, shoot, and upload philosophy allows anyone to take high-quality images with ease, upload them to a computer, and then use them for professional or personal use.[1] Prior to the age of digital photos, the process of incorporating photos within collateral material or on a website was tedious and time consuming. As digital photos started becoming more mainstream, but preceding social networks like Instagram, Flickr, Pic Stitch, and Tumblr, consumers flocked to photo-sharing websites such as Kodak Gallery.com and Snapfish.com. These types of web-based photo-sharing and photo-printing services allowed users to create a private account, upload

129

images from their digital camera, buy prints, and share their albums with others. Essentially, these websites paved the way for what we now use today.

## Show, Not Tell

At any given moment there are thousands of people on the web searching for photos. The vast majority of these photos are more than likely located on

### 5 Reasons to Use Photos in Social Media Campaigns

*People Are Visual Beings*

Photos allow a company to tell a story that they otherwise could not have accomplished through other, more traditional mediums. People like to look at pictures. The majority of people will typically stare at text when browsing online. Integrating photos as a means to inform your audience can create engagement and interaction.

*Share Photo Streams*

Instagram and Flickr make it easy to share photos across multiple social media platforms. Encourage the company's online community to distribute photos across multiple sites.

*Tag It*

Tags assigned to photos are used in SEO. Tags allow users to more easily find your brand, products, and services. This not only supports growth of your base audience but also affords a more genuine level of interaction with them.

*Creative Commons*

Employ a Creative Commons (CC) License on the photos that a company uploads. The social web is about sharing, being both transparent and authentic. CC License gives individual creators, large companies, and institutions a simple, standardized way to grant copyright permissions to their creative work.

*Chat, Chat, Chat*

Instagram and Flickr allow for users to post comments on photos that are uploaded. Take the time to interact with your consumers by replying to their comments and also share what they have to say.

photo-sharing websites that are associated with a company, brand, celebrity, hot-spot destination, must-attend event, or anything else that a person can even imagine. Think about the numbers: Flickr alone has fifty-one million monthly visitors, while Instagram boasts a whopping 150 million users who have shared more than sixteen billion photos since the platform launched in 2010.[2] Companies utilize channels like Flickr and Instagram to successfully connect with online influencers, investors, stakeholders, consumers, and prospects. Mirroring other forms of social media, photo-sharing sites allow users to share their love and affinity for a company's brand with others inside their sphere of influence. Photo-sharing websites are another example of a powerful tool that allows direct interaction with your consumer base.

The more a company shares with its consumers, the more likely that those consumers will share with others. Two-way communication is at the epicenter of social media. Sharing photos with those on the social web, while also encouraging them to share, comment, and interact with a company, supports the very spirit of social media. Instagram and Flickr allow companies to create communities, share images, build trustworthiness, and develop genuineness with consumers—just like every other social media platform that has been discussed.

## Instagram

The allure of Instagram is the ability to create, manipulate, and share photos with family, friends, coworkers, and anyone else interested in taking a peek at those sepia-tinted, vintage-style, toaster-hued digital images. With Instagram's mass appeal, unprecedented usage, and popularity, the company has

**What Is Instagram?**

Owned by Facebook, Instagram is a free photo-sharing application that allows users to take photos, apply a filter to a photo, and also share the photo on Instagram or other social networking sites, including Facebook, Twitter, Foursquare, Tumblr, Flickr, and Posterous.

positioned itself as a social network in its own right and not merely a photo-sharing app. The success and mass appeal of Instagram has not escaped the attention of many popular brands that have incorporated the platform within their social strategies. MTV, Nike, Starbucks, Forever 21, Burberry, and Victoria's Secret are among the most popular brands on Instagram, with followers numbering one million or more. Companies engage with customers by sharing snapshots of their products, culture, and people in an intimate, yet informal, manner. There are three major features that draw users to Instagram: (1) personalization, (2) lifestyle, and (3) exclusivity.

## Personalization

Nike, for example, offers its Instagram followers the opportunity to become custom designers and allows them to create their own shoes using Instagram photos. The "NIKEiD" campaign utilizes the power of the social community by providing users with a chance to design, share, and purchase customized versions of Nike gear.

## Lifestyle

Starbucks is a company that resonates well with Instagram users because followers of the company primarily control the content on this social platform. The Starbucks Instagram account predominantly features images posted by enthusiastic, imaginative fans that love and enjoy everything about Starbucks coffee. The company aims to promote the brand as part of a lifestyle choice and one that should be enjoyed with friends. It should come as no surprise that Starbucks is famous for cross promoting its social strategies. For example, the company used Instagram to promote a Google Hangout with Maroon 5. This was a great illustration of how the mobile app can be used as part of a multichannel social media campaign.

## Exclusivity

Instagram users have also become accustomed to seeing exclusive photos, including behind-the-scenes looks at their favorite company. Burberry is a company that frequently does this. Whether it is the latest commercial, photo shoot, or iconic images from London, Burberry fans always feel connected to the brand. As a company, Burberry recognizes the impact of this premier access and often rewards followers with exclusive content. This technique builds a community of loyal brand ambassadors.

With these success stories in mind, the first question that a public relations practitioner should ask might be "How might a company best look to harness the power of Instagram?" A company's Instagram account can serve multiple purposes, but, above all, it should make users feel included and part of the company culture. Some tactics to consider when planning an Instagram campaign include the following:[3]

- **New Products**: Snap a quick picture of a new product, share a screenshot, or, better yet, share an image of someone using the product on Instagram. Instagram photos should be simple and can promote the desired effect through the use of the many photo filters that are available.

- **Company Culture and Employees**: Use Instagram to humanize the company brand. Highlight the inner workings of the company culture; give followers insight into the day-to-day behind-the-scenes activity. Followers want to see who is running the company, who is tweeting them, and who is blogging—so show them. It is not necessary to post a traditional headshot. This would be too formal for Instagram. Save those for LinkedIn and the company website. Make the photo fun by using a more relaxed image. A peek behind the scenes is not a photo of someone simply sitting at their desk. As an example, Centresource, an interactive agency, uses Instagram to show the details of its company culture. The "Who We Are" page is a running feed of its Instagram account.

- **Trending Topics and Events**: In addition to posting images of company events, illustrate that the company is involved and informed on events that matter to your followers. Post Instagram photos of news, fun facts, and trending topics that followers are most likely aware of and then engage with them on that topic.

- **Photo Contests**: Instagram users love the app because they can create fun images. Use this passion to a company's advantage. Develop and launch a photo contest in which followers can submit images and earn recognition by a brand they adore. White House Black Market's Sweater Boutique Instagram Contest asked followers to incorporate their pets into a photo of themselves dressed in their favorite White House Black Market (@ whbm) outfits and upload it to Instagram using the hashtag #feelbeautiful (while also mentioning @whbm). Upon posting the photo to Instagram, participants received one entry into the contest. Three grand prize winners took home $100 store gift cards. This contest helped build followers, create brand loyalty, and showcase the new clothing line as modeled by real customers, and it also provided a platform for the company to engage with its community of users.

In taking its capabilities one step further, Instagram had social media strategists and public relations professionals buzzing as it extended its photo-sharing features to include video capabilities. This development is another avenue for companies to use in promoting products and services, building corporate culture, or interacting with their customer base. Using the video feature within Instagram allows for fifteen seconds of video recording with a built-in editing capability, the ability to decide which image to use for the cover image, instant integration with the existing Instagram app, Facebook in-line viewing, and, of course, those filters we have all come to love.[4]

Brands are already using Instagram video in some pretty ingenious ways. Charity Water, for example, brings its mission to life by capturing the story of a woman who benefited from the nonprofit organization, using a short, impactful video of her life.[5] This example has Charity Water using the video feature along with the introduction of captions, thereby maximizing both the technological features and searchability of the video. Ben and Jerry's gave fans a peek into its kitchens by showing them how it makes its dangerously delicious ice cream, while famous chef Jamie Oliver whipped up a simple how-to video teaching fans how to make salad dressing in his traditional, crazy style.[6]

The power of Instagram is that it allows companies to use this video feature in countless, creative ways. Shooting a product demo, answering some frequently asked questions, featuring events and special offers, creating a video portfolio of the company's products, or encouraging fan submissions are some examples of ways that a company can take advantage of video storytelling.[7] Both customers and fans want to see a humanized brand, one that captivates them and keeps them connected to the brand.

## Measuring Matters

Being able to illustrate results and understand metrics properly is important to all social media platforms because the analytics can drive social media strategies. Statigram, a tool specifically developed for Instagram users, allows brands to measure their efforts through viable metrics. With Statigram a company can manage both comments and the community simultaneously, and also analyze the company activity within Instagram.

## Flickr

While not necessarily at the center of every social media campaign, Flickr should not be discounted as a way to connect with consumers. Flickr's subscribers are made up of amateur as well as professional photographers who want to share their photos with others, who engage Flickr's active community of users, and who are also interested in obtaining feedback from other users. The culture and draw to Flickr is much different than for other social communities because Flickr has rules that explicitly forbid companies from uploading photos that are posted with the sole purpose of advertising or marketing of products.[8] Two of the most effective ways to use Flickr include commenting on photos that are uploaded by other users and by participating in Flickr groups. Each time that a user leaves a comment on the site, the username (alongside the comment you made) will link back to their personal profile, which in turn contains links to their photo sets, videos, and additional biographical information. Flickr groups is an area for members to upload photos and videos, and it is also a platform for users to engage in discussions with other members on a specific topic. Creating a group, adding photos, and participating in the discussions are great ways to gain exposure and establish a community with a company's followers.

### Authorized Resources on Flickr

Brands that use Flickr tend to implement strategies that help build a community base and act as a resource center for their consumers. Graco and Nikon are two companies that have successfully utilized Flickr to connect with their consumers. Nikon provides a "Digital Learning Center" allowing fans access to step-by-step tutorials, photography tips, discussion forums, and advice from Nikon photo experts.[9] With more than seventy-two thousand registered members, Nikon Flickr users also have access to a variety of hardware-related experts, as well as exposure to authentic Nikon supplies. Nikon's use of Flickr illustrates the concept that there is now an opportunity for companies to act as branded resources and can provide an additional outlet to consumers who want to hear from qualified experts.

Graco is another company that has built a community around its products using Flickr reviews. By posting photographs from members using Graco products and photos that provide behind-the-scenes access to the people behind the brand, Graco is humanizing the brand.[10] The company has even combined offline tactics into its strategy by hosting a number of community gatherings. The images from these events are also posted to the company Flickr page and contribute to bringing a more intimate and personalized feel to the brand.

Photos, and the resulting discussions they stimulate, can be an incredible way to share ideas and stories, give advice, and receive feedback from your customer base. Brands that have successfully incorporated photo-sharing platforms into their social strategy have yet to blatantly sell their products using these services. These companies have effectively found a following using various strategies, including posts of photos of recent events, employees, and customers using their products, and even introducing creative and innovative ways to do something using their brands, products, or services.

## The Upsurge of Visual Social Media

The trend toward incorporating visual has also been influenced by the uptick in mobile use. More and more people engage with one another using social media on their smartphones, tablets, or other portable devices. Research indicates that when people interact with brands on social networking sites, they are more likely to engage with those brands that post images over other forms of media.[11] The need for, and rise in, the incorporation of images will undoubtedly increase in the coming years. Consumers have emphatically shown that they would like to see what a company is made of. Whether it is a fashion house giving fans a peek behind the label or a chef welcoming you to their kitchen, photos are becoming a staple in social media campaigns.

# Theory into Practice

## Ford Fiesta[12]

### *Challenge*

The Ford Fiesta is known for its award-winning sleek, sexy design and sophisticated exterior. However, the Fiesta is not as well known for its intuitive tech-savvy features that include keyless entry, MyKey technology, EcoBoost, and auto start-up features, to name a few. Ford set out to change all of that. Nicholas Oliver and Tom Gibby of Blue Hive, a London-based marketing firm that worked with Ford to execute the campaign, were charged with creating the captivating campaign.

### *Strategy*

In October 2012, Ford leveraged the power of Instagram and launched "Fiestagram," a six-week contest in which users throughout Europe could submit photos for an opportunity to win prizes. The best photos were selected to be featured in actual photo galleries and digital billboards all across Europe. Weekly innovative hashtags associated with one of the Fiesta's high-tech features, such as #entry, #music, and #hidden, were revealed. Fans could then submit photos on Instagram, tagged with "#Fiestagram" with that week's particular hashtag. Photos needed to hold true to four criteria: (1) relevance to the theme; (2) artistic interpretation of the theme; (3) relevance to the Ford Fiesta technology; and (4) originality of the photos. Judged by Scott Monty, Ford's head of social media; James Day, an internationally renowned photographer; and Philippe Gonzalez, the founder of the Instagramers fan network, winners of the contest were selected and awarded prizes including iPads and digital cameras. The grand prize was a Ford Fiesta.

### *Instagram: The Right Social Tool*

For this campaign, the key demographic identified as participants on Instagram and within the campaign tended to represent a specific demographic—trend-setting fashion, style, and tech mavens—all of whom are committed, high-volume users of Instagram. The campaign focused on showing the story through images, rather than telling it. Images, via Instagram, became the channel to launch and execute a multinational, multilingual campaign.

### *Results*

Considered greatly successful, more than sixteen thousand photos were submitted as a result of the Fiestagram contest, and Ford gained in excess of 120,000 new Facebook fans across Europe. More importantly, Ford successfully attracted the attention of its target demographic: fashion, style, and technology trendsetters. Daily Fiestagram updates and entries were showcased on the "popular" page of Instagram, prominently featuring Ford's name and the Fiesta's technology.[13]

Ford saw unprecedented success using Instagram. Too often, brands stick to what is common, what they know, or what they see other brands doing. Rather than launch its campaign through more established platforms such as Facebook or Twitter, Ford developed and executed a successful social media campaign using Instagram. The overall success of Blue Hive's Ford Fiesta campaign can be attributed to a variety of elements, but five ingenuous tactics really stand out above the rest:[14]

1. *Ease:* Users simply had to take a picture, add a preset hashtag, and upload to Instagram for their chance to win a car. Making it easy to participate and easy to share makes participating worthwhile.
2. *Influencers:* Relying on the knowledge of previous successful campaigns, Ford again called upon its community of influencers to help promote the contest. Instagram has a vibrant network of super users—called Instagramers. Recruiting Philippe Gonzales, the Instagramers fan network founder, and tasking him with spreading the word to promote the contest to his massive audience, was genius.
3. *Community:* The contest unsurprisingly nurtured a community of supportive users. Fans encouraged their friends to add the #Fiestagram hashtag to applicable photos to help spread the word. Ford realized a fairly substantial trickle-down effect from this community participation. Participants could not wait to share the fun with others.
4. *Transparency:* Ford has a policy of transparency in all modes of social media. It should come as no surprise that the company utilized its Facebook page to share relevant information with that community as well, including contest rules, processes, and weekly challenges.
5. *Momentum:* Weekly giveaways of smaller, highly desirable items like iPads kept users engaged as Ford continued to build toward awarding the Ford Fiesta grand prize. Using this tactic, Ford was able to create continued buzz around the campaign, keep fans interested, and keep them coming back and sharing more often.

**#LRNSMPR**

Learn More about Photo Sharing on the Social Web

Quick Links

- 5 Brands That Are Doing Great Things on Instagram, http://bit.ly/1eiU7GP
- @Statigram and What It Can Do for Your Brand and @Instagram Account, http://bit.ly/18jwCXY
- Here's How You Should Be Using Flickr to Boost Business, http://read.bi/19ucyBe

# Notes

1. L. Safko, *The Social Media Bible Tools and Strategies for Business Success* (New York: Wiley, 2010), chap. 9.

2. C. Smith, "How Many People Use the Top Social Media, Apps and Services," *DMR Digital Marketing Ramblings* (blog), September 15, 2013; C. Smith, "By the Numbers: 12 Interesting Instagram Stats," *DMR Digital Marketing Ramblings* (blog), September 8, 2013.

3. B. DiFeo, "Some Tactics to Consider When Planning an Instagram Campaign," June 7, 2012, http://socialfresh.com/instagram-followers/.

4. M. Gingerich, "How to Use Instagram Video for Marketing," *Social Media Examiner* (blog), July 8, 2013.

5. G. Soskey, "10 Brands That Jumped on Instagram Video (And Rocked It)," *Hubstpot* (blog), July 12, 2013, http://blog.hubspot.com/brands-jumped-instagram-video-li.

6. Gingerich, "How to Use Instagram Video for Marketing."

7. DiFeo, "Some Tactics to Consider When Planning an Instagram Campaign."

8. C. Parker, "How to Use Flickr to Grow Your Brand," Memeburn, August 4, 2010, http://memeburn.com/2010/08/how-to-use-flickr-to-grow-your-brand-%E2%80%93-part-1/.

9. Author Unknown, "Brands on Flickr," *Supercollider* (blog), July 12, 2008, http://geoffnorthcott.com/blog/2008/07/brands-on-flickr/.

10. S. Balwani, "Presenting: 10 of the Smartest Big Brands in Social Media," *Mashable* (blog), February 6, 2009, http://mashable.com/2009/02/06/social-media-smartest-brands/.

11. ROI Research Inc., "Performics," last modified July 25, 2012, accessed September 22, 2013, http://www.slideshare.net/performics_us/performics-life-on-demand-2012-summary-deck.

12. D. Klamm, "How Ford Used Instagram to Promote the Fiesta's High-Tech Features," *Mashable* (blog), February 2, 2012, http://mashable.com/2012/02/02/ford-fiesta-instagram/.

13. Balwani, "Presenting: 10 of the Smartest Big Brands in Social Media."

14. Balwani, "Presenting: 10 of the Smartest Big Brands in Social Media."

# CHAPTER EIGHT
# VIDEO

> The introduction of video on the social web in 2003 created an area of substantial growth for public relations practitioners and social strategists alike. Approximately two hundred million people, or roughly 76 percent of the online population, will be consistently viewing video using online platforms in just a few short years.[1] Companies can step into the spotlight and generate user-specific content that resonates with their customers through creative, high-impact, well-thought-out videos.

## 1.8 Million Words

According to Dr. James McQuivey of Forrester Research, video is worth 1.8 million words.[2] Imagine this: In a single frame, a video can deliver the same amount of information as three pages of text or an astonishing 3,600 average webpages. In all, it would take a person 150 days of writing to achieve relatively the same impact that a one-minute video has.[3]

Scientifically, it is known that when people read they convert text into images and emotions.[4] So it should not come as a surprise that when people receive information directly from images as opposed to text, the mind creates more connections intellectually and emotionally because the translation from word to image is not necessary. People are drawn to video for four simple reasons: we see the face as a point for gathering information and believability; the voice allows us to convert information into meaningful content;

body language resonates; and movement grabs and holds our attention.[5] For public relations professionals and social strategists, this is great news.

Video is effective when implemented with the total communications strategy in mind. Companies can increase outreach to influencers, build credibility, promote brand awareness, enhance SEO, and, more importantly, create a loyal following of brand ambassadors.

## Idea to Implementation

Create content that is relevant. Keeping your audience in mind is essential to the success or failure of a video strategy. Videos can be shot in a variety of styles and formats. The first step for a public relations practitioner is to decide which format is right for the organization. Generally there are three overarching varieties of videos found on the web:

- Product Demonstrations: This type of video captures a product's best features and uniqueness while entertaining and engaging your audience. One of the most famous examples is the Blendtec blender.[6] To illustrate the amazing capabilities of the product, CEO Tom Dickson blends items like iPads, iPhones, golf balls, Justin Bieber CDs, and even his mother's dentures. The company posted these videos on its YouTube channel and the "Will It Blend?" series exploded. The videos not only increased brand awareness but also made the Blendtec product a household name. In fact, shortly after the video series launched in 2006, sales increased over 1,000 percent. Today, the Blendtec videos receive hits, likes, and shares totaling in the millions (http://www.youtube.com/user/Blendtec).
- How-To/Educational: This video format shares best practices and builds trust with consumers. Ranking the highest among brands, Home Depot stands out because it publishes content about topics that are relevant to its brand without blatantly promoting or advertising the specific products it sells.[7] Home Depot strategists have established their brand as a trusted expert and resource for home renovation and repair projects while at the same time humanizing the company. Videos are hosted by and feature their employees sharing a wealth of home improvement information (http://www.youtube.com/user/homedepot).

- Viral: Every brand wishes that its videos will go viral, but none can guarantee that particular outcome. Viral videos typically share two things in common: relatability and discussability.[8] People are drawn to content that affects them deeply. The videos could be serious in nature or comical. Either way, the content is emotionally stimulating and creates a connection with the viewer, so much so that the viewer wants to discuss it and share the video with others. In essence, it is the viewers that make videos "go viral," not the actual videos. Dove's "Real Beauty Sketches" (http://bit.ly/1hpZuRD), the Harlem Shake (http://bit.ly/1ccJNPU), and Pepsi's "Test Drive" prank with Jeff Gordon (http://bit.ly/19pBdq5) rank among the top viral videos—each garnering millions of views, likes, and shares.

Videos, like most forms of social media, should not "sell" anything. The most successful videos are the ones that resonate. Useful, smart, interesting, captivating, and entertaining videos tend to be most popular. Social media strategists and public relations professionals need to decide why a video should be part of an overarching strategy and then ultimately what content should go into the video. Does the company want to drive traffic to a website or landing page? Perhaps growing the number of company YouTube subscribers is the ultimate goal. Increasing blog followers, heightening brand awareness, or setting up an RSS feed (which would allow users to subscribe to your channel) are all plausible objectives. These milestones will become important in measuring their overall level of success. Content within the videos can range from a simple interview to a complex story line like Pepsi's "Test Drive" prank or Chipotle's mini–animated movie about a lone scarecrow looking for ways to provide alternatives to the unsustainable processed food world we live in.

## Producing Quality Videos

Video has the potential to spread copious amounts of information to a broad audience. Every detail is critical, whether you are shooting a thirty-minute video or a six-second video. When a social strategist or public relations professional steps behind the camera, they become a video maker and thus are responsible for every image and message conveyed in each frame of the finalized product.

YouTube, Vine, and Instagram, all video-sharing social media sites, each have their own set of rules, time constraints, and uses. When using these platforms for filming videos, the following guidelines can be used:

1. Know Your Audience and Platform: This may seem obvious, but believe it or not, it is often not the case. Knowing whether the video should be six seconds or sixty minutes means that you need to know your audience, which platform will work best for the content you plan to promote, and on which social media platform the video will make the most impact.

2. Purpose and Storyboard: Understanding the purpose, and then taking the time to storyboard the idea, is the first step toward creating the framework for a company video. Even short videos, including those being considered for Vine and Instagram, need a purpose and a storyboard. Defining the purpose helps to deliver the core message. Creating a storyboard is a technique that maps out a video sequence prior to filming. Essentially it is a written plan for the content going into the video.

3. Style and Tone: The style of the video sets the stage. Videos can be serious, funny, cheerful, professional, or even whimsical. Regardless of the style, the message needs to fit the overall tone. Some professionals have created videos many times over. To these individuals, conveying a style and setting the tone may be simple. However, not all social strategists or public relations professionals are trained videographers. By taking a look at videos with similar messaging or format on YouTube, Vine, and Instagram, professionals can catch a glimpse into how certain tones and feelings have previously been conveyed. Seeing the work of others may inspire you or give you an idea. Consider these tips:
   - *Tone*: Upbeat, carefree, serious minded, or staid
   - *Dialogue*: "Talking head" interview-style or free-flowing conversation
   - *Production Quality*: In-house studio or on location
   - *Video Quality*: Simple online, made-it-myself video or big-budget professional production

4. Script Writing: Once the purpose and tone have been decided, it is time to write the script. For longer YouTube interview/

interviewee-style videos, write out the list the questions so that you are prepared. For more conversational videos, use bulleted notes. Is it possible to pack a story into a six-second or a fifteen-second video? The answer is *yes*! The key here will be to weave in quick edits and multiple shot angles throughout.

5. Angles and Shot: How the video is made has a direct effect on whether the content will resonate. Remember that all videos need to be relatable, discussable, and sharable. When filming a video, you need to take into consideration the best angle and perspective for each sequence. For videos that require multiple frames, characters, or scenes, it is best to script out your video in detail. This includes notes related to the sets, stage actions, props, and dialogue.

6. Images, Sound, and Lighting: Graphics, music, and imagery also play a critical role in video. These elements support the tone, dialogue, and effectiveness of the messaging. When storyboarding the video, think about the types of still shots, b-roll footage, music, and background sounds that can be used. Lighting can make or break the quality of a video. Poor lighting creates dark, shadowy, discolored, or even gritty images. Never record a scene with a window in the background. The subjects will appear dark, and although some editing can happen, the quality of the shot is diminished. Viewers tend to accept ordinary, uninspiring graphics but have very little tolerance for poor sound. Invest in external microphones to ensure good sound quality.

7. Editing to Final Product: The three most commonly used desktop editing tools for YouTube videos are iMovie, Camtasia, and Windows Movie Maker. The websites associated with each of these tools provide in-depth instructions for how to use each editing product. Both iMovie and Windows Movie Maker are easy to use and have drag and drop tools, while Camtasia is an excellent tool for simple videos and screencasts.

8. Share: Once the video has achieved production-ready status, it is now time to publish the video for the world to see. Be sure that the original goals of the video are in line with the company's overarching social media goals. This can include calls to action, hashtags, clever captions, and tags. Since YouTube, Vine, and

Instagram are embeddable, the potential for innovative storytelling is limitless.

Regardless of the route, there are many options supporting inclusion of a video into a social strategy. It was not that long ago that YouTube was the only outlet for video. Not anymore. Today videos also appear on Vine and Instagram, both of which facilitate easy video capabilities and are generating quite the stir in the video creation sphere.

## YouTube

The practicality of YouTube, for the end user, is quite simple: to locate and watch videos. However, for social strategists and public relations practitioners, this platform is much more. Owned by Google, YouTube is a search engine, promotional platform, a social network, and a community site with

**Mind-Numbing YouTube Stats and Figures**

According to YouTube's statistics:*

- More than one billion unique users visit YouTube each month.
- Six billion hours of video are watched on YouTube monthly—almost one hour for every person on Earth.
- One hundred hours of video are uploaded to YouTube every minute.
- Seventy percent of YouTube traffic comes from outside the United States.
- YouTube is localized in fifty-six countries and across sixty-one languages.
- According to Nielsen, YouTube reaches more US adults in the eighteen to thirty-four age demographic than any other cable network.
- Millions of users subscribe to YouTube every day, with subscription numbers having more than doubled since 2012.
- Mobile makes up more than 25 percent of YouTube's global watch time, with more than one billion views per day.
- YouTube is available on hundreds of millions of devices.

* YouTube, "Statistics," last modified 2013, accessed October 4, 2013, http://www.youtube.com/yt/press/statistics.html.

a loyal viewership. One unique feature that YouTube boasts is the ability to create branded channels.

The YouTube branded channels allow for the creation of a specific space for all of the videos that pertain to that company. Users do not have to search to find the content they desire because these branded channels ultimately create a set destination for customers to locate the content that they seek. YouTube channels afford the opportunity for companies to engage and further shape formidable relationships with their audience using an environment that consumers know and trust.

Channels should reflect the brand itself through the use of company images, graphics, and colors. YouTube does offer an upgrade to its channel services that help public relations and social strategists further maintain company branding. Users can benefit from this by accessing templates that can be customized and personalized to complement other social sites, the company website, and even printed collateral material. Using this functionality helps create and align content with key demographics and the company's goals, products, or mission.

It may not come as a surprise that Red Bull is one company that understands how to maximize YouTube's potential. Red Bull's overarching theme embedded throughout all of its communication strategies focuses on extreme sports and extreme athletes. Its Facebook page and twenty Pinterest boards feature spectacular images and videos of Red Bull–sponsored extreme sports and extreme sport athletes, while the Twitter feed is dedicated to various events and current projects. To keep its content fresh and new, Red Bull posts between one and three new videos per day—all of which are directed toward its key niche audience.

When Felix Baumgartner took his leap from the edge of space, Red Bull's live broadcast of the remarkable video pulled in more than nine million streams of the actual dive. Aside from the historic feat, what made this video so successful was that Red Bull documented the days leading up to the jump by producing and posting more than fifteen videos that chronicled the journey. The project, "Red Bull Stratos," drew millions of viewers to Red Bull's site. In all, Red Bull Stratos garnered over 366 million content views on YouTube alone.[9]

## Mobile and Video Are Making an Impact

Video is undoubtedly effective. Consider these two facts: (1) two-thirds of the world's mobile traffic is expected to comprise solely of video by 2017; and (2) mobile makes up more than 25 percent of YouTube's total global watch time. Vine and Instagram are also mastering the mobile sphere; thus, paying attention to the results that companies are seeing on these platforms will help put their effectiveness into perspective.*

### Vine Stats
- Five tweets per second contain a Vine link.
- A branded Vine video is four times more likely to be seen than a regular branded video.
- The first day of Honda's #WantNewCar Vine campaign brought the car brand 1,020 new followers (compared to its six-month average of 242 new followers) and 2,292 mentions.
- From June 19 to July 19, Vine videos got 0.0206 percent average engagement rate and an average of twenty retweets, while Instagram videos got 0.0111 percent average engagement rate and an average of seven retweets.
- 10 a.m.–11 a.m. is the most popular time of the day to post Vine videos.
- On April 15, 2013, the day of the Boston Marathon bombing, a record 19,667 Vines were made.
- Historically speaking, three of the five most retweeted Vines made were created by musicians.

### Instagram Stats
- Instagram has roughly 130 million users, compared to Vine's thirteen million users.
- Two-thirds of the top one hundred world brands were already on Instagram before it introduced video.
- Since the launch of Instagram video, there has been a 37 percent increase in Instagram shares on Twitter.
- Instagram videos are promoting two times more engagement than Instagram photos alone.
- Lululemon, one of the first brands to use Instagram video, receives approximately seven times as many comments on its Instagram videos as it does on its photos.
- Of the brands on Instagram, 62 percent have shared at least one Instagram video.

---

* S. Weissman, "15 Stats You Need to Know about Vine and Instagram Video," *Digiday* (blog), September 9, 2013, http://digiday.com/brands/15-stats-vine-and-instagram-video/.

## Vine

If a midge (a type of gnat) can beat its wings one thousand times in one second, a rattlesnake can shake its tail in warning sixty times in a mere second, and a fast human can spring thirty-nine feet in just one second,[10] imagine what social media strategists and public relations practitioners can do with six seconds! Creating lasting impressions on Vine, Twitter's mobile video app, is fast becoming a prominent player in the social sphere.

By fusing video content, static imagery, and incorporating audio, Vine enables mobile users to capture and share miniature moments. The videos play on a loop, similar to an animated GIF (graphics interchange format). "Posts on Vine are about abbreviation—the shortened form of something larger. They're little windows into the people, settings, ideas and objects that make up your life."[11]

The Vine app is an easy-to-use, easy-to-understand tool that can support the need for video within a company's overall social media strategy. Since the videos are only six seconds in length, companies can get creative and show off some of their personality. General Electric (GE) was one of the first brands to embrace Vine. With its "#6SecondScience" campaign, the company effectively created the world's first Internet science fair. The campaign challenged its audience by asking one question: "How much science can you fit into six seconds?" During the week-long campaign more than four hundred videos were submitted, covering a wide range of topics showcasing much of the magic behind science. Some Twitter followers received a special science kit that included a thank-you card, a bumper sticker, and a 4M Kitchen Science Kit to help in the creation of the videos. Each kit included experiments on how to power a clock using lemons or to take fingerprints with flour. Within the first twenty-four hours of the campaign, more than one hundred Vine videos were created.[12] As the videos continued to roll in, GE shared them with its audience using their Facebook, Twitter, and #6SecondScience Tumblr pages, which acted as the center of the campaign. Those individuals seeking inspiration need only look to GE's Pinterest page for ideas. The company highlighted numerous Vines by retweeting, revining, and reblogging. The underlying idea of this campaign was to create a community for sharing ideas and participating in a fun, creative way.

Not every company is a science powerhouse like GE, but that doesn't mean creative campaigns are not possible to realize. The following three brands have also found success in generating creative Vine campaigns:

*The science kit from GE that was sent to fans encouraging participation in the world's first Internet science fair. (Courtesy of Regina Luttrell)*

- Oreo: Like fresh ground cookie on your ice cream? Then check out our latest Vine, #OreoSnackHacks (http://bit.ly/1e4k6iL).
- Lowe's: "Lowe's Fix in Six": Keep squirrels away from your plants with a dash of cayenne pepper, #lowesfixinsix #howto (https://vine.co/Lowes).
- Honda: Sick of your car? Use #wantnewcar to tell us why and you might get a special one of these (https://vine.co/search/%23 wantnewcar).

## Instagram Video

Instagram video, part of the Instagram photo site, is an online video-sharing and social networking service that enables users to take videos, apply those crafty digital filters (fifteen in all) to them, and share on a variety of social networking sites. In contrast to Vine's six seconds, users can shoot a slightly longer video, fifteen seconds, using this service. That's a whopping nine extra seconds to capture a customer's attention and tell your story. Another great feature of this video service is the ability to go back and add or delete scenes after you have shot some additional video. Vine does not allow for this feature. The videos on Instagram also have a defined beginning and end that may also be preferable over the continual loop offered on Vine. This feature allows content creators to capture more fully the story that they intend to share. Burberry has successfully used Instagram video to build interest surrounding its upcoming 2014 men's clothing line, while Michael Kors has launched #instakors, which showcases the life of designer Michael Kors.

## YouTube or Vine or Instagram?

Social media strategists and public relations professionals are in a great position in that they have three integratable video platforms to choose from. Knowing when to use the right platform is critical to the ultimate success of the project. Here are some general guidelines:

*YouTube*: Good for practical advice, guest speakers, case studies, conference events, and longer how-to videos.

*Vine*: A perfect platform for invitations to events, video teasers, new products, and how-to.[13]

*Instagram Video*: Nice for promotional campaigns, layered stories, video series, and commercial-style videos.[14]

As noted previously that any of these platforms can be used to showcase sneak peeks, promote an upcoming speaker or event, highlight a quick clip to demo a new product or feature, spotlight community service initiatives, or provide a behind-the-scenes look at the office. The key to success is that the video idea should be creative in a personal, yet professional, way. Relatability and discussability should be at the forefront of the campaign.

Regardless of which platform is selected to promote the videos, the same manner in which a company promotes its other social media strategies should be followed. This strategy typically lends itself to cross promotion over multiple social platforms for maximum exposure. Whether embedding the video within a company blog post, tweeting the link, including links to websites or microsites, sharing the video on the company Facebook or Pinterest pages, posting it straight to the company website, or sharing the video within Vine and Instagram, one can see that there are many options for sharing content. Cross promotion also lends itself to opportunities for further engaging in and encouraging conversations by listening and reacting to what is being said about the videos. Finally, you cannot overlook the metrics aspect. Tracking video viewership will help a company understand its audience and how they interact.

With the advent of multiple video supporting platforms within the social sphere, one can see that video is growing expeditiously. Social strategists and public relations professionals can thank smartphones, tablets, and laptops for this advance in the profession. As access to these handheld devices expands, so does the opportunity to reach your intended audience.

## Video Newcomers

Two players newer to the video scene are Keek and Magisto. Both of these platforms possess a number of unique characteristics that differentiate them from YouTube, Vine, and Instagram. Although small in scale, the features provided by Keek and Magisto may give some of the more veteran video platforms a run for their money.

### Keek

Another word for a short look, glimpse, or peek, Keek is a relatively new app and budding social networking site that allows users to create and instantly watch short video updates using any smartphone, tablet, or laptop—and then share these with their friends.[*] This platform has been described as a "new wave" in technology and even a "mini version" of YouTube. Functions of the app are similar to those seen in Vine and Instagram with other elements of YouTube interspersed within as well. Users, also referred to as "Keekers," create and post short videos—up to thirty-six seconds in length—and then share with the Keek social community. Similar to many other social networking sites, users upload their videos from the mobile app or from the user's desktop webcam. Keekers can follow other Keekers, like their videos, share them, and, of course, comment on them. Although relatively new to the social scene, Keek has already amassed fifty-eight million users. With 250,000 new users signing up to the site each day, Keek is already the top video app in eighteen countries around the world.[†] Available for iOS, Blackberry, and Android, Keek operates via a hashtag system in which users can utilize the "#" sign to unite conversations or create campaigns. Businesses can share their Keeks on other social media platforms, allowing them to incorporate their existing campaigns and magnify the results. Uses of Keek include showcasing everything from live demonstrations to even a *Keek* behind the scenes of a company.

---

[*] Regina Luttrell, "Keek. What's That?" *Gina Luttrell PhD* (blog), August 13, 2013, http://ginaluttrellphd.com/2013/08/13/keek-whats-that/.

[†] Luttrell, "Keek. What's That?"

## Magisto

Some in the social arena are calling Magisto a fresh spin on personal video that has started to set the stage for social sharing and brand curation.* Magisto is an automated online video editor: "Using artificial intelligence algorithms, the software takes 3 to 20 minutes of video and up to 20 photos, analyzes the content and condenses it down to a 1 to 3 minute narrative arc."† Using the Magisto app, users create unique and one-of-a-kind videos using photos right from a digital camera roll or computer.‡ Users choose from a variety of themes and can also incorporate a selection of music offered by Magisto or from the user's personal playlist.

Brands have already taken notice of Keek and Magisto and started using both in promoting their messages. Currently, the top users of Keek are the social media mavens—Kim, Khloe, and Kourtney Kardashian, and British Olympic swimmer Tom Daley. Since Keek plays on the strengths of quick interactions in real time, celebrities and brands that take chances will thrive on this social networking site.

A company quick to adopt the Magisto utility has been Sierra Trading Post. This company recently ran a promotion involving Magisto encouraging consumers to create and post a fun outdoor adventure movie. During the two-week promotion, two hundred Magisto videos were posted, generating fifty-four thousand views.§ As a point of reference, over a four-year period, videos on Sierra's YouTube channel have garnered a *total* of four hundred thousand views. Sporting goods maker Rawlings has also embraced the widespread appeal of video-sharing sites and recently invited baseball fans to create movies about their love for America's favorite pastime.¶ Ten winners were selected from the fifty most liked videos on the Rawlings-branded album on Magisto.

---

* Regina Luttrell and Laura Jackson, "Magisto—You Heard It Here First!" *Gina Luttrell PhD* (blog), October 10, 2013, http://ginaluttrellphd.com/2013/10/10/magisto-you-heard-it-here-first/.

† Unknown, "A Fresh Spin on Personal Video," *AdWeek* (blog), October 21, 2013, http://www.adweek.com/sa-article/fresh-spin-personal-video-153211.

‡ Luttrell and Jackson, "Magisto—You Heard It Here First!"

§ Unknown, "A Fresh Spin on Personal Video."

¶ Unknown, "A Fresh Spin on Personal Video."

# Theory into Practice

Skittles: "Smash the Rainbow. Taste the Rainbow."[15]

Skittles brand enlisted DDB Chicago, a public relations agency, to help create a promotional spot that might be considered quite different from your ordinary candy commercial. The completed commercial was released on YouTube as an interactive commercial that allowed viewers to "pick up" virtual figurines and smash them onto the ground, resulting in the figurine turning into a pile of rainbow-colored Skittles.[16] The Skittles brand tried to take a different approach at an advertisement in an effort to make its brand stand out and be more memorable: http://www.youtube.com/watch?v=ywTgLeb4458.

## *Target Audience*

For this campaign, the Skittles brand target audience included teens and young adults. By incorporating an interactive element within the commercial, the Skittles brand was banking on the fact that teens and young adults are much more likely to search videos on YouTube and, thus, would also be much more likely to share and interact with a video commercial like this.[17]

## *Objectives/Goals*

The overarching goal of this campaign was to make the Skittles advertisement stand out over those promotions from competing brands. The idea of airing a YouTube video that lets the viewer choose which figurines he or she wants to "smash" in order to get Skittles is very innovative. This promotion is very unique and unlike any other candy commercial in the market. By creating a much more personalized commercial and experience, Skittles is establishing a stronger connection between its consumers and the brand, and also allowing the consumer to feel as if they have become a part of the brand.

## *Strategies*

By using such an unorthodox interactive advertisement, the Skittles brand drew a lot more attention than just an ordinary commercial traditionally might. Since many teens and young adults spend a lot of time on YouTube, they tend to share videos with their friends and family more often than adults do. The Skittles brand took advantage of this tendency, and by posting this commercial on YouTube, they made it easier for people to share and interact, which makes people feel a closer connection to the brand.

*Tactics*

Using interactive advertising, Skittles can promote an interest in watching the commercial. Although figurines cannot actually be smashed and magically turned into Skittles, it makes the advertisement more personalized and builds a connection between the user and Skittles brand as a whole.

*Evaluation*

This commercial received two hundred thousand views on YouTube, and the Skittles' Facebook page now has over twenty-five million "likes" and over 116,000 followers on Twitter.[18]

---

**#LRNSMPR**

Learn More about Video on the Social Web

Quick Links

- Why You Need a Branded YouTube Channel and How-to Tips That Attract Viewers, http://bit.ly/1fdAXCA
- Viral Video: The Scarecrow from Chipotle, http://ti.me/GCPfyA
- Five Video Projects You Can Do in 25 Minutes or Less, http://bit.ly/1dZyvg8
- 10 Editing Tips for Making Killer Instagram Videos, http://bit.ly/16OsNhN

---

# Notes

1. Claudio Pannunzio, i-Impact Group, "SMK: Social Media Knowledge," last modified April 18, 2012, accessed September 30, 2013, http://www.i-impactgroup.com/A Video Is Worth_041812.pdf.

2. Pannunzio, "SMK: Social Media Knowledge."

3. A. Follett, "18 Big Video Marketing Statistics and What They Mean for Your Business," *Video Brewery* (blog), April 11, 2013, http://www.videobrewery.com/blog/18-video -marketing-statistics.

4. Kobus Barnard, Pinar Duygulu, David Forsyth, et al., "Matching Words and Pictures," *Journal of Machine Learning Research* 3 (2003): 1107–35.

5. S. Rosensteel, "Why Online Video Is Vital for Your 2013 Content Marketing Objectives," *Forbes* (blog), January 28, 2013, http://www.forbes.com/sites/seanrosen steel/2013/01/28/why-online-video-is-vital-for-your-2013-content-marketing-objectives/.

6. R. Parker, "Content Marketing Shoutout: Blendtec," *Resonance* (blog), January 8, 2013, http://www.resonancecontent.com/blog/bid/169002/.

7. G. Reinhard, "YouTube Brands: 5 Outstanding Leaders in YouTube Marketing," June 1, 2009, http://mashable.com/2009/06/01/youtube-brands/.

8. S. Fiegerman, "Here's Why These 6 Videos Went Viral," *Mashable* (blog), May 15, 2013, http://mashable.com/2013/05/15/viral-video-factors/.

9. G. Abramovich, "The Best YouTube Brand Channels of 2012," *Digiday* (blog), December 11, 2012, http://digiday.com/brands/the-best-youtube-brand-channels-of-2012/.

10. Steve Jenkins, *Justa Second* (HMH Books for Young Readers, 2011).

11. Dom Hoffman, "Introducing Vine," *Vine Blog* (blog), January 24, 2013, http://blog.vine.co/post/55514427556/introducing-vine.

12. L. Lacy, "GE Hosts World's First Science Fair on Vine," *ClickZ* (blog), August 13, 2013, http://www.clickz.com/clickz/news/2288357/ge-hosts-worlds-first-science-fair-on-vine.

13. A. Patel, "When to Use Vine and When to Use Instagram," *Venture Beat* (blog), August 12, 2013, http://venturebeat.com/2013/08/12/when-to-use-vine-and-when-to-use-instagram/.

14. Patel, "When to Use Vine and When to Use Instagram."

15. Rosemary Sheridan, Regina Luttrell, and Melissa Meyer, "Smash the Rainbow. Taste the Rainbow," working paper, College of Saint Rose, 2013.

16. "Video Viral of the Week: Skittles Lets Viewers 'Smash the Rainbow' with Interactive YouTube Ad," *Digital Strategy Consulting*, accessed October 3, 2013, http://www.digitalstrategyconsulting.com/intelligence/2013/06/video_viral_of_the_week_skittles_lets_viewers_smash_the_rainbow_with_interactive_youtube_ad.php.

17. "Skittles' New Digital Marketing Campaign Showcases the Trend towards Interactive Videos," *Marketing Easy*, accessed October 3, 2013, http://marketingeasy.net/skittles-smash-the-rainbow-digital-marketing-campaign/2013-08-07.

18. "Help Tommy Smash Porcelain Figurines as He Hunts for Skittles," *TrendHunter Marketing*, accessed October 3, 2013, http://www.trendhunter.com/trends/porcelain-figurines.

# CRISIS MANAGEMENT ON THE SOCIAL SPHERE

Social networks create significant opportunities for brands, but they also become platforms on which crises can develop and go viral at an unprecedented rate. In dealing with a rogue tweet, a product recall, an employee acting badly on YouTube, a disparaging review on Yelp, or a spokesperson who tarnished the brand, the ability to prepare for a crisis situation in a digital age requires a fresh perspective.

## Millennial-Era Crises

A 2013 survey revealed that more than 28 percent of reported crises spread internationally within an hour, and over two-thirds spread within the first twenty-four hours.[1] Despite having traditional crisis plans in place, companies find that they are not prepared to manage the crisis on the social sphere. In fact, 50 percent of communications professionals believe organizations are not adequately prepared to handle such situations, and 94 percent think that the failure to effectively define how to handle online issues leaves an organization open to "trial by Twitter."[2] These statistics illustrate the impact that social media has on crisis management. Governments, educational institutions, nonprofit organizations, corporations, and even private citizens are not immune. The following examples highlight this exact point:

- Governments: In 2011, social media-savvy activists across the Middle East and North Africa contributed to the downfall of two dictators, causing widespread disruption. "We use Facebook to schedule the protests, Twitter to coordinate, and YouTube to tell the world," an Arab Spring activist told a reporter during the riots.[3] These types of demonstrations force countries and governments to move into a crisis-response mode.

- Educational Institutions: Penn State University remained silent amid allegations of sexual abuse, years of cover ups, and acts of misuse and exploitation, while the larger community took to Twitter, Facebook, and hundreds of other online news and media sites to voice their opinions and blast the Penn State brand.

- Nonprofit Organizations: After admitting to doping and using performance-enhancing drugs to win seven Tour de France titles, Lance Armstrong stepped down as chairman of the Livestrong Foundation. The public lambasted Armstrong on several social sites, tarnishing the reputation of both his charity and his personal image. In the aftermath of this crisis, the Livestrong Foundation amped up efforts to detach itself from the cyclist.

- Corporations: The BP oil spill in the Gulf of Mexico spawned an oil disaster so large that the complete ramifications are still unknown almost four years later. In response to the crisis, CEO Tony Hayward demonstrated an arguable approach, landing him in hot water with the public and throughout the social sphere. During the crisis Hayward was quoted as saying, "Well, it wasn't our accident, but we are absolutely responsible for the oil, for cleaning up" (May 3, 2010); "The Gulf of Mexico is a very big ocean. The amount of volume of oil and dispersant we are putting into it is tiny in relation to the water volume" (May 14, 2010); and "The environmental impact of this disaster is likely to have been very, very modest" (May 18, 2010).[4] Hayward's attempt to apologize and mitigate the crisis led to further outrage: "I'm sorry—we're sorry—for the massive disruption this has caused their lives. And there's no one who wants this over more than I do. You know, I want my life back" (May 30, 2010). Hayward, and as a result BP Oil, became fodder on numerous blogs, and the topic continues to retain genuine staying power within the Twitterverse.[5]

- Private Individuals: Chelsea Welch, an angry Applebee's waitress, catapulted Pastor Alois Bell from private citizen to evil villainess after the pastor left an unassuming note on the waitress's receipt. The social sphere reacted swiftly, harshly, and without mercy to the Applebee's response in the matter and to the pastor herself.

These five examples represent modern-day crises that spread on social media as the events unfolded in real time. The reputation of a brand can easily be tarnished in mere moments because an active public now has the ability to take a stance, make a statement, and judge that brand based on how the company chooses to addresses (or not address) the crisis at hand.

Social media is immediate, pervasive, and widely available, and it appeals to hundreds of millions of people. However, for many of those same reasons, social media can also be dangerous for brands, especially during a time of crisis, requiring the addition of entirely new components within crisis communication. What would have been considered a "textbook" crisis situation years ago (think Johnson & Johnson Tylenol and the Exxon Valdez oil spill cases) is long gone. Today, public relations practitioners employ an amalgamation of tactics, strategies, and responses during a time of crisis via the social web. A fresh perspective is necessary to effectively respond to today's crisis situations.

## Five Stages of Crisis Management in the Digital Age

Konrad Palubicki (@konradpalubicki) from Edelman Digital in Seattle, Washington, developed what he considers the five most important stages of crisis management in the digital age:[6]

1. Prepare in advance.
2. Isolate the origin.
3. Evaluate the impact.
4. Mitigate the crisis.
5. Learn from the crisis.

### Prepare in Advance

We all love watching viral videos just as much as the next person. The Harlem Shake, Conversations with My Two-Year-Old, and "What Does the Fox Say?" are all funny, sharable, and light-hearted videos. But when a viral video is about your company, brand, or products, it may not be as funny.[7] It is unrealistic to believe that brands can prepare for every potential crisis, but pre-crisis planning is essential. Author and crisis communication professional Kathleen Fearn-Banks suggests creating a crisis communication plan.[8] The plan should list the individuals on the crisis management team, generate a crisis audit, and develop key messages, objectives, procedures, and specific guidelines. Some companies take the added step of developing a "dark" website that only goes live in the event of an emergency.[9] Prewritten messaging and critical information can be created ahead of the crisis, uploaded to the site, and launched if a crisis ever breaks.

Preparing in advance also means that companies must be paying attention to the conversations occurring on their social channels. The task of perusing through the company Twitter feed or browsing the company Facebook posts should not be considered as truly listening. Organizations need to use specific social media–monitoring software such as Meltwater Buzz, Crimson Hexagon, Sysomos, Lithium, Viralheat, or Social Mention to understand the messages that pertain to their company or brand. These software systems help companies monitor who is participating in conversations and what is being said specific to their company across multiple social media platforms, blogs, and website comments. Monitoring also aids in identifying where the crisis originated.

### Isolate the Origin

Being able to identify where a crisis initiates and on what social channels the conversations fueling the crisis are happening is paramount in controlling the crisis situation.[10] When brands understand the cause of the crisis, they can better assess how to respond. Proper identification helps a company determine whether a full social media crisis is present and is also invaluable in helping a company decide the next steps in formulating a proper response.

### Evaluate the Impact

Take inventory of the situation. Create a log to determine which stakeholders need attention first, and fast. There are two primary audiences during a crisis—those directly affected and those whose attitudes about the company could be influenced.[11] Determine whether one group is being impacted more than another and evaluate the immediate impacts of the situa-

**Social Media Crisis or Not?**

Would you know if your company was in the midst of a social media crisis? These three characteristics can help determine whether a company is in a true social media crisis mode:*

1. *Definite Change from the Norm*: Companies should watch for sudden changes in tone and sentiment that are being discussed and shared on social media sites.
2. *Information Separation*: The company is not aware of the situation any more than the public.
3. *Widespread Impact throughout the Company*: The scope and scale is so large and incomprehensible during the initial stage at which the crisis breaks that it has ramifications at every level.

---

\* Jay Baer, *Youtility* (New York: Penguin, 2013).

tion. The sense of urgency in a company's response and the tactics selected could include:[12]

- uptick in calls to the customer service hotline
- rise in media inquiries
- flurry of comments on social channels
- interest from government regulators
- inquiries from the board of directors
- disaffection toward brands or products
- drop in sales
- potential lawsuit
- vulnerability of personal, societal, and economic conditions

If a company waits too long to acknowledge and respond while a crisis breaks, the company can instantly lose credibility. Social media crises will not disappear after a few days. On the contrary, without proper management, the crisis will continue to build momentum and accelerate to a tipping point. Twenty-four hours on the social web is too long to wait to acknowledge and respond. Heck—four hours could be too long!

## Mitigate the Crisis

The more rapid the response time, the better chance a company has at limiting the total time the crisis lasts. The first rule in crisis management is "stop the bleeding." Acting fast and responding to the situation is paramount. Once the crisis team establishes an initial response, focus should then shift toward ensuring a continuity of messages throughout all traditional and social channels.

It is important to sustain real-time updates by including details that are honest and straightforward. Remember the "dark" website suggestion from earlier in the chapter? Bring that to life. A website dedicated to the crisis serves two purposes. First, the website can minimize the conversations happening on social sites. Second, the website illustrates that the company is proactive in resolving the issue at hand. A website of this nature can provide companies with a platform for providing regular updates, contact information, video or photo updates, current actions related to the crisis, and plans to ensure the incident will not happen again.

Continue listening through the monitoring tools set in place prior to the crisis. Establish an in-house crisis command center so that the crisis team can collaborate in real time.[13] Companies can track the crisis using all traditional media channels and social platforms simultaneously. Companies can use Twitter and Facebook to proactively post statements such as "We are aware of the issue. Live updates are here: [provide URL]." The URLs will drive traffic back to the company-dedicated website that contains the most relevant information.

## Learn from the Crisis

All crises are learning opportunities. Crises may not necessarily be the type of lessons that we love, but they are opportunities where we can gain valuable insights. Companies should conduct a postcrisis meeting to determine how the organization performed during the crisis. An analysis of emails sent, offline media coverage garnered, company statements, and all social mentions, including tweets, blog comments, pins, videos, Facebook updates, and any other online media mentions, should be conducted. The process of analysis is evaluative and designed to bring about change that helps prevent similar future crises.[14]

## Smart Companies, Unfortunate Crises

Some companies are better equipped to handle a crisis than others. Regardless of how prepared a company believes it is regarding how to handle a crisis, there is always something to learn from the experience. Companies can learn how to strengthen their own social media crisis management strategy by examining how other organizations, including the media company IAC, Oreo, J.C. Penney, Burger King, KitchenAid, Applebee's, Paula Deen, and British Airways, dealt with crises within the social sphere.

### Offensive Tweet *Not* a Match Made in Heaven[15]

Justine Sacco, former corporate communications director for the prominent New York–based Internet media company IAC, lost her job after she tweeted "Going to Africa. Hope I don't get AIDS. Just Kidding. I'm White!" IAC owns and operates more than a dozen websites, including the news websites the Daily Beast and CollegeHumor; dating websites such as Match.com, BlackPeopleMeet.com, and OKCupid; and other well-known brands like Vimeo. IAC acted swiftly, which illustrated just how seriously the company took the incident. In a public statement, company spokespeople were quoted as saying, "The offensive comment does not reflect the views and values of IAC. We take this issue very seriously, and we have parted ways with the employee in question." Sacco herself apologized in a written statement "for being insensitive to this crisis—which does not discriminate by race, gender or sexual orientation, but which terrifies us all uniformly— and to the millions of people living with the virus, I am ashamed."[16] This incident is an excellent reminder for corporations as well as individuals that each opinion expressed on the Internet can be heard by the millions of active users who are listening, following, and sharing. Sentiments that individuals or corporations tweet, like, or share can have grave consequences.

### Colorful Cookie

Kraft Foods, the brand behind Oreo cookies, found itself in some trouble after it posted a rainbow-stuffed cookie with the caption "Proudly support love!" in honor of Gay Pride month.[17] The backlash to this initiative came from some consumers who felt that the brand should not support gay rights. Consumers voiced their opinions on both Twitter and the Oreo

Facebook page. Kraft Foods was facing a possible boycott from the public over this initiative. Basil Maglaris, a spokeswoman for Oreo's parent company Kraft Foods, responded by saying, "We are excited to illustrate what is making history today in a fun and playful way. As a company, Kraft Foods has a proud history of celebrating diversity and inclusiveness. We feel the OREO ad is a fun reflection of our values."[18] On the flip side, there were also numerous fans who supported the campaign. Loyal Oreo cookie supporters from across the globe defended the issue on the company's Facebook page and Twitter feed. Talk about devotion! Fans who are willing to help in a time of crisis are just the kind of fans that a brand wants to attract. This example illustrates how much trust consumers have with Oreo and the type of genuine relationship that Oreo has built with its customer base. The tone and consistency with which Kraft Foods responded to the public contributed greatly to the success of its response. From email to social media, Kraft Foods consistently stood by its company values and stopped the crisis from igniting into a maelstrom of negativity.

### Teapot Debacle

J.C. Penney came under fire after a number of reddit users noted that the company's newest teapot design closely resembled the ex-German dictator Adolf Hitler.[19] An innocent mistake on behalf of the designer, yes, and some might even argue that the interpretation is a matter of personal perception. In this instance, however, perception did not seem to matter much. J.C. Penney now had a potential firestorm brewing and needed to respond quickly before the situation could escalate into a full-blown social media crisis. J.C. Penney's approach involved addressing the situation quickly and acknowledging the social references. Using Twitter, the crisis team developed and delivered a tweet response for each instance that the teapot's likeness to Adolf Hitler was mentioned: "Certainly unintentionally. If we had designed the kettle to look like something, we would have gone with a snowman or something fun :)." The tweet illustrated good intentions, acknowledged what consumers were chatting about on the social web, noted that the act was unintentional, and attempted to keep the response respectful, yet humorous. J.C. Penney had the wherewithal to discern the difference between a social media *issue*, which this was, and a social media crisis. The company handled the situation well by staying calm, responding promptly, and providing the public with the right amount of information.

## Hacked Burger

In February 2013, the Burger King Twitter account was hacked.[20] The pranksters changed Burger King's company avatar and name to that of its rival McDonald's. The hackers then proceeded to tweet numerous questionable and offensive tweets from this account. Within the first thirty minutes of the attack, the Burger King Twitter account attracted five thousand new followers. By the time Burger King regained control of its account and issued an apology, the brand had gained more than thirty thousand new followers. In this instance the response was rapid and information was proactively shared with the public during the crisis. Burger King took the proper steps to "stop the bleeding" and ended up with an increased following due to this event.

## Messy Mix-Up

What happens when an employee tweets from the company account rather than their own personal Twitter account? KitchenAid knows all too well the ramifications of a crisis like this.[21] A member of the KitchenAid social media team posted an insensitive tweet about President Barack Obama's grandmother during Obama's first presidential campaign. Rather than posting this message to their personal Twitter account, the employee posted the message to the KitchenAid Twitter account. The outrageous tweet read, "Obamas gma even knew it was going 2 b bad! She died 3 days b4 he became president." The tweet was deleted from the KitchenAid account within fifteen minutes of its original post, but countless people had already seen it, shared it, and commented on it. It only took fifteen minutes to damage the KitchenAid brand. Cynthia Soledad, the head of the KitchenAid brand, immediately apologized to both President Obama and the public. In a series of 140-character tweets and a full apology on the company website, Soledad issued the following apology: "During the debate tonight, a member of our Twitter team mistakenly posted an offensive tweet from the KitchenAid handle instead of a personal handle. The tasteless joke in no way represents our values at KitchenAid, and that person won't be tweeting for us anymore. That said, I lead the KitchenAid brand, and I take responsibility for the whole team. I am deeply sorry to President Obama, his family, and the Twitter community for this careless error. Thanks for hearing me out."[22]

Several actions on the part of the brand manager deserve applause in this time of crisis. Soledad's response was quick and sincere; she confronted the situation head on, illustrating empathy, compassion, and transparency; and she humanized the brand through her words. She also stated what the company was going to do to address the situation so that it did not happen in the future. There are many takeaways from this social crisis, but stressing the importance of keeping personal and company accounts separate is an imperative lesson for businesses and employees alike. Many social strategists use tools like HootSuite to manage their personal and client accounts, but this social media crisis keenly illustrates the ramifications of not paying attention. If a mistake like this does occur, it should be addressed immediately. What saved KitchenAid was Soledad's candid, authentic explanation and personal tone of regret. By regaining control quickly, the apology was well received, thus minimizing any long-term damage to the brand's reputation.

Oreo, J.C. Penney, Burger King, and KitchenAid are all examples of what *should* be done during a social media crisis. Not all brands understand the power and magnitude of consumers on the Internet. Just as a quickly and well-timed reaction or sincere apology can prevent a potential crisis from forming, the opposite response can have an equally rapid, disastrous consequence for a brand. With that in mind, let us examine what happened when Applebee's, Paula Deen, and British Airways faced their own social media crises.

## What's Good for the Goose Isn't Always Good for the Gander

A seemingly innocent note incited fury on the social web and set a series of bad events in motion for the Applebee's restaurant chain.[23] Pastor Alois Bell had eaten at an Applebee's restaurant and, upon paying her bill, crossed out the automatic 18 percent tip charged for parties of more than eight people and left the following message on the receipt above her signature: "I give God 10% why do you get 18?" The waitress, Chelsea Welch, was so upset that she took a photo of the receipt and posted it on the social news and entertainment website reddit. Subsequently, the waitress was fired for "violating customer privacy." Actions related to violating this policy would have been completely understandable if Applebee's had not posted a similar receipt that was *complimenting* the company only two weeks prior. As news of this incident spread and enraged people across virtually every social media platform, Applebee's responded with this short post defending its actions on its Facebook page: "We wish this situation hadn't happened. Our Guests' personal information— including their meal check—is private, and neither Applebee's nor its franchisees have a right to share this information publicly. We value our Guests' trust above all else. Our franchisee has apologized to the Guest and has taken disciplinary action with the Team Member for violating their Guest's right to privacy."[24] Almost instantaneously, the Applebee's statement precipitated more than ten thousand comments—most of which were negative in nature. At this point, Applebee's was knee deep in a social media crisis that it did not appear prepared to manage. Applebee's began posting the same message in its response to comments on multiple social media platforms. The repetitive response only garnered additional negative feedback. Applebee's then deleted all negative messages and started to block fans. The downward spiral of contempt continued as Applebee's persisted in defending its actions and arguing with, even criticizing, its fans during the crisis. Another questionable move by Applebee's involved a decision to hide the original post. Not surprisingly, this action spawned even more public fury, rage, and annoyance.

In retrospect, it may be easy to see that Applebee's broke many rules regarding crisis communication. Companies must remember that it is not about winning an argument; rather, it is about responding with empathy, honesty, patience, authenticity, and transparency. During a period in which a crisis exists, people are angry. In some instances, anger is at such an elevated level that any company response may incite added fury or rage. Make sure that employees know *not* to go "tit for tat" with upset consumers. Applebee's also failed to observe "The Rule of Three": never, *ever*, send a third reply.[25] A third reply is an argument and no longer an answer. If a company feels that it must explain its actions a third time, then it is time to take the conversation offline. In this case, Applebee's was well past having a conversation; instead, it was engaged in a full-blown argument with fans. The defensive and confrontational approach amplified the disastrous crisis condition. Intentionally hiding comments or criticisms should never be a consideration because these actions can only make the crisis worse. Simply put, arguing with Facebook fans is *always* wrong and *never* appropriate. This crisis, including the Applebee's response in how to handle it, may be remembered as one of the most ill-thought-out social media crisis communication strategies to date.

## Now in Session: The Court of Public Opinion

June 2013 was a very bad month for Paula Deen, the "Queen of Butter" and celebrity personality on the Food Network.[26] After allegations surfaced that Deen had testified under oath to using the "n" word, mistreating and harassing employees, and demonstrating an arguable level of ignorance as to what it means to have racial tendencies and tolerance, she found herself watching her career career out of control. Deen failed to obey the golden rule of crisis management—acknowledge, say sorry, and truly mean it. A company, brand, or (in this case) an individual has only one opportunity to apologize. After posting three insincere video apologies *days after the crisis broke*, and following an in-person appearance on the *Today Show* in which she emerged with a defensive persona, the Food Network, Walmart, Sears, and Kmart, J.C. Penney, Walgreens, and a laundry list of other high-profile sponsors all ended their long-term relationships with Deen. And sponsors were not the only ones who had enough. Many of Deen's loyal followers had also thrown in the towel. The Paula Deen Facebook page and Twitter feed was littered with comments from outraged fans. Deen had very quickly lost control of the crisis, and the court of public opinion had taken over. It still remains to be seen what will happen to her in the future.

## Flying the Not-so-Friendly Skies

Promoted tweets are all the rage for celebrities and businesses alike, but when an angry customer buys a promoted tweet, you can imagine that a social media crisis is quick to ensue. In September 2013 an unhappy customer of British Airways purchased a promoted tweet to complain about the lack of customer service provided by the airline. In a response to a lack of information regarding his missing luggage, British Airways passenger Hasan Syed had this to say: "Don't fly @BritishAirways. Their customer service is horrendous."[27] After what could be deemed a lifetime on social media—*ten hours*—British Airways finally responded with an apathetic tweet of its own: "Sorry for the delay in responding, our twitter feed is open 09:00–17:00 GMT. Please DM your baggage ref and we'll look into this."[28] Today's consumers are more empowered than ever before. Social networks give people immediate platforms from which they can broadcast their messages. In the case of Syed's lost luggage, consumers are now even taking the added step of buying their messages in an effort to communicate with companies. On a business level, there is really no excuse for not providing a real-time response to any type of social media issue. If a company is going to have a presence on social networking sites, it must also have a well-thought-out online strategic customer service policy in place. This plan should address and instruct employees how to respond to disgruntled customers, provide examples of messaging, and include an action plan for escalated incidents deemed potential crises for the company or brand. The takeaway here is that with any crisis situation, it is vital to respond with humility. The response from British Airways lacks any degree of understanding, empathy, or compassion. Social customer service teams should be empowered to engage in a timely, personalized manner that illustrates to customers that the brand is listening and cares about what the customer is saying.

## Today's Reality

Public relations practitioners should expect that within the first seconds or minutes after a crisis arises targeting a company, brand, or organization, conversations related to the crisis would be mentioned, shared, and talked about online. In the highly interconnected environment in which we conduct business today, the chance that a crisis can go viral has become extremely high. Knowing how to communicate with fans and on the correct social networking platforms is critical to being able to properly manage a social media crisis.

## Theory into Practice

### Burger King's Damaging Lettuce Debacle

Burger King is no stranger to crises involving employees participating in disgusting acts and then alerting the public to these incidents. In 2008, a Burger King employee posted a Myspace video of himself bathing in a restaurant sink. The company handled the crisis well and with swift action.[29]

More recently, Burger King faced another crisis after an employee posted a picture to 4chan depicting himself standing in two containers of lettuce.[30] The caption read, "This is the lettuce you eat at Burger King." Some 4chan users were so outraged that they took it upon themselves to take action. Using GPS data attached to the image, 4chan users traced the photo and were able to pinpoint the location of which Burger King restaurant that the photograph had been taken. Once the offending employees were identified, Burger King promptly fired them and the company released the following statement:

> Burger King Corp. has recently been made aware of a photo posted on a social networking site that allegedly shows a Burger King restaurant employee violating the company's stringent food handling procedures. Food safety is a top priority

169

at all Burger King restaurants, and the company maintains a zero-tolerance policy against any violations such as the one in question.

Read the full story and watch the following video: article: http://huff.to/18x5RBE; video: http://bit.ly/1gtAttl.

*Discussion Questions*

1. Could Burger King have prevented the employee from taking and posting the image of himself on the Internet?
2. What can Burger King do to prevent a crisis like this occurring in the future?
3. How sharable was this story?
4. Was the brand hurt in any way?
5. Was Burger King's response sufficient?
6. Were you surprised that consumers took action to locate where the photo was taken?
7. Would you have handled this social media crisis differently? If yes, how so? If no, what was exemplary about how Burger King handled it?

Amy Neumann (@CharityIdeas), a digital media and technology expert, recommends incorporating the following actions during a crisis:

- Stay on top of conversations about your company with simple tools.
- Watch for sudden changes in tone and sentiment, ranging from positive or neutral to negative.
- Set up and monitor keywords related to your business.
- Monitor who is talking to you across all social media platforms and website comments.
- Respond, both individually and more broadly.
- Use updates on the same platforms someone talks, and invite them to email you if deeper interaction is needed.
- Acknowledge there is a situation.
- Keep real-time updates flowing.
- Be honest and straightforward with details.
- Make sure customers feel heard by replying, directing them to resources for updates.
- Answer questions directly.

- Be gracious in receiving their feedback, and do not delete negative comments.
- Update social media platforms with outcomes, and update websites.
- Notify the media for additional outreach.
- Outline the resolution, what was learned, and how similar situations will be prevented in the future.*

* Amy Neumann, "5 Steps for Crisis Management Using Social Media," *Huffington Post*, August 20, 2012, http://www.huffingtonpost.com/amy-neumann/5-steps-for-crisis-manage_b_1791673.html (accessed October 16, 2013).

# Notes

1. Freshfields, "Half of Businesses Unprepared to Handle 'Digital Age' Crises," *Freshfields Bruckhaus Deringer* (blog), November 13, 2013, http://www.freshfields.com/en/news/Half_of_businesses_unprepared_to_handle_%E2%80%98digital_age%E2%80%99_crises/.

2. Freshfields, "Half of Businesses Unprepared to Handle 'Digital Age' Crises."

3. Philip Howard, "The Arab Spring's Cascading Effects," *Pacific Standard*, February 11, 2011, http://www.psmag.com/politics/the-cascading-effects-of-the-arab-spring-28575/ (accessed November 13, 2013).

4. Julian Hoffmann, "BP Oil Spill: Failed Crisis Communication," *My PR Master of spin doctors and mutual benefits: A PR Master student's blog* (blog), January 17, 2013, http://myprmaster.wordpress.com/2013/01/17/bp-oil-spill-failed-crisis-communication/.

5. Ian Capstick, "5 Digital PR Lessons from BP's Oil Spill Response," *Media Shift* (blog), July 12, 2010, http://www.pbs.org/mediashift/2010/07/5-digital-pr-lessons-from-bps-oil-spill-response193/.

6. Konrad Palubicki, "Friday Five: Crisis Management in a Digital Age," *Edelman Digital* (blog), June 14, 2013, http://www.edelmandigital.com/2013/06/14/friday-five-crisis-management-in-a-digital-age/.

7. Amy Neumann, "5 Steps for Crisis Management Using Social Media," *Huffington Post*, August 20, 2012, http://www.huffingtonpost.com/amy-neumann/5-steps-for-crisis-manage_b_1791673.html (accessed October 16, 2013).

8. Kathleen Fearn-Banks, *Crisis Communication: A Casebook Approach*, 4th ed. (New York: Routledge, 2011).

9. Palubicki, "Friday Five: Crisis Management in a Digital Age."

10. Palubicki, "Friday Five: Crisis Management in a Digital Age."

11. Fearn-Banks, *Crisis Communication*.

12. Palubicki, "Friday Five: Crisis Management in a Digital Age."

13. Palubicki, "Friday Five: Crisis Management in a Digital Age."

14. Neumann, "5 Steps for Crisis Management Using Social Media."

15. Ashley Southhall, "A Twitter Message about AIDS, Followed by a Firing and an Apology," *New York Times* (blog), December 20, 2013, http://thelede.blogs.nytimes.com/2013/12/20/a-twitter-message-about-aids-africa-and-race/?_r=1; Rob Beschizza, "The Tweet Heard Round the World," *Boing Boing* (blog), December 20, 2013, http://boingboing.net/2013/12/20/the-tweet-heard-round-the-worl.html.

16. Kami Dimitrova, Shahriar Rahmanzadeh, and Jane Lipman, "Justine Sacco, Fired after Tweet on AIDS in Africa, Issues Apology," *ABC News* (blog), December 22, 2013, http://abcnews.go.com/International/justine-sacco-fired-tweet-aids-africa-issues-apology/story?id=21301833.

17. Leslie Poston, "Shining Examples of Excellent Social Media Crisis Management," *Salesforce Marketing Cloud* (blog), September 21, 2012, http://www.salesforcemarketingcloud.com/blog/2012/09/shining-examples-of-excellent-social-media-crisis-management/.

18. Amy Bingham, "Oreo Pride: Rainbow-Stuffed Cookie Sparks Threats of Boycott," *ABC News*, June 26, 2012, http://abcnews.go.com/blogs/politics/2012/06/oreo-pride-rainbow-stuffed-cookie-sparks-boycott/ (accessed October 19, 2013).

19. M. Agnes, "JC Penney Handled Their Hitler Teapot Debacle Like a Pro," *Melissa Agnes Crisis Management* (blog), May 29, 2013, http://www.melissaagnescrisismanagement.com/jc-penney-handled-their-hitler-teapot-debacle-like-a-pro/.

20. Alana Horowitz, "Burger King Twitter Account Hacked," *Huffington Post*, February 18, 2012, http://www.huffingtonpost.com/2013/02/18/burger-king-twitter-hacked_n_2711661.html (accessed October 19, 2013).

21. Kristen Lee, "What a Twit! KitchenAid Takes a Beating over Tasteless Rogue Tweet about Obama's Dead Grandmother," *Huffington Post*, October 4, 2012, http://www.huffingtonpost.com/2013/02/18/burger-king-twitter-hacked_n_2711661.html (accessed October 19, 2013).

22. Brian Anthony Hernandez, "KitchenAid Tweets Joke about Obama's Dead Grandma [Updated]," *Mashable* (blog), October 3, 2012, http://mashable.com/2012/10/03/kitchen-aid-obama-dead-grandma/.

23. R. L. Stollar, "Applebee's Overnight Social Media Meltdown: A Photo Essay," *Overturning Tables* (blog), February 2, 2013, http://rlstollar.wordpress.com/2013/02/02/applebees-overnight-social-media-meltdown-a-photo-essay/.

24. Dean Spencer, "Social Media Storm Hits Applebee's Hard," *The American Citizen's Daily* (blog), February 8, 2013, http://tacdnews.com/2013/02/08/social-media-storm-hits-applebees-hard/.

25. Jay Baer, *Youtility* (New York: Penguin, 2013).

26. Melissa Agnes, "Lessons to Learn from Paula Deen's Three Crappy Apologies," *Melissa Agnes Crisis Management* (blog), June 24, 2013, http://www.melissaagnescrisismanagement.com/lessons-to-learn-from-paula-deens-three-crappy-apologies/.

27. Todd Wasserman, "Man Buys Promoted Tweet to Complain about British Airways," *Mashable* (blog), September 2, 2013, http://mashable.com/2013/09/02/man-promoted-tweet-british-airways/.

28. Katy Ryan Schamberger, "British Airways Sponsored Tweet: Customer Service Is Critical," *Business 2 Community* (blog), September 9, 2013, http://www.business2community.com/customer-experience/british-airways-sponsored-tweet-customer-service-critical-0609554.

29. Fox News, "Burger King Workers Fired over Video of Teen Bathing in Sink," August 13, 2008.

30. Andres Jauregui, "Burger King Employee Posts Photo of Himself Stepping in Lettuce, Gets Busted by 4chan Users [Updated]," *Huffington Post*, last modified July 17, 2013, accessed October 19, 2013, http://www.huffingtonpost.com/2012/07/17/burger-king-employee-steps-in-lettuce-busted-4chan_n_1679793.html.

**CHAPTER TEN**

# RULES OF ENGAGEMENT: DEVELOPING AN EFFECTIVE SOCIAL MEDIA POLICY FOR YOUR COMPANY AND EMPLOYEES

> Organizations that conduct business in today's on-demand media environment should possess a social media policy, yet surprisingly very few do. Social media policies provide a framework to carry out social strategies and implement tactics.

## Establishing the Groundwork

Similar to traditional public relations and social media planning, social media policies are part of a larger, more encompassing strategy. As a company establishes the groundwork for its public relations and social media efforts, establishing clear objectives and the strategy to achieve the objectives is paramount. Development of such a strategy fosters cross-departmental coordination and encourages synergistic cooperation throughout the organization. It also requires strategic input from the individuals tasked with drafting the document and those intending to engage in social media communications on behalf of the organization. The most successful strategies result from the combined opinions and recommendations of many individuals and, regardless of job title or level, all contribute to the larger cause.

Companies face various forms and levels of risk when engaging in social media strategies. However, the necessary steps to mitigate risks tend to all be fairly similar. Often referred to as a social media policy or social media guidelines, these parameters provide a framework for when employees interact online. Some companies may choose to implement rigid policies that spell out exactly what is permissible on company-sponsored social media channels, while others may develop policies that serve as a reference point for staff but allow flexibility in making decisions on their own.

Every company is unique; as a result, their social media policies are also unique. Social media policies tend to reflect the personality of the company. While a single template or set of standards that is applicable to all businesses or organizations has yet to be developed, most social media policies share the following characteristics:[1]

- Trust and respect: Good policies stem from mutual trust. The policy should foster a positive atmosphere in which employees are free to share personal opinions while respecting the opinions of one another without living in fear of retribution. Effective policies outline acceptable online employee behavior rather than listing the actions that are forbidden.

- Values driven: Companies should reflect upon their core values and overarching company culture when drafting their social media policy.[2] This will provide the correct foundation to build a policy that is central to the work that the company does. These values might include integrity, respect, humility, teamwork, or accountability. "Respect" is a core value often found within many organizations. It might then make sense to include a point within the social media policy, related to respecting others' opinions and valuing all contributions. A policy addressing "respect" may read as follows: "It's OK to be yourself and say what is on your mind, but do so respectfully. We want you to connect with colleagues and engage with the larger community. We just ask that when you do, you provide value, share content, ask questions, and participate in meaningful conversations politely, considerately, and without malice toward others."

- Fluid: Companies should be open to adjusting and incorporating any potential changes to their policies over time. Just as social media sites change over time, policies should be fluid enough to accommodate future modifications. If policies and guidelines are narrowly focused, they may become outdated rather quickly.[3] Successful social media policies tend to capture the big picture, are not overly complicated, and are easy to understand.

- Avoid zero tolerance: Stay away from using words such as "always," "must," "shall," and "never."[4] Implementing a "zero-tolerance policy" can be extremely tough, and even problematic to enforce. The legal restrictions within this area are currently evolving at an unprecedented rate. Consider it a best practice to consult the legal and human resources departments for guidance during severe or ongoing circumstances.[5]
- Jargon free: Eliminate highly technical language or legalese. Develop a policy that can be understood across departments. This will encourage participation and become more meaningful to employees.
- Sensible: The policy should not be so complicated that employees need a reference book to understand what to do when they need to interact on social media channels. Provide practical examples and easy-to-understand points. Encourage employees to reference the policy when they are faced with a new or unfamiliar situation.
- Friendly: Policies should be written in such a way that encourages participation. This should include all acceptable actions and employee empowerments.
- Consistent: The best policy is one that is consistent with regard to participation and enforcement throughout the organization. Consistency helps organizations keep their social media efforts on course while also avoiding accusations of favoritism or discrimination.[6]
- Clear consequences: Employees should know what actions the company will take if they violate any part of the social media policy. Should the company need to take action, make certain that the employees are afforded due process and are allowed to present their side of the story.[7] If the transgression requires serious disciplinary consequences, including termination, due process will become even more important.

Social media policies are "living" documents. This means that once the policy is created, it should not simply be put away and never referred to again. Organizations should review and modify their policies on a recurring basis—perhaps quarterly or biannually. A company might consider some of the following questions when revising its social media policy or guidelines:

- Is the policy still relevant?
- Have any social media sites changed? If so, do the changes impact our policy?
- Has the online environment changed? If so, what should we consider revising?
- Are there legal updates that need to be addressed?
- Does anything new need to be added? If so, what?
- Are there any gaps?
- Does a guideline require any clarification? Are examples necessary?

As these policies are revised, seek employee feedback. Keeping the line of communication open and free flowing will maintain continued interest among staff.

## Rolling Out the Policy

Once the social media policy is finalized and ready to roll out, take the time to communicate to employees the importance of every aspect within the policy. The company human resources, legal, and public relations departments can serve as hosts to various events to roll out the new social media policy. As with any other company initiative, create a buzz and drive excitement. Make a big deal out of the new policy.

Consider starting with a number of informal "brown bag lunch" sessions. Invite staff to come to several planned luncheons whereby a presentation of the policy is explained and employees have the opportunity to ask questions. For smaller businesses, one session may be sufficient, but in larger organizations with multiple sites, it may be necessary to schedule several sessions. Employees are more likely to participate if they are given flexibility regarding attendance at an informational session.

Once the in-person sessions are completed, companies can create and post a video online outlining the guidelines so that employees can access the information at will. This material can be posted to the company website or Intranet. A series of blog posts can also be written to illustrate examples, best practices, and case studies.[8] Employees tend to respond with the same enthusiasm that is exhibited by the company. If a company shows a low level of interest regarding the social media policy, it should expect that employees will mimic that same behavior.

## Key Sections

Social media policies have three main sections: an introduction, the main policy points, and a conclusion. The following list highlights five examples of corporate social media policies that you can review, analyze, and consider as you draft your own set of guidelines. Make note of the key sections as you read these policies.

1. Best Buy—Under the premise of "Be smart. Be respectful. Be human." Best Buy clearly presents its do's and don'ts for all company employees engaging in social media activities (http://bit.ly/HJee3k).
2. Oracle—Oracle provides a stricter approach to its social media policy. This set of guidelines includes a higher degree of specifics and also provides pertinent examples (http://bit.ly/HNDs0y).
3. Walmart—Walmart's social media policies speak to almost every area of online engagement, from intellectual property to disgruntled employees and social media engagement (http://bit.ly/18mihJn).
4. IBM—This clear-cut social media policy is specific enough to avoid mistakes created by a lack of common sense demonstrated by employees (http://ibm.co/1gDnS6i).
5. Shippensburg University, Shippensburg, Pennsylvania—This set of social media guidelines is specific to official university social media accounts. What is great about these guidelines is that they provide employees with numerous outside links that assist with everything from privacy to graphics standards (http://bit.ly/1iZyv0i).

## Ubiquitous Sphere

A social media policy is one of the most important set of guidelines that an organization can develop and execute. A well-thought-out policy will encourage employee participation and interaction with customers, build relationships, foster transparency, and minimize risks. It is unrealistic to think that any company can foresee or protect against what may happen on social media platforms used by employees. Taking a proactive and thoughtful approach when creating social media policies can help to avoid many of the pitfalls before they are realized. As long as a company has the right team in place, asks the right questions, revisits the guidelines every now and again, and acknowledges that the culture within the social sphere values transparency, trust, empowerment, and creativity, it is well on its way to creating a policy that fits its needs.

## Theory into Practice

As the presence of social media expands within business, the court systems throughout the United States are experiencing an influx of employee lawsuits against their employers.[9] Numerous court cases regarding social media within business arenas that focus on labor relations issues and related violations by employers continue to appear. For this reason, in May 2012 the National Labor Relations Board (NLRB) created a sample of a lawful social media policy for employers to use as a guideline. Take a moment to read the policy from the NLRB and then choose a social media policy presented within the chapter or one found on the Social Media Governance website, http://bit.ly/18cWVOI. Compare the two.

1. What are the differences?
2. Are the guidelines too broad?
3. Are there any guidelines that might be considered open to interpretation?
4. How might you need to amend these guidelines in order to apply them to your organization?
5. Are there any guidelines that are not clear or that could be misinterpreted by an employee?

### A Sample Social Media Policy from the NLRB[10]

At [Employer], we understand that social media can be a fun and rewarding way to share your experiences and opinions with family, friends, and coworkers around the world. However, the use of social media also presents certain risks and carries with it certain responsibilities. To assist you in making responsible decisions about your use of social media, we have established these guidelines for appropriate use of social media.

This policy applies to all associates who work for [Employer], or one of its subsidiary companies in the United States ([Employer]). Managers and supervisors should use the supplemental Social Media Management Guidelines for additional guidance in administering the policy.

## Guidelines

In the rapidly expanding world of electronic communication, *social media* can mean many things. *Social media* includes all means of communicating or posting information or content of any sort on the Internet, including to your own or someone else's web log or blog, journal or diary, personal website, social networking or affinity website, web bulletin board or a chat room, whether or not associated or affiliated with [Employer], as well as any other form of electronic communication.

The same principles and guidelines found in [Employer] policies and three basic beliefs apply to your activities online. Ultimately, you are solely responsible for what you post online. Before creating online content, consider some of the risks and rewards that are involved. Keep in mind that any aspect of your conduct that adversely affects your job performance, the performance of fellow associates, or otherwise adversely affects members, customers, suppliers, people who work on behalf of [Employer] or [Employer's] legitimate business interests may result in disciplinary action up to and including termination.

### *Know and Follow the Rules*

Carefully read these guidelines, the [Employer] Statement of Ethics Policy, the [Employer] Information Policy, and the Discrimination and Harassment Prevention Policy, and ensure your postings are consistent with these policies. Inappropriate postings that may include discriminatory remarks, harassment, and threats of violence or similar inappropriate or unlawful conduct will not be tolerated and may subject you to disciplinary action up to and including termination.

### *Be Respectful*

Always be fair and courteous to fellow associates, customers, members, suppliers, or people who work on behalf of [Employer]. Also, keep in mind that you are more likely to resolve work-related complaints by speaking directly with your coworkers or by utilizing our Open Door Policy than by posting complaints to a social media outlet. Nevertheless, if you decide to post complaints or criticism, avoid using statements, photographs, video, or audio that reasonably could be viewed as malicious, obscene, threatening, or intimidating; that disparage customers, members, associates, or suppliers; or that might constitute harassment or bullying. Examples of such conduct might include offensive posts meant to intentionally harm someone's reputation or posts that could contribute to a hostile work environment on the basis of race, sex, disability, religion, or any other status protected by law or company policy.

## *Be Honest and Accurate*

Make sure you are always honest and accurate when posting information or news, and if you make a mistake, correct it quickly. Be open about any previous posts you have altered. Remember that the Internet archives almost everything; therefore, even deleted postings can be searched. Never post any information or rumors that you know to be false about [Employer], fellow associates, members, customers, suppliers, people working on behalf of [Employer], or competitors.

## *Post Only Appropriate and Respectful Content*

- Maintain the confidentiality of [Employer] trade secrets and private or confidential information. Trade secrets may include information regarding the development of systems, processes, products, know-how, and technology. Do not post internal reports, policies, procedures, or other internal business-related confidential communications.

- Respect financial disclosure laws. It is illegal to communicate or give a "tip" on inside information to others so that they may buy or sell stocks or securities. Such online conduct may also violate the Insider Trading Policy.

- Do not create a link from your blog, website, or other social networking site to a [Employer] website without identifying yourself as a [Employer] associate.

- Express only your personal opinions. Never represent yourself as a spokesperson for [Employer]. If [Employer] is a subject of the content you are creating, be clear and open about the fact that you are an associate and make it clear that your views do not represent those of [Employer], fellow associates, members, customers, suppliers, or people working on behalf of [Employer]. If you do publish a blog or post online related to the work you do or subjects associated with [Employer], make it clear that you are not speaking on behalf of [Employer]. It is best to include a disclaimer, such as "The postings on this site are my own and do not necessarily reflect the views of [Employer]."

## *Using Social Media at Work*

Refrain from using social media while on work time or on equipment we provide, unless it is work related as authorized by your manager or consistent with the Company Equipment Policy.

Do not use [Employer] email addresses to register on social networks, blogs, or other online tools utilized for personal use.

## Retaliation Is Prohibited

[Employer] prohibits taking negative action against any associate for reporting a possible deviation from this policy or for cooperating in an investigation. Any associate who retaliates against another associate for reporting a possible deviation from this policy or for cooperating in an investigation will be subject to disciplinary action, up to and including termination.

## Media Contacts

Associates should not speak to the media on [Employer's] behalf without contacting the Corporate Affairs Department. All media inquiries should be directed to them.

## For More Information

If you have questions or need further guidance, please contact your human resources representative.

### #LRNSMPR

Learn More about Social Media Guidelines

Quick Links

- NLRB Outlines Employers' Social Media Policy Do's and Don'ts, http://bit.ly/1azPO3p
- Best Practices for Developing a Social Media Policy, http://bit.ly/1a7tN0Y
- 4 NLRB Social Media Case Studies, http://bit.ly/18mfOif
- Southwest Airlines Social Media Guidelines, http://bit.ly/1iRHNLy
- Social Media Employee Policy Examples from Over 100 Organizations, http://bit.ly/1cOaRX3

## **Notes**

1. Cision, "Developing Social Media Policies," last modified 2009, accessed November 8, 2013.

2. Andrea Berry and Ben Stuart, "Create a Social Media Policy for Your Nonprofit Elines to Cover All of Your Social Media Bases," *Social Brite* (blog), February 5, 2013, http://www .socialbrite.org/2013/02/05/create-a-social-media-policy-for-your-nonprofit/.

3. Berry and Stuart, "Create a Social Media Policy."

4. Berry and Stuart, "Create a Social Media Policy."

5. Alyesha Asghar Dotson, "NLRB Outlines Employers' Social Media Policy Dos and Don'ts," *Spilman Thomas & Battle, PLLC* (blog), April 29, 2013, http://www.spilmanlaw .com/Resources/Attorney-Authored-Articles/Labor---Employment/NLRB-Outlines-Em ployers--Social-Media-Policy-Dos-a.

6. Lindy Dwyear, Maddie Grand, and Leslie White, Croydon Consulting and Social-Fish, "Social Media, Risk, and Policies," last modified 2009, accessed November 18, 2013, http://www.socialfish.org/wp-content/downloads/socialfish-policies-whitepaper.pdf.

7. Dwyear, Grand, and White, "Social Media, Risk, and Policies."

8. Sean Gardner, "Two Great Social Media Law Cases Involving Facebook and Linked-In," *The 2morrowknight* (blog), September 28, 2013, http://www.2morrowknight.com/two -great-social-media-law-cases-involving-facebook-and-linkedin/.

9. Gardner, "Two Great Social Media Law Cases Involving Facebook and LinkedIn."

10. National Labor Relations Board, http://www.nlrb.gov/news-outreach/fact-sheets/ nlrb-and-social-media.

# ONLINE MEDIA CENTERS IN A CONNECTED WORLD

The online media center is among the highest-ranked webpages on a company website and is an integral part of a successful media relations strategy. If implemented correctly, journalists will flock to this area of a company website, potentially leading to an increase in media coverage.

## Make a Good First Impression

Research indicates that reporters continue to take on more work with fewer resources.[1] Public relations professionals can make the job of any media representative easier by creating online media centers allowing journalists a quick and efficient way to find key information necessary to pull together a story. If a reporter has to dig too deep for information on a company or to determine whether the story has any merit, they will simply leave the website.[2] An online media center helps tell a company's story. It is our job as public relations professionals to make it easy for the journalists. Developing a compelling online media center, with relevant information, is fairly straightforward. The content should be accessible, easy to share, and easy to find.[3]

### Accessible

Flashy is not necessarily better. Too often companies choose appearance over content. Grandiose images, varied logos, flash technology, video intros, and just about every social media technology out there lacks true value if a journalist cannot find the information they need to complete a story. If you recall, "content is king." Well, the same rule applies here. Content is the driving force behind long-standing, trusting relationships between public relations professionals and journalists. Content such as social media–generated press releases, executive bios, white papers, company logos, and essential photographs are all essential elements within a company's media center. These elements will be explored in more depth within this chapter.

An important aspect of accessibility to a journalist is the ability to be "found." Make sure to take the appropriate steps to maximize the company's SEO strategy and confirm that the online media center is easily located using major search engines. If done properly, web searches using Google, Bing, and Yahoo! should locate the company media center at the top of the list. Once a journalist lands on the company website, prominently feature a tab dedicated to the online media center on the website's main home page.[4] Allow journalists to subscribe to categorized RSS feeds or receive email updates when new content becomes available.[5] RSS feeds, email updates, and e-newsletters will draw journalists to the website over and over. Journalists who subscribe to the company's content are demonstrating that they are interested in the company and that the content the company is generating is relevant to them. Moreover, they see the company as a resource for future stories.

## Easy to Share

Make content easy to share and bookmark—assign each page a unique URL for easy linking, and add social media tags to allow your audience to spread the content for you. You can also embed supplemental video and photos within the media center to make your site more compelling.

## Easy to Find

Frequently journalists complain that they are unable to find necessary information. This might include a photo, an old press release, or the contact information of the media relations department for the company. In general, company websites are designed for customers looking for products, services, or information about a company. This makes it critically important to prominently feature the online media center on the home page of the website to make it easier for journalists to contact a company representative. Companies may also refer to the online media centers as a "Press Center" or "Newsroom." Regardless of the name, the focus and purpose remain the same: companies have the ability to present themselves to an expansive audience with the intent to motivate more significant participation and openness while potentially boosting organic website SEO.[6]

## Components of an Ideal Online Media Center

Online media centers should be viewed as a press kit in digital format.[7] They contain similar elements found within a physical press kit, but are clickable and sharable—both of which are essential elements of media relations in our connected world.

- *Press Releases:* Ideal media centers incorporate the most recent press releases and feature them prominently. The media center home page should list three to five of the company's most recent press releases and also link to a separate archive section. Press releases should be listed in reverse chronological order, with the most recent press release listed first. For press releases that garner media coverage, include links to the articles near the press release. McDonald's separates its press releases into corporate news and financial news and makes it easy for journalists to quickly and efficiently locate the information that they need.[8]
  - o Contact Information: Media contacts are one of the most important elements in an online media center. Journalists often complain that they cannot quickly locate the public relations contact information on a media center webpage without clicking at least five times.[9] This can potentially lead to missing out on media coverage for the company. The contact information for the public relations person should be prominently displayed. For the benefit of journalists who are working on tight deadlines and need to reach someone immediately, list the best telephone number, email address, and any social media channels that they can quickly utilize. When a company representative is not directly available to the reporter, or if the reporter cannot easily find a phone number, the journalist will move on to another source. Including a tab titled "Media Inquiries" with the phone number and email addresses of the persons responsible for

responding to journalists is simple and effective. Southwest Airlines, Lands' End, and Dick's Sporting Goods have all adopted this strategy.[10]

- *Company Background/Statements*: Include information that explains the history of the company or product(s). As the name implies, this tab should provide background information on the company: how it began, milestones the company has reached, and the mission, vision, and goals of the company. Starbucks, for example, includes a tab titled "Views."[11] Within the Starbucks "Views" tab, consumers can read about the company's stance on topics including fostering a culture of responsible self-government, comprehensive health care, the earth's changing climate, and more.

- *Leadership Team*: Within this tab, integrate short biographies of the company owners or founders as well as the top leadership team. Often the name of the individual, the individual's professional title, and a photograph is included. Make the images clickable so that a journalist can select the person they wish to learn more about. The Campbell's Soup Company provides a list of its executive team members,[12] while Hewlett-Packard (HP) uses a "yearbook"-style format: http://bit.ly/1cgZPn5. HP's format provides the journalists with the option of immediately downloading a high-resolution image of the individuals comprising the executive team, since their photos are provided as part of the biographies. Again, this tactic makes the job of the reporter easier because they now have an image to include in their article.

- *Multimedia*: The multimedia tab should include photographs of essential personnel, special events, products, and logos, as well as infographics and video snippets. White papers, reports, webcasts, presentations, and b-roll round out a well-apportioned multimedia area. Some companies create separate tabs or provide a drop-down menu to choose from related to multimedia. One of the most comprehensive multimedia centers can be found on the Coca-Cola Company's website: http://bit.ly/1ch1V6b.

- *Products*: Include a list of products or services, with a brief description of each. Include copy that illustrates why the products or services are significant in the marketplace.[13]

- *FAQs/Fact Sheets*: Many companies have a list comprised of the FAQs from media representatives. Use this portion of the online media center to answer those questions. It is also a best practice to include a fact sheet or sheets depending on the business. Starbucks provides a general company fact sheet, company timeline, and a series of fact sheets on its products (http://bit .ly/1bOJwD2).

- *Speakers or Interview Topics*: Perform the legwork for a journalist by providing a list of topics that company spokespeople can speak to. Consider this tab the company's "expert's directory"—an online resource typically developed by the public relations department for use by local, regional, and national media who seek sources for interviews, inquiries, news, and feature stories. Directories like this incorporate members from various departments and areas of expertise. In providing an avenue for a company's experts to converse with members of the media, the company not

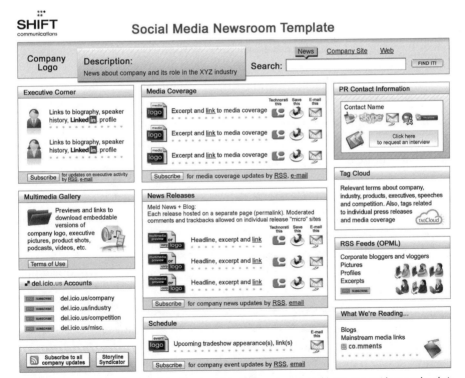

SHIFT Communications developed the first template that companies could use as a guide to evolve their online newsrooms for the "social media" age. (Courtesy of SHIFT Communications)

only gains media exposure but also enhances its public image and illustrates the wealth of expertise that the company possesses.

Additional items to consider for the company media center include an AddThis or ShareThis solution that allows the media to share content more easily.[14] It is also a good idea to incorporate a calendar of events highlighting upcoming events or trade shows, speaking engagements, or community appearances. Providing links to the company newsletter can also be beneficial and provides journalists with insights not available through press releases, fact sheets, white papers, images, or b-roll footage.

### Navigating the Online Media Center

The design of the online media center is almost as important as the content itself. A website designer can help develop the best layout, navigation, and features based on specific requirements. However, the online media center should have its own navigation tab featured on the home page of the company website. Information presented within the online media center should be partitioned into separate tabs. This will make it easy for a journalist to navigate from one tab to the next without ever having to leave the online media center.

The "Press Info" section within Apple's online media center (http://bit.ly/1eXEZwa) prominently features the company's media contacts followed by the latest news, media resources, product images, and the leadership team. The Hershey Company's media center (http://bit.ly/1jxNOQL) contains tabs that feature its newsroom, historical press releases, calendar of events, financial press releases, media contact information, and the latest featured story. Starbucks (http://bit.ly/1kmXYkX) has seven tabs within its media center—Featured, News, Fast Facts, Views, Leadership Team, Multimedia, and Contact—all with drop-down menus in each tab that provide further details.

As technology and communication channels continue to evolve, the development of online media resources is now a business essential. Online media centers are vital for the modern journalist—equally as important as a traditional or social media press release. Beyond journalists, a much larger, more demanding audience is showing interest in accessing the information found within a press release, including bloggers, citizen journalists, content creators, the general public, and various other stakeholders. As a result of this trend toward companies providing more online content, the required elements within a press release have also changed. Not only do audiences desire substantial content that communicates an overarching story, but they also expect to see video, pictures, infographics, stats, and quotes. The public in general now yearns to experience the news, not just read about it. With this in mind, it is essential that practitioners understand how an online (social) press release differs from a traditional press release with respect to content and format.

## Modern Press Releases

One of the most noteworthy events in the history of public relations occurred on October 28, 1906. A tragic accident led to the arrival of the first press release. Public relations expert Ivy Lee was working with the Pennsylvania Railroad when the tragic accident occurred. The lives of fifty passengers were taken when a three-car train of the Pennsylvania Railroad's new electric service jumped a trestle at Atlantic City, New Jersey, and plummeted into the Thoroughfare Creek.[15]

It is reported that Ivy Lee convinced the railroad company to release a statement about what occurred. In doing so, Lee set in motion what is now considered the first press release. Ivy Lee created a public statement about the accident and presented it to journalists at the location of the train accident.[16] The *New York Times* was said to have been so utterly impressed with Lee's information that the newspaper printed the press release word for word on October 30, 1906.[17] Although it is rare for media outlets to use press releases verbatim these days, they do still often act as a starting point for a journalist, bloggers, and content creators to compose a story.

Despite some backlash and criticism of the viability of press releases in more recent years, it still remains one of the most important tools in attracting the attention of journalists more than one hundred years after its inception. A press release that is newsworthy, specifically targeted, and well written is always appreciated by media professionals. In printed form, the structure of the traditional press release has not evolved considerably in format. However, press releases communicated via social media are vastly different.

In the broadest terms, a social media press release, also referred to as a social media *news* release (SMNR) can be defined as "a single page of web content designed to enable the content to be removed and used on blogs, wikis and other social channels."[18] SHIFT Communications developed the world's first social media press release template in 2006. Shortly thereafter,

# The Blog Post Heard around the World*

Influential Silicon Valley journalist and blogger Tom Foremski's now famous blog post, "Die! Press release! Die! Die! Die!," sparked a revolution in the public relations industry. The way public relations professionals announced news to the media had not changed since 1906. Our tactics were stale.

When Formeski wrote this post, the year was 2006 and the public relations industry was experiencing vast changes. The emergence of blogs, bloggers, citizen journalists, and social networking sites began to flood the scene. The long-standing rules between journalists and public relations professionals were in a state of flux. Bloggers were "rogue" and playing by different rules. For the first time bloggers like Chris Anderson were "outing" bad public relations professionals,† and the industry began its transformation. Journalists needed more from public relations profession-als, and Foremski's blog post indicated what was necessary—loud and clear!

To Foremski's credit, he did not just condemn and criticize the press release; he deconstructed what the problem was and suggested alternatives. Essentially, he put the framework together for what we now know as the social media press release. He suggested that public relations professionals should deconstruct the press release into specific sections and tag the information so that media person-nel could compile and connect useful information to aspects of the story. It was also suggested that a larger number of links should be included within the press release body and other relevant links to news articles and references. Foremski likewise proposed that a specific section of the social media press release include a brief description of the announcement, various quotes from C-level executives, and financial information in varied formats.

Today's press releases need to adhere to the requirements of a modern-day audience in response to the way that information is obtained. Press releases that are interesting, informative, and entertaining need to be nimble and fit into multiple formats in order to resonate.‡ Captivating visuals, tweetable headlines, interesting factoids, keyword-friendly text, and easy-to-share pages provide the user with an enhanced experience over a traditional press release. Take the time to examine the overall outcomes and the actions that you want to inspire from a press release hosted within the social sphere.

---

* Tom Foremski, "Die! Press release! Die! Die! Die!" *Silicon Valley Watcher* (blog), February 27, 2006, http://www.siliconvalleywatcher.com/mt/archives/2006/02/die_press_relea.php.

† C. Anderson, "Sorry PR People: You're Blocked," *The Long Tail* (blog), October 29, 2007, http://bit.ly/1bRpBRy.

‡ Magdalena Georgieva, "3 Characteristics of Successful Modern-Day Press Releases," *Inbound Marketing* (blog), October 21, 2011, http://blog.hubspot.com/blog/tabid/6307/bid/27623/3-Characteristics-of-Successful-Modern-Day-Press-Releases.aspx.

Edelman launched StoryCrafter, and the emergence of varied configurations to the social media press release soon followed. The format of the social media press release has gone through many iterations and revisions over the years; however, there are some elements that have remained constant:[19]

**Contact Information**—Prominently feature the media relations personnel contact information at the top. In addition to traditional details like an email address and office and mobile telephone numbers, include other pertinent contact information, such as other social media platforms that the company uses. Keep in mind that you should only list the outlets that you would want a media representative to use to contact you. It's OK if you want bloggers and journalists to simply call or email you, but do not list a Twitter handle if you do not intend to respond via Twitter.

**The Headline**—A good headline has always been integral to entice a journalist to read your press release. You want the headline to immediately gain the reader's attention so that they will continue to read further. Write captivating copy and include specific keywords that are likely to be picked up by search engines.

**Length:** Headlines should fall be between 60 and 120 characters in length. Shorter headlines are easier to share on social networking sites like Twitter and Facebook and are more easily read via subject lines in an email inbox. Additionally, many of the top search engines have specific headline character limits. Google displays headlines that are sixty characters in length, Bing allows for seventy-one characters, and Yahoo! displays 120 characters.

**Format:** Bold and capitalize each word except for prepositions and words three characters or less. For example, **"Consumers Find Social Media Increasingly Trustworthy."**[20]

**The Introductory Paragraph**—Using the standard inverted pyramid—who, why, what, when, and where tell the whole story. Provide a synopsis of the information contained within the press release. A succinct introductory paragraph is critical since many distribution channels only display the headline, a short summary, and a link to the news release.

**Length:** One to four sentences.

**Format:** Title case—use capital letters at the start of the principal words.

**Example:** "In line with ING's ambition to be at the forefront of developments in social media, ING is today presenting the study 'Impact of social media 2012 (#SMING12)' based on a survey among 1,500 Dutch consumers. The survey shows that consumers find social media increasingly trustworthy. 65% said they find the information posted on online media to be trustworthy. 40% of consumers find posts made on social media to be trustworthy."[21]

**Supporting Paragraphs/Details**—Develop a well-written message that resonates with your audience by capitalizing on traditional public relations writing styles and incorporating bulleted points. The information provided within this section should tell your story. Stay away from advertising or marketing speak. Integrate details that support the main points, add interest, or reinforce a message. In traditional press releases the use of multiple quotes can be frowned upon, but multiple quotes from staff, customers, or experts in the field can help round out the story in social media press releases. Bloggers and journalists like to have many quotes to choose from. Statistics and charts can provide additional research and numbers often appreciated by journalists. Be sure to include links throughout the body copy.

**Length:** Three hundred to eight hundred words.

**Format:** Title case, which uses capital letters at the start of the principal words.

**Example:** The following release was written and released by ING and is an excellent example of the critical elements used in social media press releases: http://bit.ly/1jAYgHo.

**Anchor Text Links**—Social media press releases incorporate many anchor text links. Anchor text links are keyword-rich phrases that are linked to a relevant page on the Internet, which then provides additional details related to the phrase. For example, when the American Humane Society announced the release of its documentary *Red Star™ Rescue in Oklahoma*, the organization linked the text *legendary red star* back to a webpage detailing the history of the American Red Star Animal Relief. This tactic not only provided the reader with access to additional information on the program but also helped to improve the SEO of the press release itself. You can read the social media press release here: http://prn.to/1ckCBMG.

**Facts and Stats**—Create a space where bloggers and journalists can find links to the facts, stats, research, and statements highlighted within the press release.

**Multimedia**—Provide a variety of videos, photos, and sound bites that can be used to write the story. For example, if a new partnership is being announced, include a video interview with the CEO. If a new product is being launched, give bloggers and journalists an inside peek at the product by sharing multiple images or even a short video of the product.

**Mobile Friendly Audio**—When including audio sound bites, use a service such as SoundCloud. This service is mobile compatible and allows readers to see and hear all aspects of your social media press release even when they are on the go.

**Video**—Videos can be created on any platform, but recent research has shown that YouTube is one of the best video options.[22] YouTube is fully mobile and provides one of the largest audiences available. Videos can play on a variety of devices, allowing journalists, bloggers, and content creators to view your video no matter where they are. It is also important to note that nearly all social networks recognize YouTube URLs and allow videos coming from the site to be played instantly.

**Infographics**—Infographics have exploded in popularity throughout the social media world and mainstream media outlets. They are an excellent way to highlight research, focus-group results, or survey outcomes or insights from the company's latest white paper.

**Social Bookmarking**—Incorporate buttons allowing readers to share and save webpages of interest. Digg, Delicious, and StumbleUpon are examples of frequently used social bookmarking tools.

**Sharing Tools**—Social media is all about sharing information, and so it is important for readers to have the option to digg your story, pin it, tweet it, like it on Facebook, share on LinkedIn, and email it to friends. Many of these sharing buttons can be set up to share specific content or are text enabled so that your message is disseminated in the way that you intend.[23]

**Social Commenting**—Conversations are paramount to social media. Encourage conversations by integrating common plugins such as Facebook comments, WordPress, Livefyre, Realtidbits, Disqus, or other platforms that foster discussions.

**Creative Commons License**—Disseminating news in a connected world needs new policies. Too often bloggers and other content creators will see warnings of "media use only" when visiting online media centers. This type of messaging can often dissuade these reporters from covering a company. A Creative Commons License is an online copyright release that clearly articulates how the content can be used and shared and should be considered as

---

## SHIFT Communications Social Media Press Release Live Example

**How to Make a Social Media Press Release [tweet this]**

Making a social media press release is relatively straightforward. It's nothing more than a variable width table with the shareable social content in it. Remember that the goal of a social media press release is to make every piece of it shareable.

Everything you see on this page has a sharing mechanism of some kind, from the title itself to the story to the individual pieces of content. This way, everything is separable and divisible. If a media influencer just wants to use the video on their site, they can. If a podcaster just wants to grab the audio for inclusion in their show, they can. There's no requirement that you ship the entire thing lock, stock, and barrel.

The SMPR was created entirely in a plain vanilla HTML editor like Adobe Dreamweaver or BlueGriffon, using various social networks and content networks to provide the individual pieces.

There's a third hidden piece that's not immediately obvious. This social media press release is being hosted not on our corporate web site, but by our marketing automation system. As a result, it can detect when people who are already in our marketing database are looking at it, clicking on things, and sharing stuff, so we know if it resonates or not.

Like this? Let us know in the comments:

**Video**

**Audio**

*SHIFT Communications pioneered the first social media press release. (Courtesy of SHIFT Communications)*

part of any media center content-related policies. Removing any barriers or concerns about copyright that may cause your audience to hesitate is a best practice.[24]

The takeaway here is that a company should want its social media press releases to be sharable. Unlike traditional press releases that were deliberately sent specifically to journalists, social media press releases can be found, shared, and circulated through the social sphere. Prezly (http://www.prezly.com/), MarketWired (http://www.marketwired.com/), PRESSfeed (http://www.press-feed.com/), CNW (http://www.newswire.ca/en/index), and Pitch Engine (http://new.pitchengine.com/) offer services to help create social media press releases and online media centers, as well as distribute the finalized content.

## Fostering Online Media Centers and Social Media Press Releases

Social media news releases achieve three times the coverage as traditional news releases.[25] Today's public relations practitioners need to understand that company media centers and social media–based press releases are only effective if they incorporate the right content using the right platform. The advent of new "modernized" media relations requires practitioners to embrace new methodologies and technologies and learn how to best communicate and interact with journalists, bloggers, and content creators. Incorporating interactive and multimedia content is now considered the norm and should be used to enhance a story in ways that traditional media could not do.

(Readers of the print book can find an interview with leaders at the College of Saint Rose regarding their campaign to promote the school using a combination of traditional public relations and social media efforts at http://ginaluttrellphd.com/videos/; ebook readers can use the embedded link.)

**#LRNSMPR**

Learn More about Online Media Centers and Social Media Press Releases

Quick Links

- Die! Press release! Die! Die! Die!, http://bit.ly/18w8XGt
- Social Media Release Must Evolve to Replace Press Release, http://to.pbs .org/1aObzMH
- How to Write a Social Media Press Release, http://bit.ly/19bYpgt
- What Is a "Social Media Newsroom"?, http://bit.ly/1ckGgdv
- 20+ Free Press Release Distribution Sites, http://on.mash.to/1ksuVwj

## Theory into Practice

Planning is the key to designing an effective online media center and developing a social media press release. Company webpages can be great resources and highlight many of the aspects that were mentioned in the chapter. Visit an online newsroom from the list provided:

- e.l.f. Cosmetics: http://www.eyeslipsface.com/
- Hershey: http://www.thehersheycompany.com
- IBM: http://www-03.ibm.com

After exploring the media centers, provide answers to the following questions:

1. Assess how easy it was to find the online media center from the home page of the website.
2. Once in the online media center:
   a. Is the contact information prominently displayed?
   b. Are there clearly marked tabs devoted to specific information?
   c. Are there links to rich content like infographics, webcasts, podcasts, audio files, or SlideShare presentations?
   d. How many quotes are available?
   e. Were there avenues to share the information?
3. Did the company provide contact info, names of press contacts (including contact info), RSS links, and social media platforms?

4. Was the information accessible on a mobile device?
5. Was a Creative Commons License in place, or was the information strictly for journalists?

## Notes

1. PR Newswire, "Online Newsroom Best Practices," last modified 2013, accessed November 26, 2013, http://www.prnewswire.com/knowledge-center/online-public-relations/Online-Newsroom-Best-Practices.html.

2. Elena Verlee, "How to Create a Good Online Media Center," *PR in Your Pajamas* (blog), http://prinyourpajamas.com/online-media-center/.

3. PR Newswire, "Online Newsroom Best Practices."

4. PR Newswire, "Online Newsroom Best Practices."

5. David Meerman Scott, "Online Media Room Best Practices," *Web in Know* (blog), 2005, http://www.davidmeermanscott.com/documents/online_media_room_best_practices.pdf.

6. Christopher Penn, "Social Media Press Release 2.0," *SHIFT Communications* (blog), December 2013, http://www.shiftcomm.com/2012/12/social-media-press-release-2-0/.

7. Verlee, "How to Create a Good Online Media Center."

8. McDonald's Newsroom, Press Releases tab, http://news.mcdonalds.com/Corporate/Press-Releases.

9. PR Newswire, "Online Newsroom Best Practices."

10. Southwest Airlines, Media Inquiries tab, http://www.swamedia.com/pages/contacts; Lands' End newsroom, Media Contacts tab, http://www.landsend.com/newsroom/press_contacts/index.html; Dick's Sporting Goods, Media Contacts tab, http://www.dickssporting goods.com/corp/index.jsp?page=pressRoom&ab=Footer_Know_PressRoom.

11. Starbucks Newsroom, Views tab, http://news.starbucks.com/views.

12. The Campbell's Soup Company, Executive Team, http://www.campbellsoupcompany.com/about-campbell/executive-team.

13. Verlee, "How to Create a Good Online Media Center."

14. Joel Kessel, "The Online Media Room: Why It Needs to Be Part of Our Communications Strategy," http://kesselcommunications.com/the-online-media-room-why-it-needs-to-be-part-of-our-communications-strategy/.

15. Mary Belles, About.com, "How to Write a Press Release—Invention of the First Press Release," last modified 2013, accessed December 7, 2013, http://inventors.about.com/od/pstartinventions/a/press_release.htm.

16. Belles, "How to Write a Press Release."

17. Mickie Kennedy, *eReleases* (blog), March 29, 2010, http://www.ereleases.com/prfuel/history-of-the-press-release/.

18. Ian Capstick, "Social Media Release Must Evolve to Replace Press Release," *Media Shift* (blog), April 23, 2010, http://www.pbs.org/mediashift/2010/04/social-media-release-must-evolve-to-replace-press-release113/.

19. Penn, "Social Media Press Release 2.0"; PRWeb, "Writing Great Online News Releases," last modified December 2013, accessed December 8, 2013, http://lp.prweb.com/Global/FileLib/

Guides/PRWEB_-_Writing_Great_Online_News_Releases.pdf; S. Bruce, *Share This: The Social Media Handbook for PR Professionals* (West Sussex: Wiley, 2012), chap. 16.

20. PRWeb, "Writing Great Online News Releases."

21. ING, "Consumers Find Social Media Increasingly Trustworthy," last modified November 15, 2012, accessed December 8, 2013, http://ing-group.pr.co/34147-consumers-find -social-media-increasingly-trustworthy.

22. Capstick, "Social Media Release Must Evolve to Replace Press Release."

23. Capstick, "Social Media Release Must Evolve to Replace Press Release."

24. Magdalena Georgieva, "3 Characteristics of Successful Modern-Day Press Releases," *Inbound Marketing* (blog), October 21, 2011, http://blog.hubspot.com/blog/tabid/6307/ bid/27623/3-Characteristics-of-Successful-Modern-Day-Press-Releases.aspx.

25. Adam Parker, "Social Media News Releases Achieve Three Times the Pickup," *ShowMeNumb3R5* (blog), March 22, 2011, http://www.showmenumbers.com/news-release -distribution/social-media-news-releases-achieve-three-times-the-pickup.

## CHAPTER TWELVE
# MEASURING SOCIAL MEDIA'S IMPACT AND VALUE

> The success that social media has achieved within mainstream business activities has already influenced the importance of measuring the outcomes of these campaigns. Traditionally, up to 5 percent of a typical public relations budget is allocated toward measuring and interpreting campaign-related metrics. Today, companies expect their public relations and social media professionals to quantify the impact and value.

## We've Listened, Now What?

Listening, as we have learned throughout the book, is a vital component within social media. When a company actively listens to its respective audiences, it can assess what is being said about the company, an individual, a brand, or a product in the social sphere. These conversations produce copious amounts of unstructured data, which can seem somewhat uninterpretable and overwhelming. Just ask the individuals who spend their time trolling through Twitter feeds, Facebook comments, pins, and posts, reading comments from blogs, and examining message boards or forums. *Phew! It was exhausting just thinking about that!* It is difficult enough to simply closely follow these conversations, let alone interpret the content and make sense of the information as an origin for action. Listening to and monitoring social media–driven conversations allows a company to gather data, enabling it to create metric-driven reports and define action items. As a company collects this data, it is then able to directly correlate and measure the results of its campaigns or initiatives. However, this does not mean that this task is a simple one.

Measuring a company's social media initiatives and impact is not as simple as adding up the number of "likes" or "shares." In fact, measuring the effectiveness of a social media campaign and overall strategy can be very daunting. Measuring experts like Bernadette Coleman have developed a series of equations to calculate everything from user lifetime value to impression value and social media expenditures to valuate social media efforts. For example, companies that would like to calculate their social media expenditure might use the following formula:

$$\text{Expenditures (E)} = \text{hard costs} + \text{cost/time spent} + \text{sunk cost}$$

while those companies interested in calculating their lifetime user value might instead use:

$$\text{user lifetime value (U)} = (\text{gross distribution per customer}) \times$$
$$\Sigma \, (\text{yearly retention rate})^{\wedge}i \, / \, (1+ \text{yearly discount rate})^{\wedge}i—$$
$$(\text{retention cost per customer per year}) \times \Sigma \, (\text{yearly retention rate})^{\wedge}p \, /$$
$$(1+ \text{yearly discount rate})^{\wedge}p+0.5^{1}$$

While the formulaic approach can be confusing, other models and frameworks are more straightforward. Don Bartholomew (@Donbart), senior vice president of Digital and Social Media Research at Ketchum, is largely considered one of the industry's "resident experts" on measurement. His work,[2] and the efforts by both the International Association for Measurement and Evaluation of Communications (AMEC) and the Conclave, a volunteer group representing different associations, organizations, and academia, are contributing to the development of a set of generally accepted standards within the communications industry.[3] In June 2013 the Conclave released the "Complete Social Media Measurement Standards" in an attempt to provide a framework around some generally accepted measurement principles. The full report can be found using the following link: http://bit.ly/1cKw9l4. Themes addressed within this report include the following:

1. *Content and Sourcing*: This area of the report attempts to capture information regarding content sources in order to provide transparency and ease of comparison across analyses.[4] This

section highlights an analysis of content from multiple sources (channels), including Twitter, Facebook, Instagram, YouTube, forums, and monitoring services such as Radian6, Sysomos, and so on, along with methods of data collection and analysis. Key metrics that are calculated to understand reach, engagement, influence, and opinion/advocacy are also examined during this section. Even the coding for understanding sentiment is addressed.

2. *Reach and Impressions*: This section serves as a basis for defining data collection in social media so that subsequent metrics and other standards can be calculated consistently. In-depth definitions and explanations of "item," "mention," "impressions," and "reach" are provided.

3. *Engagement and Conversation*: *Engagement* and *conversation* are words commonly used by social media professionals; yet they are rarely defined with any type of consistency to guide sound measurement. Within this section of the report, definitions and differentiations between "engagement" and "conversations" are provided. For example, the report states, "Engagement counts for such actions as: likes, comments, shares, votes, +1s, links, retweets, video views, content embeds, etc. Engagement types and levels are unique to specific channels, but can be aggregated for cross-channel comparison."[5] Conversation, on the other hand, measures items such as blog posts, comments, tweets, Facebook posts/comments, video posts, replies, and so on.[6]

4. *Opinion and Advocacy*: Since not all practitioners are experts in market research, robust parameters, and comprehensive examples regarding measuring sentiment, opinion and advocacy are provided within this section of the report.

5. *Influence*: Buzz words like *influencers* or *influentials* are regularly used in social media planning. However, consistent definitions of these words have not yet been adopted within the industry. Therefore, a common language and conceptual framework have been developed to aid practitioners in being able to quantify "influencers."

6. *Impact and Value*: It is widely accepted that both "impact" and "value" represent the ultimate outcome of any social media or campaign effort.[7] Too often, these terms are interchanged and confused with return on investment (ROI). Descriptions and

metrics related to "impact" and "value" are provided within this section of the report that enable practitioners to understand the difference between the three terms (ROI included) and how they relate to measuring outcomes.

## The New Frontier: Social Media Models and Framework

For decades, communication models have been linear and almost formulaic in nature. There are countless examples that support this claim, of which we will look at three of the more widely adopted models. John Marston's R-A-C-E Four-Step Model for Public Relations is one that is considered very straightforward.[8] The components include research, action, communication, and evaluation. Practitioners commonly begin with the *research* phase, continue to the *action* and *communication* phases, and then ultimately end with the *evaluation* phase in a linear fashion. R-O-P-E, another commonly adopted model used in communication planning, follows the same blueprint—practitioners start with *research*, create *objectives*, *plan*, and finally *evaluate* the outcomes. Schramm's Communication Model is the final example we will examine. Again, this model follows a linear process. Wilber Schramm is a pioneer in communication theory. He developed the one-way linear model of communication, which sought to explain how meaning was transferred between both individuals and corporations. Meaning, in the context of this model, includes five basic elements: source, encoder, signal, decoder, and destination.[9] Schramm's model emphasized that the source and receiver continually encode, interpret, decode, transmit, and receive information while also filtering out noise.

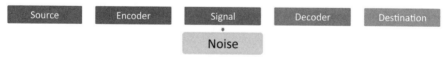

*Wilber Schramm proposed the model of communication in the 1950s.*

Schramm's model revolutionized how individuals thought about communication between senders and receivers.[10] Now, each of these three models continues to be taught in universities across the globe and is still widely used in public relations planning and practice today. However, in today's digital age of communication, these models continue to provide challenges when tasked with measuring outcomes. There simply are no standards.

Since public relations activities are regarded as a series of actions, changes, and functions that generate results, the same can also apply to social media and social strategies. Social media impacts the way that content is created, distributed, and consumed. It should not come as a shock that measuring these efforts takes great change.[11]

## Social Media Metrics Model

Google searching "how to measure social media" will result in hundreds of pages of advice. In this text you are presented with the framework for what one day may be generally accepted practices. Using the Conclave Report and approximately fifteen other social media and communications models, Don Bartholomew and members of AMEC set out to develop a social media metrics model that takes into account the different stages of social media measurement.[12]

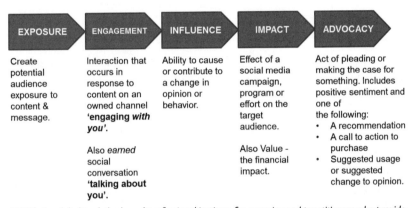

| EXPOSURE | ENGAGEMENT | INFLUENCE | IMPACT | ADVOCACY |
|---|---|---|---|---|
| Create potential audience exposure to content & message. | Interaction that occurs in response to content on an owned channel 'engaging *with you*'. | Ability to cause or contribute to a change in opinion or behavior. | Effect of a social media campaign, program or effort on the target audience. | Act of pleading or making the case for something. Includes positive sentiment and one of the following: |
| | Also *earned* social conversation 'talking about you'. | | Also Value - the financial impact. | • A recommendation<br>• A call to action to purchase<br>• Suggested usage or suggested change to opinion. |

*AMEC, the global trade body and professional institute for agencies and practitioners who provide media evaluation and communication research, and Don Bartholomew, Ketchum, developed the suggested Social Media Metrics Model. (Reproduction of the images is by kind permission of AMEC, the global trade body and professional institute for agencies and practitioners who provide media evaluation and communication research, and of Don Bartholomew, Ketchum)*

The social media metrics model presented can be considered a recommended approach that strives to create standard metrics for measuring social media. Incorporating models and developing intuitive frameworks are integral to properly conducting any measurement. A five-step social media measurement process accompanies this model to integrate all aspects:[13]

1. Step one of the social media measurement process begins with practitioners establishing measurable objectives that are aligned

with desired business outcomes and key performance indicators (KPIs).

2. Step two digs deeper and further defines the specific metrics required to assess performance against any/all measurable social media objectives. Performance targets should be set for each metric during this step.

3. Step three requires populating the selected social media model with the metrics specified and defined in the previous step.

4. Having previously defined the measurement approach earlier in the planning process, step four focuses on the gathering and analysis of data. Practitioners should always strive to evaluate the performance against the objectives and targets.

5. Finally, report the results to stakeholders and interested parties as step five.

## Social Media Valid Frameworks

Throughout the process of developing a set of accepted metrics and consistent definitions to aid in measuring the success of a social media initiative, Bartholomew and others have proposed a less complicated arrangement that captures social media metrics from three specific areas: programmatic, channel specific, and business. Bartholomew explains that "programmatic metrics directly tie to social media objectives while channel-specific metrics are the unique metrics associated with specific social media channels—tweets, RTs, MTs, Followers, Likes, Diggs, Talking About This, Pins, and Re-Pins, and finally, business metrics illustrate the business impact of the campaign or initiative."[14] Additionally, paid, earned, owned and paid, earned, shared, owned media metrics were also considered and enable businesses to measure integrated programs containing a variety of differing elements.

One can now see why the creators of social media–based measurement models have abandoned the one-size-fits-all framework that could be instituted across differing business platforms. Business goals and objectives vary, therefore a flexible and easily adaptable, one-size-fits-*most* approach is appropriate.[15] This approach allows for companies to focus the framework to their specific business objectives. Within the fifteen-plus models that were studied by Bartholomew and AMEC, the ideas related to postpurchase engagement and advocacy were repeatedly identified. As a result, these elements are also included in this recommended approach. Finally, engage-

## Understanding Media Platforms: Paid, Earned, Shared, Owned

Seasoned public relations professionals can have difficulty distinguishing between various forms of media in the digital age. An easy way to remember and understand the differences within the media landscape is by using the acronym PESO: *paid, earned, shared, and owned.*\*

**Paid** refers to the social channels a company pays to leverage its message. For example, promoted tweets, banner ads, Facebook or LinkedIn advertisements, pay-per-click search ads, sponsorships, and ads in magazines or radio are all considered paid media. The company did not *earn* the coverage; instead, it *paid* for it.

**Earned** is when the customers become the channel for a company through word of mouth (WOM) or achievement of viral status. Think traditional public relations efforts. The resident public relations manager writes a narrative around the company's latest product launch and then pitches that story to both new and traditional media channels, including blogs. The resulting news coverage, broadcast hits, or blog posts are deemed "earned" media, since the company did not pay the news writers, bloggers, or other media outlets for coverage in both online and offline media channels.

**Shared** refers to the instances in which consumers are working in conjunction with a brand to create, share, and promote the brand's content. This occurs only when a brand cultivates passionate and loyal followers who want to engage not only with the brand but also with a larger audience.

**Owned** is a term for channels that a company owns and controls. These include the company website, a Facebook brand page, blog, ebooks, infographics, an official Instagram account, or pinboards specifically maintained by the company or Twitter accounts.

---

\* Lee Odden, "Paid, Earned, Owned and Shared Media—What's Your Online Marketing Media Mix?" *Online Marketing* (blog), 2011, http://www.toprankblog.com/2011/07/online-marketing-media-mix/.

ment and influence have always been key concepts in social marketing and measurement; consequently, these elements are explicitly used in this mode.

The following images illustrate the two routes of metrics used.[16]

The methodologies and guidelines surrounding social media measurement is still evolving. When attempting to establish a measurement strategy for your company's social media efforts, expect moments of trial and error. But do not panic. Over time you will begin to see correlations between your

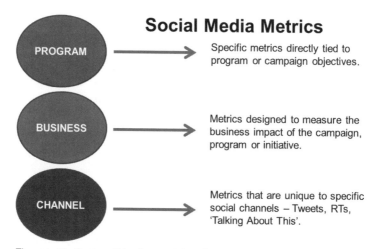

# Social Media Metrics

**PROGRAM** ———→ Specific metrics directly tied to program or campaign objectives.

**BUSINESS** ———→ Metrics designed to measure the business impact of the campaign, program or initiative.

**CHANNEL** ———→ Metrics that are unique to specific social channels – Tweets, RTs, 'Talking About This'.

*The conceptualization of the three social media metrics as developed by AMEC and Bartholomew. (Reproduction of the images is by kind permission of AMEC, the global trade body and professional institute for agencies and practitioners who provide media evaluation and communication research, and of Don Bartholomew, Ketchum)*

|  | EXPOSURE | ENGAGEMENT | INFLUENCE | IMPACT | ADVOCACY |
|---|---|---|---|---|---|
| **PROGRAM METRICS** | Total OTS for program content | Number of interactions with content<br>Interaction rate<br>Hashtag usage | Increase % association with key attributes<br>Change in issue sentiment | New subscribers<br>Referral traffic to website<br>White paper downloads | Recommendation/ Total Mentions % |
| **CHANNEL METRICS** | Number of items<br>Mentions<br>Reach<br>Impressions<br>CPM | Post Likes<br>Comments<br>Shares<br>Views<br>RTs/1000<br>Followers | Net promoter % by channel | Unique visitors to website referred from each channel | Organic posts by advocates<br>Ratings/Reviews |
| **BUSINESS METRICS** |  |  | Purchase consideration %<br>Likelihood to recommend %<br>**Association with brand attributes** | Sales<br>Repeat sales<br>**Purchase frequency**<br>Cost savings<br>**Number leads** | Employee ambassadors<br>Brand fans/advocates |

*The AMEC Social Media Valid Framework: Program, Channel, Business. (Reproduction of the images is by kind permission of AMEC, the global trade body and professional institute for agencies and practitioners who provide media evaluation and communication research, and of Don Bartholomew, Ketchum)*

| | EXPOSURE | ENGAGEMENT | INFLUENCE | IMPACT | ADVOCACY |
|---|---|---|---|---|---|
| **PAID** | **Impressions** Reach **CPM** Active GRPs | **Interaction rate** Click-thrus **Time viewing** Completed plays | **Purchase consideration** Change in opinion | **Visit website** Attend event **Sales** Download coupon | **Mentions in Earned channel** |
| **OWNED** | **Unique visitors** Page views **Reach** Impressions **CPM** | **Return visits** Interaction rate **Duration** Subscriptions **Links** | **Tell a friend** Change in opinion **Association with key attributes** | **Download paper** Download app **Sales** Request info **Cost savings** | **Recommendations** Ratings |
| **EARNED** | **Number of items** Number of mentions **Number of Followers** OTS | **Comments/post** Shares **RTs/1000** **Followers** Number of inbound links | **Purchase consideration** Tell a friend **Likelihood to Recommend** | **Visit store** Attend the event **Sales** Vote for issue | **Ratings** Reviews **Recommendations** Recommendations rate |

*The AMEC Social Media Valid Framework: Paid, Owned, Earned. (Reproduction of the images is by kind permission of AMEC, the global trade body and professional institute for agencies and practitioners who provide media evaluation and communication research, and of Don Bartholomew, Ketchum)*

social media strategies and the company's key performance indicators. Use the models presented within this chapter to help your organization develop a powerful measurement strategy that meets the specific needs and provides the necessary metrics.

#LRNSMPR

Learn More about Social Media Measurement

Quick Links

- The Conclave: Complete Social Media Measurement Standards, http://bit .ly/1cKw9I4
- Thought Leaders Identify Priorities for Integration across Paid, Earned, Shared, and Owned Media Channels, http://bit.ly/UrEUfR
- Defining Earned, Owned, and Paid Media, http://bit.ly/1ajx4WH
- Five Social Media Measurement Questions I Hope (Not) to See in 2014, http:// bit.ly/1aWZOoj
- A Digital Leader Looks at the Agency of Tomorrow, http://bit.ly/1dI16OI

# Notes

1. Bernadette Coleman, "The Real Social Media ROI Formula," *SEJ Search Engine Journal* (blog), August 27, 2013, http://www.searchenginejournal.com/the-real-social-media-roi-formula/66047/.

2. Don Bartholomew, http://metricsman.wordpress.com/about/.

3. International Association for Measurement and Evaluation of Communications (AMEC), http://amecorg.com/; The Conclave, http://www.smmstandards.com/about/the-conclave-members/.

4. International Association for Measurement and Evaluation of Communications (AMEC).

5. International Association for Measurement and Evaluation of Communications (AMEC).

6. International Association for Measurement and Evaluation of Communications (AMEC).

7. International Association for Measurement and Evaluation of Communications (AMEC).

8. John Marston, *The Nature of Public Relations* (New York: McGraw-Hill, 1963), 161–73.

9. Wilber Schramm, *Mass Media and National Development* (Stanford, CA: Stanford University Press, 1964).

10. D. Wilcox, G. Cameron, B. Reber, and J. Shin, *THINK Public Relations* (Upper Saddle River, NJ: Pearson Education, 2013).

11. Don Bartholomew, "The Digitization of Research and Measurement in Public Relations," *Social Media Explorer* (blog), May 12, 2010, http://www.socialmediaexplorer.com/online-public-relations/the-digitization-of-research-and-measurement-in-public-relations/.

12. Don Bartholomew, "A New Framework for Social Media Metrics and Measurement," *MetricsMan* (blog), June 12, 2013, http://metricsman.wordpress.com/2013/06/12/a-new-framework-for-social-media-metrics-and-measurement/.

13. D. Bartholomew and AMEC, *Unlocking Business Performance: Communications Research and Analytics in Action*, presentation delivered at the European summit on measurement, Madrid, June 2013. Retrieved from http://amecorg.com/wp-content/uploads/2013/06/Social-Media-Valid-Framework2013.pdf.

14. Bartholomew, "A New Framework for Social Media Metrics and Measurement."

15. John Marston, *The Nature of Public Relations* (New York: McGraw-Hill, 1963), 161–73.

16. Bartholomew and AMEC, *Unlocking Business Performance: Communications Research and Analytics in Action.*

**Part III**

# THE SOCIAL MEDIA PLAN

## CHAPTER THIRTEEN

# THE ROADMAP TO SUCCESS: DEVELOPING A SOCIAL MEDIA PLAN

The development of a social media plan helps create a roadmap for companies to follow in achieving their social media–related goals. This chapter outlines how to develop a step-by-step social media plan that can be easily implemented within your organization.

## Path to Success

Research illustrates that more than 50 percent of small businesses are not regularly engaging their targeted audiences using social media sites.[1] Various reasons could contribute to this lack of engagement, but the development and implementation of a proper plan with specific metrics can directly address many of these oversights.

Social media plans are a series of proposed actions that produce specific results. They are akin to a marketing or communications plan, only specific to a social media strategy. Companies that plan out their social media efforts prevent haphazard, meaningless actions being overlooked or executed that add little value to their organizational goals. Social media plans can be used to outline a specific campaign or plan the entire year. Presented within this chapter is a hybrid model including elements from a traditional public relations plan. This example not only includes the some basic elements conventionally implemented within a public relations plan[2] but also incorporates the fundamental premise inherent in the Circular Model of SoMe for Social Communication as well as pieces from Marketo's tactical social media planning template.[3]

# Strategic and Tactical Social Media Plan Template

The following hybrid model provides an easy-to-follow template that aids in the creation of a social media plan by aligning the outcomes directly with important organization's goals. The idea of incorporating social media within a business strategy is something that requires a large investment in planning, support, and execution. When correctly implemented and properly maintained, a social media plan becomes a tangible driver for new leads and also provides a platform for customers to participate in important conversations related to the brands that are important to them.

> **Step 1: Situation Statement**—Develop a statement that outlines what the company wants to achieve and why. Valid objectives cannot be set without a clear understanding of the situation that led to developing a social media plan.[4] Some questions to ask when writing the situation statement include: Why is a plan necessary? Are we trying to overcome an issue or challenge? Is this a one-time product launch? Are we introducing new services? Are we looking to engage more genuinely on our social platforms? Is this long-term planning?
>
> **Step 2: Objectives**—Once you have a clear situation statement, setting objectives is the next logical step. What is your strategy for the social media plan? Describe your organization's objectives for your social media plan using the SMART strategy: specific, measurable, attainable, relevant, and timely.[5] Describe how these objectives support your organization's mission. Objectives are stated in terms of program outcomes. For example, "position XYZ company as a leader in premium athletic wear by getting people to recognize the brand name and associate it with specific product(s)." The objectives here are overarching in nature, not to be confused or intermingled with the specific objectives located within the tactics section of the social media plan.
>
> **Step 3: Define the Audience**—Whether the company has cornered a niche area or your products or services target the general public, social media efforts should be directed toward a specific audience. For example, Axe body spray, a brand of Unilever Global, targets males eighteen to twenty-four years old,[6] while the wildly popular British television series *Downton Abbey* targets women

aged thirty-four to forty-nine.[7] Some campaigns have multiple audiences depending on the objectives set forth in the campaign. Make sure to take the time to properly understand the demographics that you are interested in connecting with.

**Step 4: Strategy**—Describe how and why various campaign components will achieve the overall objectives. Guidelines and key messages are often included in this section. The Susan G. Komen Foundation uses four key messages in its national breast cancer awareness campaign: (1) know your risk, (2) get screened, (3) know what is normal for you, and (4) make healthy choices.[8] These four messages are emphasized throughout its public relations campaign and social media efforts.

To this point, the format that we have followed mirrors that of a traditional public relations plan. This is where the social media plan begins to diverge from a public relations plan. In general, most of the platforms that are used within the social sphere are included in this plan. However, as we have previously read, not all social media channels are appropriate for every business. Tactics can be unique for each business and consumer. Companies must decide which social platforms are right for their audience. It is okay if Instagram is not part of your plan. If a company's audience is not engaged on Instagram, then it might not be a smart use of resources to maintain an Instagram account. Knowing your audience and their social habits is paramount to successful implementation of a social media plan.

**Step 5: Tactics**—Tactics have been divided into several social media areas.[9] Let us examine how each could be included within a larger social media plan. Each tactic takes into account the measurement strategies that were presented in chapter 12 and the Circular Model of SoMe for Social Communication—*Share, optimize, Manage, engage.*

- Social Press: Just as public relations professionals pitch traditional journalists, public relations professionals and social media strategists must pitch bloggers and other online influencers.
  - Time Spent: Consider how many hours per day, week, and month will be devoted to this tactic.

- Objectives
  - Regularly update bloggers about products and services.
  - Conduct interviews, conferences, and networking events.
- Metrics
  - Posts and referrals from the social press
  - Engagement and conversation
  - Influence
  - Opinion and advocacy
  - Impact and value
- Blogs
  - Time Spent: Consider how many hours per day, week, and month will be devoted to this tactic.
    - Remember, a good rule of thumb is to post one blog a day (if possible) or at a minimum three blogs weekly.
    - Create an editorial calendar for your blog to stay motivated and to have a guideline for content.
  - Objectives
    - Increase recognition: for example, X number of posts.
    - Increase engagement: for example, encourage comments, add social sharing buttons.
  - Metrics
    - Engagement and conversation
    - Influence
    - Opinion and advocacy
    - Impact and value
    - Number of posts
    - Number of social shares—Digg, Twitter, Facebook, etc.
    - Audience growth—unique and returns
    - New subscribers
    - Inbound links clicked
- Social Networks
  - Time Spent: Consider how many hours per day, week, and month will be devoted to each social networking site.
  - Facebook
    - Establish a goal for the number of posts per day.
      - Share a mix of relevant links, engaging content, videos, and polls.

- Make sure to promote upcoming events.
- Create special event pages.
- LinkedIn
  - Establish a goal for the number of posts per day.
  - Create a group.
  - Cultivate the LinkedIn company page.
  - Identify other groups to follow and participate.
  - Encourage employee participation.
  - Monitor and participate in Q&A.
- Google+
  - Establish a goal for the number of posts per day or week.
  - Optimize for SEO.
  - Share meaningful content, videos, images, and relevant links.
  - Host a Google Hangout.
  - Create and promote upcoming events.
- Pinterest
  - Establish goals for the number of pins per day.
  - Create boards to leverage content, company culture, and behind-the-scenes atmosphere.
  - Promote consumer boards that illustrate their passion for the brand.
  - Follow other boards such as businesses, thought leaders, customers, and partners.
- Metrics
  - Engagement and conversation
  - Influence
  - Opinion and advocacy
  - Impact and value
- Microblogging
  - Time Spent: Consider how many hours per day, week, and month will be devoted to Twitter.
  - Objectives
    - Compile list of company Twitter users—follow them, have employees follow the company.

- Compile a list of vendors, customers, users, or members—follow them, RT when appropriate, and engage frequently.
- Customer Service: communicate support issues from social media to customer service team, ensure follow-up.
- Cross promote other social networking activities and sites through Twitter, the company blog, Facebook, and any other social networking site the company uses.
  - Metrics
    - Engagement and conversation
    - Influence
    - Opinion and advocacy
    - Impact and value
- Bookmarking/Tagging
  - Time Spent: Consider how many hours per day, week, and month will be devoted to social bookmarking and tagging.
  - Objectives
    - Illustrate the company as a thought leader and promote conversation using:
      - Delicious
      - Sphinn
      - reddit
      - Digg
      - StumbleUpon
      - FriendFeed
    - Participate in communities and conversations
  - Metrics
    - Engagement and conversation
    - Influence
    - Opinion and advocacy
    - Impact and value
- Social Apps, Voting, and Crowdsourcing:
  - Time Spent: Consider how many hours per day, week, and month will be devoted to social apps, voting, and crowdsourcing.

- Objectives
  - Add a social element to every campaign to expand reach and increase engagement.
  - Share videos, reviews, ratings, and polls.
  - Use promotions and contests to spread your message, such as refer-a-friend or flash deals.
  - Promote content when applicable via social crowd-sourcing and voting sites.
  - Let consumers have a say through crowdsourced events or interactive voting.
- Metrics
  - Engagement and conversation
  - Influence
  - Opinion and advocacy
  - Impact and value
  - Watch for trends over time
- Blog Commenting/Q&A Sites
  - Time Spent: Consider how many hours per day, week, and month will be devoted to comments on the company blog, as well as other industry blogs. Take into consideration the time necessary to participate in question and answer sessions.
  - Objectives
    - Participate on relevant message boards, blogs, and Q&A platforms.
    - Provide insight and thought leadership within your comments.
    - Only include a link-back when relevant.
    - Work positive comments into your posts and then follow up.
    - Focus on building authentic relationships—share, optimize, monitor, engage.
  - Metrics
    - Engagement and conversation
    - Influence
    - Opinion and advocacy
    - Impact and value

- Brand awareness
- Link-backs
- Referring traffic
- Online Video
  - Time Spent: Consider how many hours per day, week, and month will be devoted to creating, posting, and managing online videos.
  - Objectives
    - Create video series.
    - Upload videos to website, YouTube, Facebook, Vine, Instagram, and other video platforms.
  - Metrics
    - Engagement and conversation
    - Influence
    - Opinion and advocacy
    - Impact and value
- Photo Sharing
  - Time Spent: Consider how many hours per day, week, and month will be devoted to creating, posting, and managing images for the company.
  - Objectives
    - Encourage employees to share any interesting and public relations/marketing–related photos from social marketing or company events.
    - Take pictures at relevant company-sponsored events like trade shows, product launches, or community happenings.
    - Invite influencers to take photos and share with their followers.
    - Utilize photo-sharing sites to highlight images that link back to blogs and core sites:
      - Instagram
      - Pinterest
      - Flickr
      - Facebook Photo Gallery
      - Company blog
      - Google+ Photo Albums

- Metrics
  - Engagement and conversation
  - Influence
  - Opinion and advocacy
  - Impact and value
- Podcasting
  - Time Spent: Consider how many hours per day, week, and month will be devoted to development of podcasts.
  - Objectives
    - Create a list of podcast directories.
    - Repurpose webinar content (when applicable) for resource section; promote through podcast directories and iTunes.
    - Record relevant phone conferences for use as podcasts; promote through podcast directories.
    - Interview and record company thought leaders— share their insights with your community.
  - Metrics
    - Engagement and conversation
    - Influence
    - Opinion and advocacy
    - Impact and value
- Presentation Sharing
  - Time Spent: Consider how many hours per day, week, and month will be devoted to developing content to share on sites (such as SlideShare).
  - Objectives
    - Highlight company thought leaders—if someone from your company is presenting at a conference, post to SlideShare.
    - Determine the number of SlideShare presentations that need to be created on a monthly or quarterly basis.
    - Post webinars, slide decks, and infographics.
    - Optimize for SEO.
    - Generate views and leads.
  - Metrics
    - Engagement and conversation
    - Influence

- Opinion and advocacy
- Impact and value

**Step 6: Timeline**—The objectives, complexity, and timing of the campaign will dictate the timelines. Some campaigns last six weeks, while others can last six months. Campaigns can be seasonal or targeted to a specific product or event. For example, the Lay's® Do Us a Flavor™ Choose Your Chip Contest accepted entries for new potato chip flavors between January 13, 2014, through April 5, 2014. Once entries were submitted, the public had the opportunity to vote on their favorite chip from July 28, 2014, through October 18, 2014.

**Step 7: Budget**—Every social media plan requires a budget. Companies want to know all of the expenses related to the campaigns. Budgets should take into consideration both staff time and out-of-pocket expenses. Allocate at least 10 percent of a budget to unexpected costs.

After completing these seven steps, an organization has developed a complete social media plan. This plan can now be incorporated into an existing public relations plan or used as a stand-alone depending on how the plan was developed. A couple of examples of how companies successfully implemented social media plans are highlighted below. Ben and Jerry's and Oreo have both done a wonderful job of executing their social media campaigns.

As you read each case study, think about the seven steps described in this chapter, along with elements from the Circular Model of SoMe for Social Communication, and try to identify which section the information would likely fall within the framework of the social media plan. This will provide you with a chance to practice populating a plan, as well as a source for quick reference.

## Theory into Practice

Ben and Jerry's City Churned[10]

In 2013, Ben and Jerry's implemented one of the most successful social media campaigns on record. In an effort to explore and create new flavors that represent a more local flair, 360i Digital Marketing Agency and Ben and Jerry's targeted residents residing in New York City, Seattle, Portland, Washington, D.C., and

San Francisco with their "City Churned" campaign.[11] The campaign incorporated crowdsourcing to actively engage residents in both the development of flavor ideas and voting for each city's new flavor. Tactics included a variety of social media and direct interaction with the Ben and Jerry's ice cream truck. A "City Churned" microsite served as the communication hub.

### Objectives

The objective of the "City Churned" campaign was to:

- Cultivate a deeper relationship with fans.
- Capture the flair of each city within a pint of Ben and Jerry's ice cream.
- Show its continuing commitment to being eco-friendly, good to local business, and willing to work with fair trade.

### Target Audience

Ben and Jerry's focus has always been on community and wellness. The target audience for this campaign was identified to include local residents in each of the targeted cities, small business owners, social media users falling between sixteen and thirty-five years of age, and all other eco-loving citizens.

### Strategies and Tactics

By creating a flavor unique to that city, Ben and Jerry's looked to empower the local residents with a sense of pride for helping personalize the flavor that best represents their city. Incorporating social media within the campaign allowed Ben and Jerry's to reach a wider audience, but it also helped mobilize residents to vote for their favorite flavors at the Ben and Jerry's ice cream truck throughout the area.

Ben and Jerry's used multiple social media platforms within the campaign and provided residents with a number of ways to vote on their favorite flavor. Voters could use social media by checking in on Foursquare or tagging photos on Instagram. Individuals could also show up in person at a Ben and Jerry's ice cream truck and participate in the voting process by simply showing up and highlighting their individual styles. To get a better handle on the flavor of each city, Ben and Jerry's also partnered with local businesses and fair trade organizations for an even better "taste" of the local culture and feel.[12]

### Execution

- Ben and Jerry's utilized the power of crowdsourcing to communicate with residents and encourage them to visit the ice cream truck within each city to vote and help create the ice cream flavor for their city.

- Each city had several different ways that residents could vote and help shape the flavor. No two cities used the same means of determining their favorite ingredients. However, some methods were not conscious choices. For example, whether a Seattle resident could see Mt. Rainer, or which direction a New Yorker's taxi was traveling, seemed to influence particular flavor votes in specific cities.
- After the voting process was complete, locals had the opportunity to try free samples of their city's new flavor; however, they did have to first locate the Ben and Jerry's ice cream truck.
- Using Flickr, Ben and Jerry's posted photos from its ice cream truck for followers to see and share.

*Results and Evaluation*

The Ben and Jerry's "City Churned" campaign wrapped up on September 28, 2013. It reached several thousand people in each city. The campaign was aimed to create a buzz for the Ben and Jerry brand in Washington, D.C., Seattle, Portland, New York City, and San Francisco. This was achieved in part by using social media and crowdsourcing as supporting platforms and activities. The city with the lowest reach was Washington, D.C., with roughly five thousand residents deciding between Greek frozen yogurt and ice cream. In contrast, New York City had the highest reach, with over fifteen thousand residents taking part in voting between the same two base flavors. Ben and Jerry's Instagram channel reached over sixty thousand people in New York City and over twelve thousand in Washington, D.C. When the campaign shifted to using crowdsourcing, over nine thousand Washington, D.C., participants came out to cast their vote for chocolate or vanilla. Not one to be outdone, over twenty-three thousand New York City residents used turnstiles to cast their votes between coffee and chocolate. The metrics generated by the City Churned campaign confirmed that both 360i Digital Marketing Agency and Ben and Jerry's had successfully created buzz around their brand in a unique way.

Oreo "Daily Twist" Campaign Case Study[13]

In 2012, Oreo enlisted the public relations firm 360i Digital Marketing to help create and execute a campaign designed to celebrate Oreo's one-hundred-year anniversary, while drawing consumer attention back to the brand.[14] Specifically targeting the millennial generation through the use of social media sites (i.e., Pinterest, Facebook, Twitter, and Tumblr), Oreo created the campaign "Daily Twist." It ran from June 25 to October 2, 2012. By connecting the Oreo cookie with pop culture, the campaign was aimed at making the one-hundred-year-old snack food relevant again.

*Objectives*

In rolling out the "Daily Twist" campaign, Oreo was looking to highlight the Oreo cookie as a relevant, household name, even one hundred years after it was first introduced. Oreo aimed to:

- Use creative and timely content, "with a twist," to encourage conversation and interaction between Oreo fans and the brand.
- Showcase the brand as more than just a snack food; it is a brand involved in and committed to partnering with many different interests in society (e.g., images relating to Hispanic Heritage Month, LGBT, Shin-Shin/Asian culture, Comic-Con, the Emmys, Shark Week, Bastille Day).
- Bring out the "kid" in Oreo consumers and fans.

*Research*

Research supporting this campaign was largely demographic in nature, focusing on the millennial generation, or generation Y (individuals born between 1980 and 1999). A 2012 study conducted by the US Chamber of Commerce noted that "Gen Yers connect to a brand through affiliation with a cause. This is more important to Gen Y than to previous generations. A brand that shows it cares is attractive to this generation."[15]

A separate study completed by the Pew Research Center in early 2012 highlighted statistics in support of a rise of news consumption via social media channels: "On top of the increase in social network use, the poll finds that news is also more prevalent on social networking sites. The share of users who saw news there yesterday nearly doubled from 19 percent to 36 percent between 2010 and 2012."[16]

*Execution*

360i developed a number of strong tactics in order to promote the one-hundred-year birthday of the Oreo cookie.

- Brand Newsroom: A team was created to identify all top and trending headlines in the news, and from these, custom Oreo images were designed.
- Pinterest Board:[17] For one hundred days, Oreo posted a new image related to pop culture on the Daily Twist board. Each image would relate to an event or anniversary specific to that day or week. Oreo also integrated each Pinterest post with Facebook and Twitter.
- Live Event in NYC: For the finale—the one hundredth day of the campaign—Oreo held a live event in Times Square. To build hype for

the event, Oreo utilized the Times Square "spectaculars" and created a live Brand Newsroom, encased with glass. Oreo invited the online community that it had identified using its Pinterest page and other social media channels to vote on what the final image should be. When the winner was decided, the Brand Newsroom team created a related image in real time, while fans watched the action unfold before their eyes. The winning image was "Anniversary of the 1st High-Five."

- The Oreo Blackout Tweet: During the 2013 Super Bowl, Oreo capitalized on the temporary blackout that occurred during the game. With the Brand Newsroom ready to go, the company created an image relating to the blackout and put it on Twitter. The image followed the same style as the 100 Daily Twist images, but read, "You Can Still Dunk in the Dark."

*Results/Evaluation*

The campaign resulted in a 280 percent increase in Oreo's Facebook shares and a 510 percent increase in its Twitter followers. Oreo's Facebook page received more than one million likes during the campaign, while each image posted resulted in an average of ten thousand likes per post. More importantly, the campaign garnered more than 230 earned media impressions.

According to Cindy Chen, Oreo's marketing director, since the campaign's launch, "Oreo has seen a 110% growth in fan interaction per social media post—defined as any combination of shares, likes or comments. The company averaged 7,000 per post before the 'Daily Twist' launch. After, they reached an average of 14,700."[18]

Being both tactical and strategic when creating a social media plan allows for a business to successfully use social media to achieve objectives, while at the same time engaging authentically with consumers. Planning ahead ensures that the time spent on social media efforts reinforces company messaging and engagement while building brand awareness, driving traffic, and ultimately engaging.

## Discover Everything That Is *Pure Michigan*

Year after year, the Pure Michigan campaign has won top awards for promoting Michigan's state tourism by incorporating television and radio advertising, a large social media presence, a partnership advertising program, and public relations efforts into its campaigns. In fact, the state of Michigan's social media program ranked first in a study conducted by Gammet Interactive.[19] The comprehensive study evaluated fifty state tourism offices and their use of social media including Facebook, Twitter, Flickr, YouTube, and others. The state of Michigan topped the list based on its active Facebook community of almost six hundred thousand fans and the more than eighty thousand Twitter followers along with its popular, and active, blog at PureMichiganBlog.org.

An interview with Chad Wiebesick, the director of social media for Michigan Economic Development Corp. and the brains behind the Pure Michigan campaign, outlines the social media strategy approach that was followed (print readers can locate the interview at http://ginaluttrellphd.com/videos/; readers of the ebook can use the embedded link).

By using what has been described in this chapter, can you accurately identify and populate a social media plan using tactics implemented by the state of Michigan? Consider the Circular Model of SoMe for Social Communication—*Share, optimize, Manage, engage*—and ask how a public relations practitioner can thrive in a world inundated with multiple social channels and new influencers.

#### #LRNSMPR

Learn More about Creating Social Media Plans

Quick Links

- 10 Awesome Infographics to Guide Your Marketing Plan for 2014, http://bit.ly/1grloqv
- 14 Tips for Developing a Smart Marketing Strategy in 2014, http://bit.ly/1b5fUPY
- Content Marketing Editorial Calendar Template 2014, http://bit.ly/1b8abWL
- A New Year, A New Strategy: PR and Social Media Planning for 2014, http://bit.ly/1al5gkK

# Notes

1. Constant Contact, "Constant Contact Small Business Pulse," last modified December 2013, accessed January 27, 2014, http://news.constantcontact.com/sites/constantcontact.news hq.businesswire.com/files/research/file/SMBPulseReport3-26-13.pdf.

2. Dennis Wilcox and Glen Cameron, *Public Relations Strategies and Tactics, 10th ed.* (Boston, MA: Allyn & Bacon, 2012), chap. 6.

3. Marketo, "Sample Social Media: Tactical Plan," last modified 2013, accessed January 27, 2014, http://www.marketo.com/worksheets/social-media-tactical-plan/.

4. Wilcox and Cameron, *Public Relations Strategies and Tactics.*

5. Jennifer Kyrnin, "SMART Goals," *About.com* (blog), 2012, http://webdesign.about .com/od/strategy/qt/smart_goals.htm.

6. Unilever Global, http://www.unilever.com.

7. Scott Collins, "PBS Reveals Who's Really Watching *Downton Abbey*," *Los Angeles Times*, March 28, 2012, http://latimesblogs.latimes.com/showtracker/2012/03/pbs-reveals -whos-really-watching-downton-abbey-.html (accessed January 27, 2014).

8. Susan G. Komen Foundation, http://ww5.komen.org/BreastCancer/BreastSelfAware ness.html.

9. Marketo, "Sample Social Media: Tactical Plan."

10. Rosemary Sheridan, Regina Luttrell, Alyssa De Gilio, et al., "A City Churned," working paper, College of Saint Rose, 2013.

11. 360i Digital Marketing Agency, http://www.360i.com/work/ben-jerrys-city-churned/; Ben and Jerry's, http://www.benjerry.com/.

12. Christopher Heine, AdWeek, "Ben and Jerry's Lets Subways, Cabs, and Spoons Help Vote for Ice Creams," last modified June 3, 2013, http://www.adweek.com/news/technology/ ben-jerrys-lets-subways-cabs-and-spoons-help-vote-ice-creams-149965.

13. Rosemary Sheridan, Regina Luttrell, Hannah Mosher, et al., "Oreo: Daily Twist" (unpublished working paper, College of Saint Rose, 2013).

14. i360, "OREO: Daily Twist," last modified 2013, accessed January 27, 2014, http:// www.360i.com/work/oreo-daily-twist/.

15. National Chamber Foundation, "The Millennial Generation," US Chamber of Commerce, http://emerging.uschamber.com/sites/default/files/MillennialGeneration.pdf (accessed November 4, 2013).

16. "In Changing News Landscape, Even Television Is Vulnerable," Pew Research Center for the People and the Press RSS, http://www.people-press.org/2012/09/27/in-changing -news-landscape-even-television-is-vulnerable/ (accessed November 4, 2013).

17. Oreo Daily Twist Pinterest Board: http://www.pinterest.com/oreo/daily-twist/.

18. Ann-Christine Diaz, "Ad Age Digital," Advertising Age Digital RSS, http://adage .com/article/digital/oreo-s-daily-twist-campaign-puts-cookie-conversation/237104/ (accessed November 4, 2013).

19. "Michigan Tourism Takes Over No. 1 Spot in Social Media," *CBS Detroit* (blog), 2010, http://detroit.cbslocal.com/2010/08/05/michigan-tourism-takes-over-no-1-spot-in -social-media/.

# CONCLUSION
## The Burgeoning Horizon: A Look Forward

We have come to the end of our journey. I have taken you back in time to the first instances of people using social media all the way to its use today. We've covered much ground and explored the good, bad, ugly, and many of the finer points of social media and public relations. However, I have yet to answer the question of where the profession is headed. I'm sure you are wondering what's next, so let's peek into the future!

The past several years have been explosive for social media. 2013 marked a great transition within our profession and for social tools. Google+ took the #2 spot for most active users, Instagram launched video because Vine sprang onto the scene and was an instant hit, Twitter went public, Pinterest rose to great heights, Facebook plummeted in popularity among teens, and mobile usage increased by 71 percent, beating forecasted metrics.

What does all of this mean exactly? It's all good news for public relations professionals and social media strategists. Fantastic news, in fact. And before we part ways, I'll share with you a few of my final thoughts and predictions for the future of social media. But remember, I'm eager to continue our conversations. Let's chat and connect through Twitter (@ginaluttrell) and my website (www.ginaluttrellphd.com). There you will find tidbits, case studies, new research, articles, and some video footage that didn't make it into the book. It is my hope that our relationship will grow and mature in the years to come.

On to the good stuff now!

## Executive-Level Support

First, I strongly believe that public relations and social media have finally gained the attention and recognition they deserve of C-level executives. These executives not only understand the importance social media brings but also are responding with bigger budgets and dedicated resources for social strategies. Reports indicate that 93 percent of communication professionals intend to increase or maintain marketing budgets focused on customer engagement in 2014, and 46 percent plan specifically to increase social media spending for the year.

## Listening, Listening, Listening

Because consumers' likes and dislikes change continually (and unpredictably), companies need to—*now more than ever*—listen and engage with their audiences on the platforms that their audiences use. This brings challenges and opportunities to public relations practitioners, social media strategists, and marketers alike. Attempting to figure out how to maintain meaningful conversations with consumers on various platforms will be an ever-present theme as we move forward with social media.

## Mobile, Mobile, Mobile

Increased efforts on the mobile front will continue. Considering that accessing social media is the number one mobile activity that consumers engage in today, companies will need to react and enact sustainable strategies that keep consumers engaged. People predominantly use mobile devices to obtain a myriad of information, including what's happening on their social sites. Social media strategies need to automatically include paths to ensure that campaigns are mobile friendly for smartphones and tablets.

## Images, Images, Images

We've consistently seen a steady uptick in sharing through images and video as opposed to text-based content. Central to any social strategy will be visual elements. Pinterest, SlideShare, Tumblr, Path, Animoto, Keek, and Mobli will grow; thus, companies will need to take action by incorporating these social tools into their planning. Along those same lines, micro-videos will erupt and alter the video exchange occurring on the web.

## Content, Content, Content

To achieve a deeper, more meaningful connection with consumers, companies must provide content that is engaging and sharable. Therefore, content will become richer and more personalized. Brands are emerging as publishers of their own content, sharing messages across multiple media-rich channels. Company websites, white papers, case studies, e-newsletters, blogs, and videos will integrate seamlessly with social media platforms managed by the companies. Infographics, polls, photos, and strategies that probe the consumer and make the consumer part of the plan will rise to the top. Public relations practitioners and social media strategists must also rise to the occasion and develop innovative campaigns that increase brand exposure and engagement through social channels.

## Balance and Trust

Finally, companies will continue to update social media policies and brand guidelines. Companies currently struggle to understand and accept the balance between the professional and personal lives of their employees. In today's socially and digitally connected world, clear-cut policies are a must.

The future of public relations and social media is exciting. When I look at where our profession has come and where it's headed, I am filled with anticipation. Public relations practitioners have always been at the epicenter of building relationships with consumers. Social media has not changed that—it has only enhanced what we already knew. Companies ache for professionals who can combine social media understanding with tried-and-true public relations strategies. It's a good time to be in public relations—truly it is!

# GLOSSARY

**Authenticity**: Being trustworthy, genuine, and real in online interactions.

**Authority**: A person who is a recognized expert on a particular subject.

**Bitly**: A free URL shortening service that provides statistics for the links that users share online. Bitly condenses long URLs, making them easier to share on social networks such as Twitter.

**Blog**: Created from two words—"web log." Blogs are maintained by individuals or businesses with regular entries of commentary, descriptions of events, or other material such as graphics or video.

**Blogger**: A person who blogs.

**Blogroll**: Typically found on blogs, a blogroll is a list of links to other blogs or websites that the blogger commonly references or is affiliated with. Blogrolls help bloggers establish and build their blogging communities.

**BlogTalkRadio**: A free web application that allows users to host live online radio shows.

**Bookmarking**: Saving content that you found important or enjoyed, or where you left off, to continue reading later.

**Chat**: Communication over the Internet.

**Circles**: Clusters of a user's friends on Google+, meaning that you can group certain people you choose to connect with on Google+ into a specific circle—such as colleagues, college connections, family, and so forth. When you want to share content with only these individuals, you include that circle in your post's sharing options.

**Citizen Journalism**: Any type of news gathering and reporting (including writing and publishing articles, posting photographs, or creating video of a newsworthy topic) that is done by members of the larger general public rather than the mainstream media.

**Cloud**: A network of servers that exist in data centers across the world, which allows people to conduct simple activities like checking email, logging into social networking sites, or accessing applications.

**CMO**: Chief Marketing Officer.

**Comment**: A response that provides as an answer or reaction to a blog post or message on a social network. Comments are a primary form of two-way communication on the social web.

**Creative Commons**: Creative Commons Licenses help creators retain copyright while allowing others to copy, distribute, and make some uses of their work, at least noncommercially.

**Crowdsourcing**: The practice of obtaining needed services, ideas, or content by soliciting contributions from a large group of people, and especially from an online community, rather than from traditional avenues. Wikipedia is the most prominent example of crowdsourcing.

**Dashboard**: A user interface that organizes and streamlines online activity so that a person can publish content, respond, monitor, update, and listen from one central place.

**Ebook**: An electronic version of a printed book.

**Engagement**: To participate in the online community via direct conversations.

**Facebook**: A social networking site that connects people with friends, colleagues, family, and other people across the globe. Facebook is currently the largest social network in the world.

**Favorite**: Can be used to bookmark information or illustrate to the online community that you like what you are reading.

**Feed**: Feeds contain frequently updated content published by a website. They are usually used for news and blog websites, as well as for distributing a variety of digital content, including pictures, audio, or video. Feeds can additionally be used to deliver audio content. They are commonly referred to as RSS feeds, XML feeds, syndicated content, Google Reader, Twitter feed, or web feeds.

**Friends**: Individuals you consider close enough to see your Facebook profile and engage with you.

**Google+**: Google's social network.

**Hangout**: A video service on Google+ that allows individuals to video chat with multiple Google+ users at one time. Users can name the chats, watch YouTube videos together, open Google Docs with colleagues, and much more.

**Hashtag**: A word or an unspaced phrase prefixed with the hash or pound symbol "#" (for example, #LRNSMPR or #PRStudChat). Hashtags link a conversation between people with similar interests.

**HootSuite**: A social media management system that allows brands to streamline social media efforts and campaigns across social networks that include Twitter, Facebook, LinkedIn, WordPress, and Google+ pages. Social strategists collaboratively monitor, engage, and measure the results of social campaigns from one secure, web-based dashboard.

**Instagram**: A photo-sharing application that lets users take photos, apply filters to their images, and share the photos instantly on the Instagram network and other social networks, including Facebook, Flickr, Twitter, Pinterest, and Foursquare.

**Keywords**: Specific words used to describe content that ultimately boosts visibility and rankings on the web.

**Klout**: A measure of social influence. Klout allows users to connect various social accounts and then provides users with a Klout score. The score is out of 100—the higher the score, the more influence a user has in the social world.

**Like**: An action that can be taken by a Facebook user to illustrate appreciation of content shared by others.

**Link-back**: Authors, such as bloggers, obtain notifications when other authors link to one of their online publications. This enables authors to keep track of who is linking, or referring, to their articles, blogs, and other online publications.

**LinkedIn**: A business-oriented social networking site.

**Listening**: Monitoring conversations and activity occurring on the web.

**Livecast**: Streaming video or audio so that users can experience the event together via the web.

**Mashup**: The combination, visualization, and aggregation of webpages and applications that use and combine data from two or more sources.

**Meme**: An image with text above and below it (although it can also come in video and link form). A meme on the Internet is used to describe a thought, idea, joke, or concept shared online.

**Participation**: Engaging in online activity while contributing content.

**Permalink**: An address or URL of a particular post within a blog or website.

**Podcast**: A series of digital media files, either audio or video, that are released episodically and often downloaded through an RSS feed.

**Real-Time Search**: The method of indexing content being published online into search engine results with virtually no delay.

**Retweet (RT)**: Sharing another person's Tweet. This is a great way to spread links exponentially. A best practice is to credit the Tweet that you are retweeting. Clicking on the "Retweet" button on your newsfeed page of your Twitter account will make this happen automatically. Use the RT symbol and copy and paste, simply adding a (via @username) after the RT.

**RSS Feed**: RSS (really simple syndication) is a group of web feed formats used to publish frequently updated content such as blogs and videos in a standardized format. Content publishers can syndicate a feed, which allows users to subscribe to the content and read it when they have time, and from a location other than the original website or blog, such as a reader or mobile device.

**Search Engine Optimization (SEO)**: The process of improving the volume or quality of traffic to a website from search engines via unpaid or organic search traffic such as Google.

**Sentiment**: The attitude of user comments related to a brand online.

**Skype**: A free program that allows for text, audio, and video chats between users.

**SlideShare**: An online social network for sharing presentations and documents.

**Social Media**: Media designed to be disseminated through social interaction.

**Social Media Monitoring**: A process of monitoring and responding to interactions occurring on social media sites.

**Social Sphere**: The entirety of one's connections on the web, through social media and various networks.

**Tag**: A keyword used to describe content on a blog or in social networks.

**Tag Cloud**: A visual collection of the most frequent tags produced by a user, blog, profile, page, or descriptions on webpages.

**Transparency**: Honest, open, authentic participation in social media.

**Tweet**: An update shared on Twitter.

**Tweetup** or **Twitterchat**: Events organized on Twitter.

**Views**: Number of times content (including text, photo, and video) is viewed by people.

# INDEX

# ABOUT THE AUTHOR

Before becoming an educator, **Regina Luttrell** spent the first half of her career in public relations and marketing. Her extensive background includes strategic development and implementation of public relations and social media, advertising, marketing, and corporate communications. She has led multiple rebranding campaigns, designed numerous websites, managed high-level crisis situations, and garnered media coverage that included hits with the *New York Times*, the *CBS Evening News*, and the Associated Press. Today she is assistant professor at Eastern Michigan University, where she researches, publishes, and speaks about public relations, social media, and the millennial generation in both the classroom and the workforce. She received her BA in journalism and English from Utica College of Syracuse University, her MA in public communications from the College of Saint Rose, and her PhD from the California Institute of Integral Studies.